BREAK THE PATTERN...

BREAK THE PATTERN

CONNECTING TO THE POWER WITHIN TO CREATE THE LIFE YOU WANT

A 30-DAY PROGRAMME

ROBIN BELA

A catalogue record of this book is available from the British Library.

ISBN: 978-0-9928210-0-5

Also available on Kindle, ISBN: 978-0-9928210-1-2

Printed by CreateSpace, An Amazon.com Company

Acknowledgements

I am very grateful to my Dad, Mum, Sister, friends, clients, teachers and work colleagues who have helped me shape this book to what it is today. It wouldn't have been the same without everyone's support and contribution. Words here cannot describe how each one of them has enriched this book and what it has meant to me. I would like to specially thank all the participants of the various 30-Day Programmes conducted so far, which started as an e-course in 2011, for sharing their experiences and allowing the same to be incorporated in this book. And lastly, I would like to especially thank – Margaret Hewitson for editing support, and Patricia Blomberg for the cover design.

CONTENTS

This Book is dedicated to my Dad, Mum and Sister.

PROLOGUE

Just as my ex-husband and I parted for good, things started falling apart, bringing to the surface my long-standing fears about security. My power was in utter disarray when suddenly the very next day after our decision, my bank balance plummeted to an unexpected zero. Having been in the field of healing and inner soul work for a while then, I was able to step aside and observe myself dispassionately, away from the drama. I knew that my feelings and thoughts had instantly manifested into reality. This instant manifestation ability is inherent in all human beings, which should hopefully be used to create positive outcomes, of course, but if our feelings and thoughts inadvertently focus on the negative, Universe responds accordingly by manifesting the negative reality.

My speed of manifesting positive outcomes has increased over the years, as I have been really focusing more intensely on looking at the brighter side of life. I consciously endeavour to focus on words and thoughts, which reflect that. But if you focus your attention on fears constantly, then they would just manifest into your reality all the time. And now, I was seeing a reflection of my inner fearful thoughts in my bank balance, as I was focusing on my fears of insecurity at that moment. This was not good at all! I knew I had to start thinking and feeling differently right away. As soon as I realised this, it just took me a couple of days to get my bank balance back to normal.

At times, I could see my fears regarding my business and my recent personal life changes resurfacing, and reflecting in my life through incidents such as my heating system boiler breaking down, home keys not working, and so on. When we carry the energy of fear within us, it permeates into our everyday life. I kept pulling myself back as soon as I realised that I was getting engulfed by the fears that were illusions, and were not real, and were unnecessary to keep. Our reality is always in our hands to shape.

1

If we can learn to 'not lean against or push towards' our past fears and the doubts of future, and rather just 'stand upright' enjoying this present moment, then God or Universe (the Supreme Energy creating life), just supports us. We are in the state of least resistance at that moment. When we ask God or Universe for our needs and patiently focus on one main priority in life - 'To think only positive', then life just takes care of us. Anytime I am feeling stuck, I always check within, to see if I am leaning against something or someone for support or pushing for results or approval, or am I standing upright in my power, for life to offer me everything naturally? When I ask this question to myself, and if I see myself leaning either way in my vision, I then instantly correct my self-image to upright, independent and free. And by doing this, internally I correct my energetic response to the situation, where I may have been too attached to the outcome. I am then in the natural flow of life, and not blocking things from manifesting naturally.

When you let go of control, you allow trust in the abundant flow of Universe to grow in you. And being in that flow, there is nowhere to rush, nothing to fix. Feeling the need to fix is usually a state of anxiety. On the contrary, the natural flow of life is about just 'being present joyfully, enjoying this moment', and allowing all that you asked Universe to flow to you.

Manifestation cannot occur when in doubt or fear, but through trust and being grateful to Universe or God, even before you have received what you have asked for. And in my experience, when I do that, I have witnessed miracles, synchronicities, happiness, and most importantly, freedom, that I can create and manifest my life the way I want. Many a times, we are simply holding ourselves back or pushing too hard for results, and struggling. But in truth, life is always here to support us. Whenever you feel stuck, and are neither moving forward nor receiving what you asked for, you may keep checking with yourself whether you are leaning backward or pushing forward too hard, under some fear.

I knew that the key to changing the negative experiences was by intentionally tuning into positive frequencies, and changing my thoughts and feelings to the state that I wished to be in, through the application of the principles relating to 'Intent' as described in this book. The transition in my personal life thus went on smoothly, helped by this practice.

These days, I "Intend" and things magically happen, from little things as, a pleasant journey, finding money when I need it, or receiving what I want as a gift, and sometimes it has come from people I have never even met before. I once met a lovely woman named Arya who sells a beautiful flower essence mix called, 'Blessings' at cielessentials.com. I told her I really loved it, and would buy it from her later, as I didn't have 100 dollars in hand at that moment. The next day I saw Arya from a distance talking to a woman named Margaret, whose name I found out later, and I saw her with some money in hand. I just stood there and heard Arya saying, "Oh, this is for Robin and I have only one bottle left." When I heard that, I came to them and said not to worry as I could buy later. At that point, Margaret just gave the money to Arya saying she wanted to pay and let Robin have it, and just left. I was so amazed. I had never met Margaret before and she touched me with Blessings! Arya reminded me of something that my friend Vivian had always said that 'In the Giving is the Receiving'.

I have realised that when I focus on giving love, I also receive back two-fold, and sometimes, in amazing ways. In fact, to grow my work, I just focus on the joy of giving love and service to people. And 'receiving' part, Universe just takes care of. I just ask for my needs and let Universe take care of them. Having a management background, I might have earlier thought more strategically about money making, but I have realised that I do better when I am focusing on work passionately, rather than just looking at it as a way to make money. I have created much better strategies for my work I do now, as these come from a place of meaningful, authentic alignment to who I am at the core, and the receiver feels the benefits.

I have found that by Intending, I also meet the right people who are most helpful or really the people I like to meet. I Intend that quite often when I am in large groups. I have found that the right people just appear for help when

I pray or Intend that. Once when my shoulder was sore, I happened to meet my friend's friend just when I Intended for help. She worked as a pharmacist, and instantly gave me some soothing gel that was just perfect for the aching shoulder. Generally, in my life, such working through Intents has become my full-time occupation of serving and helping others.

I have come to realise that if Universe, Source or God, whatever you like to call it, has given us life, it is also there to take care of us, and it has also given us all the resources within us to reach out to all outside when needed. We just need to trust, Intend for ourselves, and Ask. As we work our Intent muscles, the speed of manifesting over a period becomes much quicker. Universe wants us to receive everything in life as quickly as possible, that alone is the truth! But at times, the society we live in teaches us that life is meant to be hard and a struggle, and that we need to be born lucky.

The Universal truth is that we are here to enjoy life, and that choice is really in our hands to decide, to Ask, and that we are thus blessed! The more you Ask and Intend, the stronger you get in receiving. The key in the beginning is to not lose faith in the Asking, and also to not dwell on the fears that may arise in the process as it only impedes the same. Just focus on the flow of enjoyment of the process. This book is about breaking away from old ways of thinking and patterns that are based on fear, and to find true power from within.

True power does not come from college degrees, money or clothes, it comes from the kind of thoughts and feelings you carry within you, about yourself, others and life. What is outside you is a reflection of what is inside your mind. If you face any issues in life, all answers are within, even whom to connect with, to receive more answers and support. We hear of very many stories these days of how people realised what they needed to change in their lives and beliefs, and how they regained complete health or found great success. True power comes to you when you are accountable to yourself and meet your fears along the way. That is when you can break free from old patterns and create what you want. You cannot find power from external

4

things. I've seen people who dress well and have lots of money, but really think very poorly about themselves and have no confidence in going after what they really want to do in their hearts.

Real power grows from Self-love and Self-acceptance, and knowing that you are always in charge of change in yourself! If Self Love can be attained, everything including confidence, money and relationships grows abundantly in life because you would then feel deserving of it all. And if you cannot love yourself enough, how would you expect someone else to love you in a relationship, for instance, and the same goes with respect to a business. If you think poorly of your business and are fearful about it, that is going to reflect back on you through the eyes of your clients! It is crucial to remove those fears before you plant any seeds of prosperity to grow in life, and as a teacher of this work now, I will show you in the 30-Day Programme in this book, just how to do that.

So at times, simply Intending doesn't work because there are fears or core beliefs holding you back. I teach under Day 2 and Day 3 chapters a process called 'Soul Clearing Technique' that can help you break free from the patterns blocking you. You can question yourself now to see where you stand with regard to fulfilling your desires. Are you growing your desires in the fertile soil of love or in a fearful war-zone? What do you feel deep down: can you really make your desires come true? Or are there any fears bubbling up? If there are fears, you know you've got to find a fertile ground of love and excitement for your desires, and remove the beliefs and fears that limit and bind you. You will be guided in this book day-by-day in 30-Days, on how to find your state of unconditional joy and happiness as you work at your desires fearlessly.

Over the years, I have been stepping into my power through various changes I consciously made in my life by being authentic and true to myself. I came from India to the UK at the age of 23 and settled here. I then made a quick career transition from my corporate job in management and marketing to self-employment in the field of healing, coaching and teaching. Again, this was a scary transition for me, but I knew back then that if I did not stay true to my feelings about my career, I would just suffocate and be extremely unhappy staying in that situation. I felt afraid but still went ahead, and I am so glad that I followed my heart then. And I cannot think of doing anything else today! Later, I had to pass the test of being authentic or true to myself in my relationships. This resulted in my parting ways with my ex-husband, which took place peacefully.

Change doesn't have to be dramatic, and I explain in the book how you can bring in changes easily and as peacefully as possible for yourself. My new posture in self-employment made me come face-to-face with Money issues, and I learned to correct my relationship with Money to overcome this. In the book, I reveal how I created this authentic relationship with Money. Being authentic or true to yourself and all your relationships is vital for connecting to the power within. We will be talking in-depth about some all this and more in the book. I will also be talking about some simple exercises or techniques for leading a stress-free and peaceful life, and for finding deeper perspective and meaning in life. Throughout the book, you will be offered a choice of alternative words to use to connect to your Inner Self, so that you feel most comfortable choosing the way of thinking that suits you. The exercises will offer tools on how to easily bring balance in mind, feelings and body, and consequently, in our outer life, as our inner well-being reflects in the way we function in our daily lives confidently, peacefully and happily.

There is immense power that you take back when you let go of what is not true in your life anymore. You can be taking power back from situations, people, or also from the way you have limiting beliefs about yourself. You can ask yourself, 'Am I living with an aspect in my life just because it's a convenient and safe arrangement, while deep down I wish to be something else or somewhere else?' If yes, you probably are stuck and fearful of making the changes you desire at the moment, for you are still wondering if you are powerful enough to accomplish them and change. Well, how long would you avoid recognising the truth of who you really are deep within? No one but you can take the steps.

One of my clients once asked me if it was really possible for everyone to genuinely feel confident about themselves. She was so sure that it's just an act some people put on. I explained to my client that as a child I was very shy but what connects me or anyone to confidence and true power, is being connected to who we really are, which is defined by our 'likes' and 'interests', doing what we love and 'speaking exactly how we feel', without feeling the need to prove ourselves in any way, for instance, out of guilt or to please someone. In other words, really being honest and authentic with self is the key to self-love and true power. And not allowing yourself to be fake, or to stand for something you don't like or believe in, or that is not true, are some basic requirements for being authentic with self. When you know yourself, you can stand in front of a crowd and speak confidently, authentically, and not put on an act on stage. This is when you will just be who you are and what you believe in.

If you have seen the film *Runaway Bride* that came out in 1999, Julia Roberts plays the role of a girl who doesn't have a clue about how she likes her eggs to be cooked: poached, boiled or fried. She would change her food needs to whatever her current boyfriend would like. It could be that she just liked pleasing everyone, and so she would say yes to anything. So in the end, she also had a hard time trying to figure out who was really the right man for her as she had no clue of what she wanted in a relationship and hence she kept running away from the wedding altar of all her planned weddings! Connecting to true power means knowing what you like and do not like, for a start. This book is about teaching you to understand your inner needs and to learn to find all your answers from within.

True power also comes from not really wanting to change people around you to accept your beliefs. Remember that amounts to 'leaning and pushing'. As you accept yourself, accept others too. And if change has to happen within others in accepting you, it will in time. When I was unauthentic in relationships and 'leaning and pushing' for what I needed, and most of the time did not know what I really wanted in a relationship, I had started putting on weight. Now, 20 kilos and almost 3 stones lighter, I am happier too, of course. I can tell you, losing weight was much easier when I made the right choices in life, and the weight I had put on suddenly was because I had made the wrong choices which caused stress, low self-esteem, unhappiness and over-weight. Think about which areas in your life may be going wrong for you. And question yourself why, and since when.

Eating in the right way to suit your lifestyle and metabolism is so crucial. No one but you can really tell what suits you, as everyone is unique! So, getting authentic with one's body means understanding which foods suit you. It can take some time, but you can begin doing by being conscious of how your body feels when you eat. The same goes for the type of exercise needed. I will talk more about this later in the book.

Living a conscious life means you invite what feels right into your experience. One of my purposes in writing this book is to help you connect to this. I have seen people getting very spiritual, spending time in mountains, but when they get back into their normal lives in the city, it's all gone! Or it can be the other way round, that when someone begins to live a more spiritually conscious life, he/she actually stops living the materialistic life or simply struggles to find a balance. And that's where the poverty consciousness comes from. People who think that they can be either spiritual or live a normal human city existence but not both, are the ones who are also most likely to suffer in making money and achieving happiness. Truly, I have come to learn that when you are completely tuned into your Divine Spirit, your most authentic Self, you are powerful enough to live your best in the human world with all material comforts, look your best and also have peace and love in your heart.

If you are thinking that change has to take a long time, well I would like to tell you it had just been 10 months since my separation from my ex-husband, and I had already lost 20 kilos, expanded my business even further, and written this book, initially as an e-course, not forgetting the immense amount of healing and inner work I went through too in that period. So, age, whether young or old, and time, are all meaningless when you want to connect to the person you truly are. And the process doesn't have to be hard either. I had a great, in fact quite peaceful 10 months, just as I Intended. I was mindful of all the changes taking place within and around me and I allowed them without any resistance.

For some years now, I have been doing energy healing work, coaching, and have been teaching this work to those who wish to take it up as a profession, and be practitioners and teachers. I always felt I wanted to bring healing and empowerment to people in a simple form and reach out to people who have no knowledge of any kind of healing modalities. The result is this book. My aim here is that as you read the words, you feel the changes you desire and need energetically within you and realise them in your reality. I will be giving you daily work to do through this 30-Day Programme, so that you can incorporate the changes you wish to bring right away into your life through guided practical steps.

I would like you to think of this book as a Workbook that you work with. I have held out my hand to you, but you have got to come halfway and grab it by making a commitment to bring conscious change for yourself. The words and examples I have used in this book will only make you feel as if I am leading you forward personally. So, I am truly connecting with you through this book as if I am with you now. I invite you daily for the next 30 days to work with me, so that I can help you change your life to the way you want. That would truly be my greatest joy. The book is an easy and practical step-by-step Workbook on bringing 'Change' in Personal life, Relationships, Career, Money and/or Health within 30 days.

I am really looking forward to this book bringing changes within people's lives just as I have seen in the people who completed the 30-Day Programme as a part of my e-course, through which I initially introduced the content of this book. I have been really overjoyed to see the participants make remarkable changes within their lives. I also worked closely with my first batch of participants in this Programme to ensure that the book carries all that is needed in the final draft that you now hold in your hands. I thought I would share a few comments from some of them representing the initial group of 100 odd participants below, to get you excited about your journey ahead.

The Feedbacks:

Rosie Glass, Therapist, Bristol, UK :

"I am not afraid of change – I believe in dreams now! What an amazing Programme it has been. And you are an amazing person and teacher Robin! Since I have started this e-course, people have been telling me that I look younger. I made peace with my father by saying the Intents and knowing that it wasn't my fault or his that he died, and this was the most powerful affirmation I have ever done, and the first time I have ever had the strength to acknowledge that it wasn't my fault and I wasn't abandoned. My partner said that as he was looking at me last night, I literally have started to look younger. Also, since starting this course I have really wanted to do the creative things I did as a child and was good at. I have got a real desire to play the piano again, (I was very good at it), sing, paint with oils and dance! It's amazing. I am feeling younger and more vitalised and people are noticing! I have not done anything creative since my father died, which was in 1988! I feel more alive and it's fantastic. My friends have noticed a change in me. These are some of their quotes: 'Your aura is completely different at the moment,' 'You seem so peaceful with the world,' 'Have you made peace with something?' 'Your business head has come to life!' (I now have 6 clients for massage instead of one) 'You seem to be able to glide through your problems at the moment.' I LOVE IT!!"

And later Rosie, offered a video testimonial where she said: "As I worked with Robin, it has been life changing. **The healing transformation that takes place has been completely noticeable and things I wanted for years have come to light.** For example, I met my Soul mate and managed to conceive for the first time, which I thought I would never be able to. I'm more energised and has opened doors for me."

Penelope Blissenden, Therapist, Coach, Teacher and Artist, London (www.penelopeblissenden.com):

"Hi Robin, thanks so much for this empowering 30 day course. **It has been a real turning point for me. I really am feeling so focused.** Ideas are coming and coming! So many now that I have to sit and prioritise and see it as work now. Before I just thought I was playing around and nothing would come of it. Now, I really have faith in setting-up classes in spiritual development and so many different things to develop my work that my heart wants and help others. My friends are noticing the change. I feel full of excitement. Another great thing has been offered to me – an exhibition space! So, I am now organising to have an Art Exhibition to show my paintings in a month, here in London. I haven't had one for 13 years, so I am really excited. I have so much to look forward to and am moving forward with confidence."

Lucile Christophe, Travel Agent, Paris:

"Yesterday, I came back from work all upset. My stomach was completely tied, it was like a ball of anger inside me. Dad had cooked dinner but I told him I wasn't feeling well. I sat in my bedroom and for more than an hour I listened to Snatam Kaur mix of songs on YouTube. I sat in the lotus position, closed my eyes and let it go. I breathed deeply. I sometimes sang with the music. Finally after an hour, the ball-like heaviness was gone, my back pain was less, my body was relaxed and I was feeling a bit hungry. I then realised what this Programme brought me. It brought me the knowledge of my inner strength. Thanks for all you brought me and taught me. Really Robin, this month was a gift, a beautiful gift. I can say that now, I say "I LOVE YOU" to myself in the mirror and believe in it truly. I feel lighter in my body and happier with it. I am still working on being confident with food but I've lost this "guilty" feeling I had while eating. I feel stronger with all the new Intentions I have been working with. I feel I have created a shelter inside me. I needed it so much, now I feel so safe. **I am not scared anymore of my emotions because I know, I can sit to find peace and calmness inside me.** This is the most beautiful gift of this course for me. So THANKS Robin. I am now preparing my trip to India and Nepal and I won't miss giving you news and feedback of this adventure."

Tammy Tidmarsh, Derbyshire, UK (www.equinepassion.co.uk):
"I have really enjoyed working with you Robin and I am sure I will be doing more soul coaching and courses with you in the future. I feel you have brought about tremendous changes within me – not least my poor hip, which after the second distance healing session you did with me early this year has not bothered me since! I love the way you guide and teach and bring about profound changes within and also externally. I always look forward to your course lessons, and often **I can feel the energy strongly in the words as I read**."

Linda Grieg, Speech and Language Therapist in UK and UAE before retiring in 2008, Edinburgh, UK. *(Words taken from a video testimonial):*
"The **30-Day Programme demands a lot of introspection, self analysis** but boy it cleared out a heap lot of rubbish that has been there for a long time. I felt much better afterwards. Robin somehow gives you confidence in the knowledge that she imparts about the theoretical stuff. I am a very logical person. I need to know that what I am doing has some basis and facts. And **Robin seems to have the ability to provide that theoretical framework but at the same time allows us a lot of practice and shows a lot of practical work on top of that.**"

*****

Please note that there are various examples and case studies used in this book from experiences shared by my clients, with their permission. The ones above are real names of my clients, but in the later examples, I have changed names to ensure privacy as they have shared some of their intimate experiences.

I am very grateful and excited for everything new that awaits you now, dear reader, as you are about to turn to the next page! Are you ready to bring in the change you truly want in your life? Are you ready to work with me and break all your old patterns to connect to your true power within? If the answer is 'Yes!', then let's begin!

GUIDELINES FOR THE 30-DAY PROGRAMME
PART A : GENERAL GUIDELINES

Welcome to the Programme!

I am very excited that you have decided to embark on this journey with me to bring change in your life! Before we start, I would like you to read the following carefully, as this is what my advice would be to you in person whenever you stray away from your path during this Programme. If you keep the points below in mind, you will be just fine!

This is a practical Programme that requires action on your part daily or at least regularly. If you really want to bring in the change you want for yourself in life, then it's important for you to try to apply what I talk about in this Programme in your everyday life. If you are doing one lesson per day, you may read your lesson in the morning, so that you have plenty of time in the day to ponder over the same, imbibe the new way of thinking consciously, and practically apply your daily exercises offered in lessons. This is done through regular reminders to yourself and writing answers to all questions asked at the end of each chapter. Writing is the key to getting clarity about your issues at a deeper level. You may re-read each lesson at different times of the day so that the words get firmly anchored within you.

If you dedicate each of the 30-Days to working on yourself, you will see a really quick change and a positive shift in the way you feel about yourself, your goal, and life in general. Please note that: if for any reason, you miss a day or more during the Programme, you are fine as long as you are consciously reminding yourself of the new way of being you are focusing on. It's ok to go slow in completing the Programme, rather than completely giving up or starting to feel guilty for the same. In fact, you may complete the Programme at your own pace as long as you are devoting some time to it on a regular basis. You don't have to be perfect with each lesson to move to the next one. Keep applying the previous lessons to your everyday life and they will just grow and anchor within your lifestyle with time and practice, and your life will start shifting towards the change you desire.

I would like to encourage you to have a journal or notebook for this Programme, where you write down your daily experiences at the end of each day. This is after you have applied during your day what was talked about in that day's lesson. This can help you check your progress yourself, and it can be the key to staying motivated and going deep into your own personal soul's journey. It will also cultivate a beautiful habit for you to keep in touch with your feelings and help you understand yourself better when you might be moody or feeling emotionally unstable. It will also help you to stay focused on your goals. Journaling about inner thoughts is a great self-help tool to help clear away any blocks on your way. Remember, only you would understand yourself best. If you can learn to do it, you won't need counselors most of the time. I am thus helping you to tune into your true power within.

Also, before you start the Programme, it'll be desirable to have a clear idea about any 'one' main goal or objective you would wish to achieve from this Programme. Before setting this target, you should keep in mind that it ought to be achievable in one month. You can do this Programme again at a different time with a completely different goal in mind.

In this book, for anything we wish to achieve, we form a statement called 'Intent' to help us focus on the desired goal. We will delve deeper into the topic of Intent a bit later. But before that, I would like to explain below about the one statement used before each 'Intent' and its purpose. The statement is:

'I call on the I AM Presence and ask it to direct my Higher Self that...'
The above statement helps us to remain open to receiving, as Asking opens doors just like the saying goes, 'Ask and you shall Receive'. *'I AM Presence', is a general term used to refer to Source or God or Universe - whatever you feel comfortable calling this Supreme Energy that supports life on Earth.*

Here, I would like you to commit that you will go through this Programme to achieve the goal you have in mind with the following Intention. Please read aloud or in mind: I call on the I AM Presence and ask it to direct my Higher Self that:

"I AM at the stage in life where I have completed this Programme and have reached my goal through focus and commitment in this one month. I AM excited as I have allowed the needed changes, healing, growth, empowerment and opening of my heart to take place beautifully for me. I now embrace the amazing Self that I AM. I AM grateful." (Breathe and feel its energy sink within you).

The next few pages will give you guidelines on setting the right words for the 'Intent' you have decided to achieve this month. It is important to word it accurately, so that it expresses precisely what you desire to happen in your life next.

I started working with the idea of 'Intent' since quite some time and soon realised that when goals are affirmed starting with words 'I AM', it means I already am that what I am wanting to be. **In my opinion, if we care to believe that we are already where we are meant to be, then all this fight and rush to achieve things just disappears, and we actually start relaxing into enjoying the experience of life, which I feel, is our sole purpose in life. When we are in the place of contentment, God or Universe, just offers what you are energetically Asking and reflecting, which is contentment in every area of life. Fighting to be somewhere is the state of 'being limited' or 'not having enough'. If we focus on that, we remain in a state of lack in life.** What we choose to think and feel, is what becomes our reality. Life is meant to be enjoyed and to receive everything we want. The only block usually is us when we believe that since we do not know the 'how', it is going to be hard, and perhaps impossible at times. This world is quite a magical place to be in, only if we care to believe that. Answers, solutions and miracles become common when we place our firm faith and trust in that energy of 'contentment' that all is given to us by Universe or God or Source.

I believe that it is crucial to really be able to talk in the language as if you already have got what you want, to connect to the frequency of what you like to create in life quickly. It keeps you away from the 'lack mentality' and helps you to start moving energetically and consciously towards your goal. I started asking my students in my healing courses and also clients to start saying their Intents this way. This was along with energy healing work I did on them to bring complete healing as they really needed to believe in their mind's eye and imagine and feel, how it would be to be healed, to be able to achieve it in reality, whether it is healing or anything else they want. They should be able to Intend 'I AM healed' or 'I AM wealthy' or 'I AM at peace' or whatever they need to achieve.

Many a time, I realised that energy healing, and also saying 'I AM healed' Intent, wasn't enough. It is because sometimes, people have certain core beliefs connected to some 'fears' that would inhibit full healing and acceptance of complete recovery as even a possibility. And sometimes, these core beliefs stemmed from past incidents, perhaps in their childhood. So, while I was able to heal and make the receiver feel good through energy healing sessions, some of their problems emerged again, which was due to their deep-seated core patterns of thought, habits, beliefs and behaviour, which had not been consciously changed by the receiver. After some time, they would return with the same healing issues, distressing emotions and physical pains that had once been cleared completely from their bodies and energy fields. In this situation, I would help them look within to find the reasons as to why they were repeatedly bringing back the same healing issues.

For example, if someone is having problems with legs, I would help him or her to look within, which may reveal that he or she is perhaps afraid to 'move forward' to leave his/her job and do what he or she really wants in life, may be to start a business. I then ask such persons to start shifting their thinking and life towards the situation where they want to be, through conscious reminders with the ' I AM ' Intents and teach them to clear old patterns of thought. You will learn in detail under Day 2 and 3 chapters. I have later found that the 'I AM' concept has been really important in many religious texts too but I choose to not work with any religious connections for the I AM statements as I never connected to these through that way.

I have experienced that it is simply more powerful when we call on the Source or God or Universe and our Higher Self to work along with us when we read our Intents. Therefore I suggested that one statement above to be said before reading all your daily Intents. And as you say your Intents that you form during the 30 days, simply breathe and allow the Intentions to anchor within. Reading Intents may just be for a few seconds. But you will notice the power and energy as you say this, and focus on your Intents. It is simply bringing in the energy of the I AM Presence to support you through a more focused Intent.

Please note that when I am asking you to say the Intents regularly, it does not mean, you have to say them hundreds of times. The process of doing this regularly is to help you focus on your desired direction in life. If saying it a few times is all that was needed, you have then really approached your Intent from your heart. It is not a 'thinking' process, but a 'feeling' process. But each circumstance and individual is different and may require different processes. The underlying factor will always be the belief within that you have already achieved what you are intending.

I am not going to give you ready-made affirmations in the next 30 days, as all of you are different and unique. And truly, each of your individual needs is different. Instead, I am going to empower you by teaching how to write your own Intents to focus on your unique needs, and only you will know where your core belief is stuck about a situation. You really cannot affirm 'I AM now in a job position through a promotion,' when deep down you believe that you are not good enough. So, your Intent would be to get a promotion – 'I AM good at my work and deserve to do this work "__" and I am grateful I have received the promotion at work.' And perhaps there was even a deeper layer of a core belief where you felt not good enough because your classmates made fun of you at school once, and you always felt not good enough since then. In this case, your final Intent would be worded as -"I AM always good enough to be doing whatever I choose even when I was young at school and also today. I AM always connected to my true self that is unique and powerful. I AM fully recognising it. I deserve to get the promotion at work that I received. I AM grateful.' So, you really take full control of your life through the Intents you formulate for yourself.

I will guide you especially during the Day 2 work on how to really dig and find the core issues you need to release and change.

So next, let's go through how to set your Intent or goal for the month and how to write your personal Intents as you work with this book.

Love,

Robin Bela

GUIDELINES FOR THE 30-DAY PROGRAMME
PART B : CREATE YOUR INTENT

INTENT, for the purposes of this Programme, means to consciously make a decisive statement about having reached a goal, and to start experiencing the goal as already present in this moment through repeated 'visualising' and 'feeling' in order to become an energetic match to receive it in our physical reality. This is through any known or unknown possibilities that become naturally available to us. Intents work best when any fears related to what the goal is, are released. (Steps to clear fears are first explained in Day 2 and Day 3 chapters.)

Before the Programme begins, I would like to help you write your goal in terms of Intent for the purposes of this Programme. Again, let me remind you that it is best if you focus on just one main goal for this month, although we may touch upon various other relevant issues along the way.

When I check within myself to see what I should like to create next in my life, I am not deciding on the basis of any chance or guesswork but really looking from within my soul to what I 'feel' I should like to happen next in my life without any 'ifs' and 'buts' or even the 'how'! Looking at my desires from a soul level is the opposite to what your intellectual mind might like, which is all about what you 'should' do or 'can do' and tries to control and stop all creativity and desires from flowing easily to you.

You could be saying that there are motives like 'money for safety' that you may wish to create, but the real question should be, 'How best would you see yourself making money' and not 'where to get the money from'. It's important to understand this, as your will or capacity for creating money will diminish within your soul soon, unless you are fuelled with passion to create something that you love doing. You need to find out what are the real reasons for what you want. For example, sharing love in a relationship as opposed to fear of being alone, or living your purpose rather than just making money for security or to prove yourself to others. Creating anything out of fear and any agenda other than 'unconditional' joy will only result in fear, failure, stress, and definitely, unhappiness. You are literally 'pulling' energies from outside to make yourself feel safe and fulfilled, when instead, your powerful self should come from within.

It is important to create what you desire for the sheer love of creating. You feel joyful and excited at the thought of its creation. It is from this moment that you are connected to your true power. When you talk about it, you will feel animated and alive. For example, my friend, Uta kept saying that she needed to start coaching practice and other things that would be safe in terms of making money; but when I asked her what she would do if money wasn't an issue, she instantly said that she would like to start a Cafe! Her eyes just lit up with excitement and her hands seemed to be talking along with her! Well, Vivian, my other good friend who was also there and I had then said to Uta, 'there you go, that is what you need to focus on!' The best part is that she didn't realise herself how she was so excited about it until we made her reflect upon it. As I now sit in the Starbucks Cafe in the Canongate on the Royal Mile in Edinburgh writing this, I overhear this conversation that I feel is God-sent for me to add here! A lady is sitting with her friends and saying, "The job you do should be what feeds you, gives you the drive, motivates you and not drains you at the end."

It can take some time to do the soul-searching needed to set your Main Intent for the month. Just be open to allowing that process to take all the time it needs. For some of you, your goal for the Programme can even be, 'to look for what you want next in your life'. I would like you to connect to what you desire to create next in your life without the fear of knowing what the outcome could be like or how you might manage it, and to do it just for fun. This month can be a safe cubicle for you to experiment with your creativity and also work on building and strengthening your manifesting skills.

As you begin with this joyful creation, the process and the result are always joyful too, rather than being a struggle with extreme fatigue at the end for mind, body and, most importantly, for your soul. You really don't want to be consciously creating anything new in life through this book that will bore you! You want to create something that will lift your spirit when you think of the completion of its creation. And with this passion, you also tap into your intuition and guidance within your soul to understand where all your support lies during this creative process.

It's better to have an Intention which is specific and allows you to take action steps and measures your progress. So, instead of thinking too far ahead, see what you would like to create in the next 1-3 months at the most. For example, for building a house, your instant goal may be to get all the right people for the house construction and organising finances. But the building of your house may take up to a year or more. So you want to be very specific what you wish to work on for the next 30 days.

If you are still wondering what your goal is, place one hand on your heart and ask, 'My Heart, what is it that you want to create next that will bring me happiness and abundance in all forms?' And without stopping, you just see what comes to you. It may just be a 'feeling', or a 'knowing', or 'actual words' or a 'visual image'. Speak it aloud or write it down, else you will just forget and the information will get lost. In my experience, sometimes re-reading things later makes even better sense.

HOW TO WRITE YOUR MAIN INTENT NOW AND MORE INTENTS LATER:

First, a few reminders of what we have already discussed previously:

Now, when you write your Intents, these should be written in the present tense, as if you have already achieved them. For example, you shouldn't say in your Intent, 'I will achieve, or hope to achieve, my ideal weight' but instead you will say 'I have achieved my ideal weight'. **You will not use**

21

words like –'will not', 'do not' etc. that actually emphasise the 'lack' in the present moment. If you want to not be depressed any more, you Intend, 'I AM happy and peaceful within'. You wouldn't focus on the negative words in an Intent e.g., 'I AM not depressed' etc., but instead on what you want to feel. Most importantly, you will also avoid speaking like that in your conversations in normal day-to-day life by constantly reminding yourself. Your 24 hours a day in life should slowly start reflecting the new way you are starting to perceive yourself now.

Also, you will be adding the 'I AM Intent' before that as you will see in the examples below. Again, a suggested reminder to say/read the following I AM statement before you start saying all your Personal Intents - 'I call on the I AM Presence to direct my Higher Self that.." before reading all your Intents. It is literally Asking your Higher Self and Universe/God/Source to work with you, and you are then bringing in the energy or healing needed right then and there for yourself. You become open to receiving by simply 'Asking'. Many people have told me that they can feel energies in their body as they read their Personal Intents. Also, sometimes breath gets warmer if some healing starts taking place, especially if you repeat a particular Intent a few times as you breathe along. Now, reading any Affirmations or Intent may not be so powerful as compared to the ones you yourself need to work on. That is why you need to work with me and write your own words for the Intent relevant to your personal circumstances.

Some examples of forming your Main Intent for the 30-Days are below. These are examples of Intents by people with whom I have worked with during this Programme on a one-to-one basis:

EXAMPLE 1: Work/Business

When Susie first put her goal down, it looked like this:
"My goal is to develop an idea for my own business that will bring me fulfilment and financial abundance, and which will positively impact the lives of others."

Then I helped her set the Intent with the right words. So her 'Intent' was formed as:

Intent: I AM calling on the I AM Presence (Source/Universe/God) to direct my Higher Self that:

"I AM having a clear idea of my business that is positively impacting others' lives and brings me fulfilment along with financial abundance in return. I AM full of love and joy as I start my business. I trust and follow my heart in every little step I take towards it. I AM staying focused with love in my heart. I AM very grateful to God/ Universe."

Now, the above statement was about having a clear idea of business. If you want another example of setting your goals for your business, then see below. The Intent changes according to exactly what you would think and write first.

EXAMPLE 2: Work/Business

When Mary first put her goal down, it looked like this:
"I want to work with passion and enthusiasm, drawing on my many skills and talents in order to provide a secure financial situation and a happy home environment for myself and my daughter."

So her 'Intent' was formed as:

Intent: I AM calling on the I AM Presence (Source/Universe/God) to direct my Higher Self that:

"I AM passionate and enthusiastic about using my skills and talents to help others and have developed a successful business through it. I AM having complete faith and I listen to my inner guidance. And I AM trusting and taking action with little steps, one at a time. My business keeps me financially abundant, so I have the perfect lifestyle that I like for me and my daughter. I AM very grateful to God/Universe. I AM simply joyful and excited at every step."

I have helped her to include the words such as "listen to inner guidance" and "have faith", as I felt that they were important for her. You will know which words you need which excite you about your goal as you write your personal Intent.

EXAMPLE 3: Self-Development/Spiritual Growth

When Caroline first put her goal down, it looked like this:
"As for my Intention, I think it will have to be to improve my communication and self-confidence skills. It seems to affect several of my relationships after a while."

So her 'Intent' was formed as:
Intent: I AM calling on the I AM Presence (Source/Universe/God) to direct my Higher Self that:
"I AM confident in speaking through my Heart in what I always believe in. I AM open to communicating and sharing my thoughts and my love with others. I AM joyful in this experience as it has opened me to expressing my true authentic self, and I enjoy being Me openly and confidently. And I AM absolutely safe in this process. I thank God/Universe for this."

EXAMPLE 4: Health/Weight

There have been several Intents on weight that I have seen from those who participated in my e-course. I have put a general one below that will give you an idea.

Intent: I AM calling on the I AM Presence (Source/Universe/God) to direct my Higher Self that:
"I AM my ideal weight of __Kg now and I have reached it easily and quickly. I love my body and treat it with respect by feeding it nutritional food and regularly exercising. I AM having healthy eating habits now, and listen to all my inner guidance at all times to maintain a perfect weight that is right for my body. I AM grateful for my healthy and beautiful body. I AM feeling great, slim and happy with the way my body looks better and better, lighter and stronger with each passing day. I AM grateful and full of joy. Thank you God/Universe."

EXAMPLE 5: Health/Weight

Michelle is another example I'd like to share under health/weight topic. She wrote to me:
"I tried to see which one is the most important, and I found out that the most important aspect for me is to be at peace with food. And to find back the pleasure of eating and lose the guilt of feeding myself, as well as to accept my body."

So her 'Intent' was formed as:
Intent: I AM calling on the I AM Presence (Source/Universe/God) to direct my Higher Self that:
"I AM at peace with food. I AM enjoying eating food as much as my body needs. I AM aware what and how much food my body needs. My Body and Soul deserve this pleasure, nourishment and care. I AM grateful to God/Universe for this peace within me."

EXAMPLE 6: Relationships

When Pete first put his goal down, it looked like this:
"I would like to connect to my inner joy and to rekindle a very happy relationship with Brenda. We are currently having a month out to have a think about whether there is a way for us to be together and both be happy – so, in fact, that is what I would like to create: a solution for us."

So his 'Intent' was formed as:
Intent: I call on the I AM Presence (Source/Universe/God) to direct my Higher Self that:
"I AM connected to my Spirit that is full of joy within me and that this brings further love, peace, understanding, trust and joy in my relationship between Brenda and Me, and we have found the best way to live happily together. I AM open to all support from within and outside me to bring this balance and harmony in my relationship. With this I AM getting a clear understanding of my relationship."
Months later, they are now together!

*****

So, now you can write down your Main Intent for the month. Please do not copy any of the goals above for yourself as it will not be personal to you. I have given examples only to show you how to first think of a goal and then form into an Intent using the I AM statements. You may feel inspired to use some lines from above and that's ok. For example, you may use some common statements like 'I AM grateful and full of joy' from the above examples.

You may use the Intents mentioned within examples throughout this book as your personal Intents too, only if you feel you are relating to them and benefit from affirming them regularly as well along with your personal Intents that you form for yourself as you read each chapter.

Remember these are words that you are not used to saying normally, and these may need deeper anchoring within your soul, so that they start clearing your old patterns as you speak out the new ones regularly. But let me emphasise again that repeating all the time is not essential unless you feel that you need to gain more faith and belief in this new way of thinking. I have seen that sometimes, it can take a few weeks but at times, it can happen in seconds just by realising the change that is needed. It is how quickly you say 'yes' and allow the 'change' or the 'healing', or the 'shift in thinking and feeling', to take place within you. Sometimes, it is just a decision. Every situation you work with can require different focus and time.

Congratulations once again on making the decision to jump-start on connecting to the New Exciting Powerful Self of You! Now that you are ready with your Main Intent, see you shortly with the Day 1 Lesson! You are welcome to check out the table at the end of this book, with some common day-to-day Intents for ready reference and use as and when required. You have the power to change everything in life.

Much Love,
Robin Bela

DAY 1
FEEL AND APPRECIATE YOUR VISION

If you can enjoy life in the present and simply 'be', you can then truly embrace your life. Creation of future begins by embracing the present fully. You are ready to be who you are meant to be right now, because you are already perfect at this very moment. In this acceptance, you stop the search and start living. You then come face to face with fears, and inevitably the truth, and become one with the real you. Things will come naturally, as you realise that you already have God-given peace, confidence, answers, and love within you. And that you deserve everything naturally as a child of God.

You may now remind yourself regularly of your 'Main Intent statement for your goal', which you had formed in the previous lesson. You can write it on the first page in your journal to remind yourself of it regularly, and do keep at least 5 empty pages to keep adding more Intents as we progress. In the remaining part of your journal, I expect that you will be writing your daily experiences in response to each Day's lesson. It is this process of focusing and reflecting on your daily experiences, which may lead you to discovering your 'blocks'. By 'blocks', I mean internal psychological barriers preventing your progress.

While writing your daily experiences, you may also be giving expression to your heart's desires, vision and intentions regarding the life you want, and making the first drafts of the Intents you choose to focus on. From these Intents, you may select the ones which have a bearing to or are important for the achievement of your Main Intent/Goal. You may decide to rewrite such Intents in the first 5 pages of your Journal as discussed earlier under Guidelines. All such Intents can be read regularly so that you remain focused on the changes you wish to start experiencing now in your life by appreciating your Intents through focused positive 'feelings' and 'vision'. This is the beginning of turning your goals into reality.

When you have the spark to create something, it is very important that you continue the process of achieving it from the very place where you first found your goal, which is your heart, and out of love! And definitely, we don't want any goals to come from a fearful, worrying mind, for that will only produce unhappy results. Instead, you have to 'love' the idea of having your goal achieved. You should 'feel' the joy in its creation. So, trust your heart to show you the next steps too. It's where your intuition comes from. In your Heart, you will always 'feel' or just 'know' what is right, and you will always 'feel' or just 'know' what is wrong too. For example, you might just feel uncomfortable when you make a wrong choice. I once heard someone say that his 'chest just feels tight' when he is uncomfortable with a situation or choice. It is how you might feel too when you are not connected to your heart centre and are not doing what your Heart wants, maybe you are perhaps not devoting more time for self etc.

Your job for today is to keep going deeper into your Heart to 'feel' and 'dream' and comprehend how it 'feels' to have your 'dream as a reality'. I would like you to appreciate how wonderful your goal is, to 'feel' and 'appreciate' its completion in your Heart, and not just say or think about it. As you focus on this inner work, whatever you are feeling, you will soon start radiating that on the outside as well. For example, seeing yourself in positive light brings you across in others' eyes positively too. If you feel content and peaceful within, you are reflecting out your inner radiance naturally.

There is a thin line between 'desperately wanting' something and 'simply Intending' in a focused way. In the first instance, you get too attached to the outcome mainly because you give your power away to the outcome, and as a result, you just don't live your present moment. You are then in the energy of 'lack' as you remain focused on what you lack. Please appreciate that 'desperately wanting' would be based on the 'fear' that you may not get there. Anything done out of fear, will not lead to the best result, as it will only create a fear-ridden or negative reality. And in the second instance of 'simply Intending', you actually already accept and live as if you are where you want to be. You trust that you will get all you Ask for as you have a wonderful, productive 'today'. So, the key to happy outcomes is to enjoy this moment and also feel and visualise a successful future with excitement, and without any doubt. You become quite carefree and relaxed in this process.

There is a certain amount of Asking, surrender and faith that is needed in the process of Intending too. Do not wait for your perfect life to start, decide that it starts now! Feel and know that you are that new person already! **The only difference between a person who has reached somewhere and the one who remains where he or she presently exists, is in the change of their attitude to the way they think about themselves, and in the faith that they deserve to 'Ask' and to 'receive' from Universe, naturally.**

And why is it important to 'feel and appreciate' your vision?

Only if you can imagine, feel and appreciate something in this moment can you really achieve it later. If you cannot imagine it, you still believe that it's not real or possible. It's ok if in the beginning it feels as though you are dreaming and is not real. Just keep Intending, feeling and seeing the joy of having it. It doesn't have to be for hours, instead give yourself frequent reminders, even if it's just for a few seconds each time, but perhaps 3 to 5 times a day. This is a great way of making your new Intents feel more believable and real. An example of this would be whenever you get doubts about achieving your goal, tell yourself to stay positive and simply exhale out your worries as you breathe, reminding yourself of the Intent you are reading daily. Remember, 'imagination' is the key, the seed to any creation.

YOUR WORK TODAY

1. I have mentioned this exercise to you previously: 'Place one hand on your Heart and Ask your Heart about your Intent.' I would like you to place your

hand again on your Heart and ask yourself the questions in the next paragraph. And when you do so, I want you to speak it aloud and write it down so that you do not lose the information. Then simply say, 'My Heart, this is the question...', and then follow it with, 'my Heart says...' The answer can flow as simply as 'a feeling', 'an image', 'just a knowing' or 'actual words'. Just be open to any channel by which you may receive the signs and messages. It may not even make sense immediately. Just note it down as well in your journal.

Answer all the questions below in the present tense, starting with 'I AM'. Initially you can write in any words you like, and later change them to positive I AM statements.

Here are the questions for you:
* How does it 'feel' to have what you wish to create in your life now?
* What are the benefits of having it in your life?
* Do you feel different? Do you look different?
* Is your environment different?
* How would you be as a person with this creation in your life? Would you change? For example, would you become more confident? Write down all you get as if it has already taken place. For example, I AM feeling confident in the way I look. Or I AM peaceful as I AM connected with my soul mate.

2. From today onwards, for a few minutes daily, I want you to appreciate the presence of your goal already there in your life and just say, for example, 'I appreciate that I AM always connected to the love of my life' or 'I AM appreciating the presence of money in my life always, and the beautiful relationship I have with it' etc. Appreciating and feeling the goal on a daily basis is very important in order for you to stay connected to it and to increasingly manifest it into your life. **When you read your daily Intents, just pause, appreciate and see how it feels exciting in your heart to experience it now. It is the energy of love that propels your dreams to reality!** You can imagine yourself in the future looking back as if you already have it. How does it feel when you do? Feel free to do this appreciation

exercise regularly or every day for a couple of minutes to keep your Intent strong. *Repeating what I said earlier*, the key to happy outcomes is to enjoy this moment and also feel and visualise a successful future with excitement, and without any doubt. And as you do so, you become carefree and relaxed.

3. Now based on the answers you get for the questions above, you can articulate your additions to your daily Intents by simply ensuring that these are written as if you have already achieved them, in accordance with the Guidelines given in the earlier chapter about creating Intent.

EXAMPLE : Pauline's answers to Day 1 work:

" * How does it 'feel' to have what you wish to create in your life now?
It feels great, feels free and light and I'm able to do anything.

* What are the benefits of having it in your life?
Benefits are manifold. I can do anything that I set my mind to, no doubts, and no fears.

* Do you feel different?
Feel more confident and stronger.

* Do you look different?
Taller. Happier. Smile more.

*Is your environment different?
It feels free, more creative, more open.

* How would you be as a person with this creation in your life? Would you change?
I would be a more fun-loving confident person, people would respond to that and it will be a more open two-way street in all of my relationships. I would feel happier in expressing my true feelings, confident in not hurting other people, as I'm hurting them more by not speaking in my old life."

Then I helped her formulate her I AM Statements, which she now reads along with her main Intent. This helped her to add more details or secondary Intents to her original Main Intent and make it even more real and believable. She is experiencing the result already in her body and mind by imagining, feeling and reaffirming them.

Intent: I AM calling on the I AM Presence (Source/Universe/God) to direct my Higher Self that:

I AM feeling great about myself.

I AM feeling the freedom.

I AM fearless in doing what my heart wants always.

I AM feeling the strength and confidence within me.

I AM feeling tall, happy and I'm smiling right now at myself!

I AM totally connected to my creativity.

I AM in an environment that allows me to feel free and creative.

I AM a fun loving person.

I AM accepted as I AM by people.

I AM connecting to people from my heart to their hearts.

I AM speaking from my heart and speak only from the place of love.

I AM forgiving myself for having hurt anyone.

I AM safe to speak authentically and peacefully, and it all comes from the heart, even if it is a disagreement. I AM staying honest to my feelings.

I AM peaceful about my past.

I AM full of joy and at peace as I create and build relationships around me.

I AM grateful for this.

***

Now, you can write your answers in your journal and form your new I AM Statements or secondary Intents that you wish to focus on, and put them under your Main Intent within the 5 empty pages you left in your journal in the beginning. Enjoy 'feeling and appreciating' your dream today. See you tomorrow!

Love,

Robin Bela

DAY 2
BREAKING PATTERNS THROUGH THE 'SOUL CLEARING TECHNIQUE' : PART 1 - COMING FACE TO FACE WITH FEARS AND CORE BELIEFS BLOCKING YOU

Welcome to DAY 2 of the 30-Day Programme

How are you doing today? I think by now, you will be getting a feel of how the Programme goes each day.

Today, I would like you to delve deep into identifying and understanding your real feelings about any internal blocks that you may be having towards achieving your goal. I would like you to ask yourself, "What is it that you fear most when you think about your goal or the Intents that you are creating?" I would like you to be real with your feelings and make sure that they do not remain buried somewhere deep down. Sometimes, to release the pain, you just have to feel some pain. Check if you are simply scared to acknowledge something because you are scared to face the truth or even failure? Really, no amount of Affirmations or Intents will work if you have some fears still hiding deep down within you, functioning as your core beliefs. Your Inner Self will simply reject unconsciously any new ideas that you try to accept, because it doesn't believe in them deep down!

The steps in the following paragraph can help you face and overcome your deep-rooted fears, and help you break away from old patterns. You can use this process anytime you feel that you are internally blocked to achieving something as you go through this Programme, and even later. This process is really about getting real about your goals and not living in some fantasy world about these. It is time to face your fears of not losing weight, getting a new relationship or job, or whatever is on your mind. You also need to go into the reasons for such fears, and later, look for solutions to eliminate them from your make-up.

We call this process Soul Clearing Technique because the fears/blocks are deeply seated in our subconscious, and often, in the unconscious realms of our being. This technique helps us reflect deeply within us to see why we are stuck in the same pattern repeatedly in our lives.

PART 1 OF THE SOUL CLEARING TECHNIQUE: COMING FACE TO FACE WITH FEARS:

1. Notice <u>what your fear/s might be for your goal</u>, and then see <u>where the fear/s is present in your body</u>. Have a dialogue with that part of the body.

You can think about what might be stopping you from connecting to your goals. Simply assume something if you are not sure what might be stopping you. For example, are you fearful that this is all new for you and you have never done this before? Or, since you are not getting someone's approval for your work, you're lacking the confidence to develop your business or idea? Or are you scared that you may fail and lose touch again with that spark you are connecting to? Or are you afraid to check your weight fearing you have put on weight again? It is important to stay real about your goals and face your fears and find solutions whatever the case might be. It is the process to get really honest with yourself and come face to face with all your fears. Sit with an open mind and heart for sometime, and simply breathe and allow the answers to come to you. Your mind and body are all interconnected. The fears/issues in your mind get reflected in your body.

Look or feel into your physical body with your eyes closed if needed, and try to see or feel where the fear maybe stuck within to move forward towards your goal. You may feel it actually physically present. Our body always stores unprocessed emotions within, and if not dealt with for long, may cause physical problems in the future. So, as you tune into your body, you may just feel your attention go somewhere, just take a guess. Notice if it is heavy there? Painful? Or simply have a feeling that something is there. <u>Now question that part of Body or Self for answers as: Why am I here? What is the message for me? Why am I blocking myself to move forward?</u>

2. Ask yourself and write 'why' till you find 'when' and 'where' it began first.

Then, I would like you to dig deeper into the root cause of 'why' you believe in these fears. Why are you lacking in confidence? May be because, as a child, you were told that you were not good enough? Try and pin-point the time this pattern began first for you. Keep asking 'why' to every answer you get, till you really know within your heart the root cause of fear, and when and where it began first. You will usually feel an energetic/emotional, or even a physical clearing in the body, as you acknowledge the fear. You will feel a sigh of relief, and experience an 'aha' moment! Unless you've done this process, you really haven't faced your true fear, which keeps recurring in your life in different forms. To complete the clearing, you may need to go through some breathing technique taught in the next chapter, Day 3. But for simplicity in understanding, we are only focusing on uncovering the root cause that is blocking you to move forward for now.

3. Write your new I AM statements to see yourself in the changed light.

As you come across these fears, I would like you to simply write them down and convert them into a positive I AM statement/s. For example, if your fear is, 'I am lacking in confidence', you may want to question why? And you may get the answer: 'Due to my appearance'. You would then change your I AM Statement into, "I AM confident about my appearance and accept and feel the beauty within and outside me. It just grows more and more, and I feel the love within my heart for me! This confidence reflects on to every sphere of my life." You would in this scenario start growing comfortable with the idea of looking at yourself with kindness and appreciation and make it a habit by saying your Intents daily or regularly. It would be your way of clearing the old pattern and reversing it. Along with this, you may also need some breathing work taught in Day 3 at least once for the old patterns to completely clear from your energy field and body. This would allow the new Intent/s to start sinking easily within your conscious mind.

4. Listen to your Heart for your answers.

If you feel you aren't getting the answers, place one hand on your Heart and ask your Heart the question you need the answer for. And then reply as 'My Heart says...' Heart is where really your Soul lives. All answers truly are there and never in the head. Head is where the ego lives because it analyses, over-thinks at times, and creates worries, fears and doubts. Heart is where peace comes from. Our main purpose in life is to start living through an open heart, which includes unconditional love and acceptance of Self and Others.

YOUR WORK TODAY

Think of all repeated fears and blocks that may come up as explained above with regard to your main Intent/Goal. Question 'why' as explained above in detail, and search for the root cause of your core limiting belief/s stopping you from reaching your goal. Then write in your journal a positive Intent/s to wipe it off as a limiting belief or a core pattern. Simply acknowledging a fear and being aware consciously, breathing as you observe, allows it to be released. We will do more of the clearing process tomorrow on the fears that you have listed. But today, let's just get the list of fears and delve deep into the reasons for them. You may notice that clearing has already begun or perhaps even taken place already as you do this exercise.

SOME EXAMPLES FROM THE PARTICIPANTS OF THIS PROGRAMME:

EXAMPLE 1: Emotional Healing – Fear of opening the heart to love.

Reena wrote about her fears: "My body felt numb when thinking about fears. I think it was because I was thinking about opening up my heart.' My heart is open' – just saying that, I feel the fear. My heart says, 'open up'. That is scary as I guess I have it all very controlled. I still feel I am sabotaging this as I am not making the time. "

Reena needs to dig further as to why and when she started feeling this way first and be open to releasing it. In the mean time with the information she sent, I helped Reena form her I AM statements as:

Intent: I AM calling on the I AM Presence (Source/Universe/God) to direct my Higher Self that:

I AM open in my heart.

I AM safe to open my heart to receive and give love.

I AM opening my heart to love myself and others more unconditionally.

I AM open to love.

I AM accepting love from others.

I AM open feeling the love of life.

I AM supported by life to receive all I need and I keep my heart open to receive.

I AM feeling love as I breathe in.

I AM gentle on myself with my spiritual growth.

EXAMPLE 2: Business - Fear of starting business

Kirsty wrote about her fears and these were then changed to I AM positive statements, as if already achieved in the present moment:

What I fear:

"I fear how hard I will have to work." It changed to - I AM working as much as is comfortable for me physically, emotionally and financially.

"I fear that people will not trust in me." It changed to - People like and trust me because I am living from my heart centre, which is full of love.

"I fear I will not earn enough money." It changed to - I AM earning the money I deserve for my excellent skills and for the time and intention I put in for work.

Where do my fears come from?:

"My family is scared to try new things career-wise and don't trust business.

My family worries about me not succeeding.

My family doesn't believe in me, they still treat me as a lost child."

Based on the above, there were more Intent statements for Kirsty to create and read daily as well:

Intent: I AM calling on the I AM Presence (Source/Universe/God) to direct my Higher Self that:

I AM compassionate about my family's concerns and I Intend/Pray, that they in time understand my work, but in the meantime I AM peaceful about it.

I AM good at creating a successful business due to clients' positive results and interaction with me, and I have a firm belief in my capabilities. I am confident in what I do.

I AM focusing on how I can help others and I know in return that Universe is taking care of my needs.

EXAMPLE 3: Self Confidence Issues - Fear of not connecting to your authentic powerful self.

Rohit wrote about his fears:

"My heart says the fear is that I will start on this goal and then a few months down the line, I'll go back to my usual ways and revert to old habits. The fear is that my opinions once voiced will be laughed at, that I can't hold an argument on a belief as my brain shuts down, and I don't have the confidence to back-up with any force. Being the youngest of 6 children, I've been treated as a young kid all my life, and I am still treated like that subconsciously by the family, and the fear is that I will just revert back to that position once I meet with them again. The fear is that I will become submissive again. I lack the confidence to go forward."

Rohit's I AM statements, which he Intends regularly, were formed as:
Intent: I AM calling on the I AM Presence (Source/Universe/God) to direct my Higher Self that:

I AM always kind and generous to myself and I AM joyous at every little step I take for my happiness.

I AM always joyful and loving in expressing my opinions, and it's always received joyfully, and with love.

I AM always speaking my truth, from my heart, and I know when it comes from that place of divine love, I AM able to stand-up for my truth.

I AM a mature adult who is responsible.

I AM connected to my true authentic self and with that I am truly always connected to my true power and confidence.

EXAMPLE 4: Relationship/Marriage – Fear of never being in a relationship and marriage:

Many times I get pages of written information from my clients, and then I help them write their Intents to help them focus in the right direction. So, briefly Lorraine had issues with trust in seeing herself and her partner in a marriage, and it stemmed from lack of value for herself in general, and for her appearance since her school days. So in order to feel deserving of being loved by someone, she needed to connect to first loving herself. Her I AM statements are:

Intent: I AM calling on the I AM Presence (Source/Universe/God) to direct my Higher Self that:

I AM happy and joyful within and I feel that in my heart.

I AM authentic to my feelings, and respect and do what I feel. I first give myself time before others, whenever I need to.

I AM respecting my energies and feelings, and acknowledge them.

I AM deserving of all pleasures like everyone else, to be happy, be married.

I AM always in my own energies and breathe out deeply and disconnect if any energies of others bother me.

I AM responsible for my life first, and for others I care and pray the best for them.

I AM at peace as I have forgiven the people involved in my past experience at school.

I AM accepting who I AM and the way I look and I AM appreciating that.

I AM accepted as I AM.

I AM beautiful and as I believe this more and more daily, it's what people around me feel and see too now.

I AM beautiful and attractive!

I AM loving myself.

I AM deserving of a loyal, loving partner, and I AM having one.

I AM blessed with love and peace in the relationship with my life partner.

I AM relaxing into this new-found peace to just accept happiness more and more. And that alone is my Soul's job, to accept and say yes.

EXAMPLE 5: Health and Healing

Anne wrote about her fear:

"There are 3 main fears that I feel are always there – I will list these and give you what I worked out to be the reason why:

1. I fear my cancer will return and stop my progress towards my goal of spiritual growth and healing work. WHY? Because it has in the past and it totally blocked my intuition.

2. I fear I do not have the energy for moving forward with healing and helping people. WHY? Because always for the past 5 years my energy is low, it is very easy for me to overdo things and be unable to function.

3. I fear I cannot trust my intuition for receiving messages – especially for others for doing intuitive healing and reading work. WHY – because whatever I do, I think it is my ego and I would give people (and myself) wrong messages."

So her I AM statements are:

Intent: I AM calling on the I AM Presence (Source/Universe/God) to direct my Higher Self that:

I AM always connected to my intuition no matter what, as it always comes from the connection to the Heart.

I AM connected to a state of love and Divine in my Heart and this allows me to stay peaceful, centred, mindful and intuitive.

I AM strong, healthy and radiant as ever, easily and effortlessly.

I AM who I believe to be and I now know I AM in perfect health always.

I AM always aware of my level of strength and work around it.

I AM having strong boundaries and know when to say 'No', and do only what is comfortable for me.

I AM now with fully revitalised strength and energy and I know it just keeps getting better and I AM so excited to see my new self feeling so good, like never before.

I AM led to all the things that strengthen me and keep me in my best energies (For this, you can pause to see if you get any message right away, else note during the days in a pad).

Also, I asked Anne, "I would like you to question yourself more about why you fear the cancer will return, and why do you fear cancer and affirm instead 'I AM in complete good health' and anything else you pick up in answering the 'why' should be changed to positive form and include clearing from Day 3."

In response to that, Anne sent me the message on email:

"I did make some progress with my cancer fear. Firstly was the obvious and more recent fact that it simply had returned a second time - but I realised the reason this affected me so badly was the fact that at the time I was feeling happy and well and it never occurred to me that it would return and, it did! However, going deeper into this when I was meditating I realised that all of my adult life - going back 40 years every time life was good something bad always happened and as the years went by I think I always expected the good times to end with bad things happening - and of course - it always did. Anyway, I have breathed this through (using Day 3 technique) and I feel that this is under control now.

I am finding the Intentions very powerful, and it all feels very positive for me. A lot of the things you talk about I am already doing from your previous mentoring over the past few years."

I am happy to say today Anne is cancer free, and has trained under me and is practising as a therapist and a teacher too.

***

I would like to impress upon you again to look at this book as a workbook to bring in change for yourself. When you put new Intents into writing, you are bringing in change for yourself consciously and deliberately. Else, reading through the book, might be interesting, but would simply remain at a theoretical level. One of the participants just read through the Programme and she came back to me saying how overwhelmed she felt after completing it, as she realised all the changes that she needed to make in life. When you complete the Programmme, you should also have taken action steps and completed the process of change or be in the process of confidently moving forward. So I asked her if she did any of the Soul Clearing work or wrote down any Intents for herself. She told me, she never picked up the pen and paper or gave herself the quiet space to do the Soul Clearing work as she was travelling, and was only able to read emails, but regrets that now. She is looking at it again in detail.

Please do allow yourself the luxury of time and space, especially in the beginning chapters of Soul Clearing Technique. And if you feel, you are struggling to find time and space to do this, simply start Intending regularly:

'I AM having all the time and space easily and effortlessly to complete this book in the most relaxed way, and I AM enjoying the process with excitement of feeling the new changes step-by-step. As I Intend from within, the reality is created outside for me.'

Tomorrow, I will be showing you how to release the fears you discovered today even further, as needed. And remember to keep your 'Vision' and 'Feeling' of having your Intent as already achieved in your Heart. Keep writing your daily experiences in your journal. And we will connect again tomorrow!

Love,
Robin Bela

DAY 3
BREAKING PATTERNS THROUGH THE 'SOUL CLEARING TECHNIQUE' : PART 2 - HEALING AND CLEARING THE FEARS OR THE CORE BELIEFS

Welcome to DAY 3 of the 30-Day Programme

Soul Clearing Technique is identifying fears or core beliefs creating repeated unwanted or negative patterns blocking your progress in life. And then, with focused breath and Intention, releasing the identified fears and beliefs till you feel at peace and relaxed in heart, mind and body.

I would like to suggest that Day 2 and Day 3 are perhaps the most challenging topics of this Programme. So please take your time with them.

Today, I should like you to go through the list of fears you came up with in your yesterday's exercise, and keep it alongside the re-framed Intents, in front of you. In Part 2 of the work for the Soul Clearing Technique, I want to talk about consciously facing your fears and letting them go. You may feel that you have already cleared your fears after yesterday's work. And it is quite possible, you have. You are welcome to go through the exercise in this chapter, and see if any further clearing might be needed. Usually, deep-rooted fears that have been repeatedly surfacing in your life, may require Part 2 of the Soul Clearing Technique.

Most of us have not cleared deep-buried insecurities because we are afraid to 'feel' the fear in them, and often, simply ignore them or don't like to talk about them. I am telling you here today that the only way to clear them is to allow yourself to 'feel them and come face to face with them'. Allow the feelings to flow through you like a river, through breathing, rather than holding onto those feelings. This is how your emotional being can process and create the space for your new goals and Intents to germinate unhindered and easily.

Breath is the natural and most ancient powerful healing technique given to us by nature/God. When we are in fear, we hold our breath! The only way to allow fears and undesirable core beliefs to be processed and released is to face them, feel and breathe through them. You will be learning below as to how to do it, and you will find that it's not that scary or difficult at all. In fact, you start feeling better the instant you acknowledge your fears and are ready to release them. It's like your energies would shift to an 'aha' moment, and frankly, it would be quite a relief that you are at last letting it go!

PART 2 OF THE SOUL CLEARING TECHNIQUE: THE BREATH-CLEARING PROCESS TO LET GO!

Soul Clearing Technique Part 2 is focused breathing with the intention to release the identified fears till we feel peaceful and lighter in heart and/or body. The technique consists of the following 4 steps, which you may first read carefully before beginning to apply these to clear your fears or undesirable core beliefs that may be blocking your progress:

1. State what you are clearing in your body and mind and affirm the positive Intent, thereafter.

To start the Soul Clearing Technique, remember where you felt the fear blocked in your body during yesterday's work, and put your awareness there, and notice how it feels, perhaps heavy with fear about moving forward, or just some nervousness, or feeling the sense of procrastination, or just some emotions, as you do this process. Now I would like you to breathe in specifically with the intention of clearing and letting go the fear or the undesirable core belief holding you back from achieving your goal, e.g., I am letting go: 'Fear of speaking my truth out of guilt of hurting the other person.' You will then also speak out your specific Intent with the positive assertion after speaking out what you are clearing, e.g., 'I AM speaking my truth always through peaceful means where all understand the truth.' Say it all together.

2. Breathe for a few minutes with the intention to clear an undesirable core belief until you feel peaceful and relaxed about it in mind, heart and body.

Start your breathing slowly as you are processing 'letting go' and 'change of thinking and emotions', for what you have intended in Step 1. Breathe normally in and out through the nose, and if you feel like, you can exhale out through the mouth at times. Through your Intention and breath, you can clear toxic negative energies in your energy field and body. You can choose to remind yourself, what it is that you are focusing on to clear at every inhalation, or when you feel like deepening the clearing work as you continue to breathe in and out.

As mentioned earlier, just allow the feelings to flow through you like a river, through breathing, rather than holding onto those feelings. Breathing is a natural God given process to let go of emotions and stress. When you just observe a problem and breathe through it by simply being brave enough to feel it, you have started clearing it. We can deepen the process by focusing on it more through some continuous breathing.

You would do the breathing for a few minutes for each goal. You can do it for a longer or shorter period, as needed, but you cannot really estimate the time it may take before you start; you will know as you go along when to stop. Normally, the moment you feel relaxed and peaceful about the situation in heart, mind and body, you would stop. In fact, your whole intention is to "clear" as soon as possible, maybe a minute is all you need. Your breath may feel heavier when you start, or perhaps you may have shorter or longer breaths, and sometimes, may feel the breaths feel warm too. Or you may notice some heaviness in a part of your body, e.g., your abdomen may tighten etc. Don't try to control it; just go with the flow. It is all a natural clearing process. Clearing process at times can connect you back to your old grief, pain, and trauma. So be patient, if it needs time. You then continue to breathe till it feels lighter and comfortable in the body or simply feels peaceful and positive in heart. That is how you know when your clearing is complete.

3. Time is not a constraint. Stay focused on fears already being cleared and strongly feel the new positive self to expedite the clearing.

You can help expedite this clearing process by staying focused on 'fears as already cleared' and strongly feeling the new positive self. You don't have to get entangled in any play of emotions, of 'why' and 'who' etc., as that will prolong the process. <u>The quicker you let go, or forgive and move to positive thoughts/Intents about the situation, the better</u>. So just observe the breath, and focus on working on clearing those fears. It's not at all important to shed tears, but if tears do come, it's a natural clearing process. Just allow them to flow for that moment, and then continue to focus on breathing, on your breath becoming peaceful and relaxed.

And please remember, time is never a constraint in the Process. This process can generally be done within seconds or a few minutes, but may take longer in certain cases. Sometimes, our willingness or perception on how quickly we can do it, and like to move forward to the new way of thinking, also can help speed up the process of clearing the pattern. But if you feel that your case requires more time to release and settle, please be gentle with yourself and respect that.

4. Asking The Universal Life Force Light/Universe/God/Divine Helpers' Support, if you like.

To get a focused awareness to your inner work, you may do this visualisation exercise before Step 1, <u>if you like</u> - In general, you can imagine the Universal Life Force as white light coming from Universe/Source from top of your head towards your heart and then Universal Life Force light coming from Earth to your feet and reaching your heart. Imagine the light engulf you and getting larger than you and your house, Country and the Earth. You may feel

46

very light and energised in mind and body with this exercise. You cannot go wrong, as the more often you do it, you would just feel good. In that expanded state of consciousness, if you Intend the clearing, in my experience, it will be very deep. The whole process, each time as you do, should take up to 10 seconds to a minute at the most. It is the Intention to be in the expanded awareness, that we reach there quicker. You may use this visualisation exercise at anytime even otherwise, to feel energised and balanced.

I always find great support in healing and clearing work for myself when I invite Divine helpers to oversee my healing process. You are welcome to call upon God or Divine helpers to be with you during this process. I personally like to call upon Angels specially Archangel Michael to clear fears and Archangel Raphael for healing work. Angels are messengers of God and are not connected to any particular religion. They are here to help you for anything you Ask. The only requirement is that you 'Ask' and it doesn't matter how you Ask or in what words you Ask. Archangel Raphael is particularly the Angel for healing and has green emerald light. Just breathing into their light can be additional support when you are working on some clearing. Also, Archangel Michael helps remove old fears, cut unhealthy cords with people and situations, and offers protection. Michael's colour is purple. To connect to any Angel, you just say the name or visualise their colour in and around you as you breathe.

***

You could use this Soul Clearing technique also to question 'why' you are not **healing anything specific in body or emotions.** Notice where you are feeling the presence of a block in your body. And breathe through it, while affirming the well-being for yourself in its place. Do the breath clearing work until you feel lighter physically. And then later, continue to say the positive Intent of being healed, regularly, as needed.

YOUR WORK TODAY

1. Clear all your fear/s with the above Soul Clearing Part 2 exercise. You may ask, how do I know if I have undesirable/negative recurring core beliefs related to my Intents that I wish to work on now or anytime in the future? You will know this if you feel that what you are saying every day as your Intent, still seems fake and you are resisting moving forward. That is when you would begin asking 'why' as explained in Day 2, and see where and when this recurring pattern began in your life first. You would then clear it with breath and Intent work daily in the manner explained above. You may see the summary of all steps for Day 2 and 3 together at the end of this chapter.

2. You must now regularly read the Intents formed in Day 2, after the Day 3 clearing work. No amount of Intent and Affirmations would have worked until you had accepted and let go of your fears completely. Till this clearing was done, you may have felt that the new Intents were fake. Now you should consciously start feeling the new beliefs sink in and anchor better within you, as you read and affirm your Intents, regularly.

You may need to work on today's exercise again if you have more fears to clear. For me, it has become a habit to keep clearing such negative patterns on a regular basis whenever I notice I am fearful of anything, which is blocking the free flow of energies in my body and obstructing my progress in any field.

EXAMPLES AND EXPERIENCES OF SOME OF THE PARTICIPANTS:

"In my breathing exercises, I am doing better, sometimes my mind shows me chapters of my life that are done, and don't let me re-concentrate. The fear is showing less during my exercises on breathing. When they appear I affirm, I can do it and it's my turn to be very happy. My heart says go go go, don't let the fear appear again."
[Simon]

48

"I find it hard to breathe out by the mouth and feel more comfortable with breathing in and out by the nose. Is that all right? This breathing exercise makes me dizzy. I feel kind of headache shortly after I've started to breathe and I do have some pain on my left side, at the bottom of my left breast. I tried to think those feelings were the expression of the clearing process that my breath will carry them out of me, but they stick to me all along. I feel more comfortable if I lay down and breathe."
[Susan]

My reply to Susan was:

"Yes breathing is causing healing within. After all, the Day 3 work is about clearing some deep-rooted issues. So feel free to lie down if it's tiring you. Being out in fresh air will help you strengthen your lungs. Also, do drink water a lot and whenever you feel dizzy. Doing Meditation (as taught later in Day 5) simply without the need to clear any issue will also strengthen your energy field further. You may be used to holding your breath and not doing deep breath work. You will be strengthened as you keep working on yourself slowly. And you needn't keep breathing through mouth. It's good to simply exhale a few times out of mouth for Intending a deeper clearing and then you can just breathe through the nose."

"I have done this exercise and have found that by changing my fears to a positive mantra, it feels so empowering and makes the fear seem insignificant. I am going to do more of this exercise over the next few days."
[Mary]

"The fear clearing was good. I find myself looking at people and a voice in my head telling me I am as important as them, equal, not inferior in anyway and that is really good!"
[Olivia]

***

SUMMARY IN 5 STEPS OF THE SOUL CLEARING TECHNIQUE *(DAYS 2 and 3)*:

STEP 1: IDENTITY FEARS/BLOCKS AND DEEP-ROOTED REASONS BEHIND, BY **ASKING 'WHY'**, TILL YOU REACH THE ORIGIN PERHAPS, OR GET A BIGGER PICTURE.

STEP 2: WRITE THE POSITIVE INTENTS FOR ALL FEARS DISCOVERED.

STEP 3: CLEAR THE FEARS THROUGH BREATH **UNTIL YOU FEEL PEACEFUL** IN MIND AND BODY ABOUT THE SITUATION BY SIMPLY INTENDING. YOU MAY LIKE TO CONNECT TO THE UNIVERSAL LIFE FORCE LIGHT AND ALSO CALL ON SUPPORT FROM GOD/UNIVERSE/ GUIDES/ANGELS, IF YOU PLEASE.

STEP 4: FIRMLY AFFIRM THE CORRESPONDING POSITIVE INTENT OF WHAT YOU JUST CLEARED.

STEP 5: PLANT SEEDS OF NEW INTENTS AFTER CLEARING FEARS, BY READING THE POSITIVE INTENTS DAILY OR REGULARLY AS NEEDED.

Anytime you feel you may be still stuck about your new Intents, go back to asking 'Why', and repeat the whole process.

You will need to revisit Day 2 and Day 3 chapters throughout this Programme, as you would most likely want to clear any blocks, as you notice them, as you read each chapter and form new Intents.

Have a wonderful healing day. Keep working with new additional Intents. Speak to you tomorrow!

Love,
Robin Bela

DAY 4
BECOMING AUTHENTIC :
CREATING THE RIGHT RELATIONSHIP WITH
EVERYTHING IN LIFE

Welcome to DAY 4 of the 30-Day Programme

If you consciously Intend to connect to the energy of trust, love and peace within you, your outer experiences will naturally start to reflect these energies. I am suggesting, that instead of trying to make yourself feel good, loved and powerful, by pulling in artificial energies from 'outside' you, most likely from others, you should instead search inside yourself for these energies. For instance, looking for power, love, peace and joy outside you from others, creates inter-dependency in relationships, when instead, relationships should just be about sharing love and joy, rather than being a reflection of your insecurities.

Feeling 'insecure' within, can affect the way money and abundance flow into your life, and also, feeling 'not good enough', can affect your progress at work. The power within comes, when you let go of the fearful reasons of being connected to some things in life, for support, for protection, to make you feel important and needed. It may mean clearing fear-based or un-authentic relationships, experiencing unsafe phases in life, but that is how you begin rebuilding the trust and your true power from within, in yourself. To get any relationship right, the relationship with 'self' first needs a check, because all relationships outside you, are really a reflection of your happy self or your insecurities.

I was once watching a cookery show, when an Italian cook was learning some traditional secret recipes from an old Italian couple. The man in the couple was later asked to explain the secret of their happy marriage. He pointed his finger upwards, indicating God, and said that when things go wrong in their relationship, one which has been full of love for more than 20

51

odd years, he looks within himself to see what's missing, rather than searching for reasons outside.

It's important that you create the relationship with self, out of love and compassion, first of all. How do you see yourself? Do you feel you are important enough? Do you respect yourself, and love the way you live and look? If you don't believe in yourself, how do you expect someone else to do so? Relationships with others should be about unconditional love, and should not be dependent upon any 'conditions', or on balancing your insecurities, such as, because 'he's got money' or 'she's taking care of you' etc, because any day, if he or she loses the aspect on which you are depending, you will simply lose interest in the relationship. Or perhaps, if one day, you have healed the issue, which was a condition of your love, you may discover that the so-called love interest is gone too. When that happens, you will feel that you are trapped in a wrong relationship. It is, therefore, very important to become authentic in your relationships.

You are also required to be honest about your career. Are you happy there, or are you bored? And what's your relationship with money like? Do you fear it? How can anything you fear come to you? You have to love it like a family member or better still, like a friend or even lover whom you entirely trust! If you focus on bad relationship with money, all the time, by making statements as, 'I am always short of money', 'I will never be rich' etc, then that is exactly what you will attract. Just as for developing any relationship, you need to show love, you need to feel with love and gratitude, of how joy in life increases with more money. Money should excite you for all the things it brings to you, and can bring to you. You will thus be showing love and appreciation for money in your life. But if you focus on fear of how life would be if you did not have money, you are literally disconnecting the love energy between you and Money energy.

I have also seen many people having guilt in receiving money, as for some reason, they associate it with sin or wrongdoing, or believe that it is not ethically correct or spiritual. Many people feel shy to ask for money even for the work they have done! It is just that they are not used to asking, and this usually stems from lack of self-worth. There is nothing to feel guilty about legitimately acquired money.

In any job, self employment or salaried, it is always important to receive pay in proportion to the quality and quantity of time and work that you put in, else you will not be happy with 'Money' in your life and will, in general, remain dissatisfied. If you feel you are getting less than you deserve in return for your work, it is important to start focusing on Asking for more from your employer or clients, and you can start by asking Universe/God through your Intents, to help you achieve that first. It is possible that you will start stepping up to improving your skills at work, or simply voice out your needs, if that alone is needed. All you do is, Ask Universe, just state what you want and don't offer the road-map to God/Universe through your I AM statements on how you should get it. Just leave the 'How' and simply 'Ask' with gratitude as if already achieved, and just focus on the Intent. As you do that, Universe starts connecting you to the best options and opportunities around you naturally.

I would like to share My Story to help you understand the journey to authenticity in all areas of My Life:
I have had to experience all this myself, to learn to be authentic in all areas of my life, I had to break all my old patterns. I have changed myself and my image to such an extent, that people are now saying that I look years younger and happier. I lost about 20 kilos/3 stones of body weight in less than a year. I also separated from my ex-husband after some years of being with him, once I realised that I was with him simply because of a feeling of guilt, out of fear of hurting him and to feed my own insecurities. I later realised, that he also had his own reasons. I am glad that we both had the courage to face the truth, and to understand that we were nothing more than friends, and had made a mistake.

In my career, I was authentic from quite an early age. I am an MBA/Post-Graduate and have worked in different Multi National Companies but in my early 20s, I left a so-called lucrative job, and all those career dreams of the ego, to instead follow my heart, and become an Energy Therapist, Coach and Teacher. It has been a shock for the people around me, each time I have made an authentic decision in my life. But I have really learnt that true happiness comes only when you are true and honest with your feelings, and the others around you are also happier when they see you happy and doing well. Only then will you be truly powerful from within.

I have also learnt that we don't necessarily need to look for security in a regular monthly salary. That is a fear-based concept which didn't even exist a few hundred years ago. We used to have such systems as barter, and people were usually doing skilled work, labour or work in the fields. And no one worried about where the money would come from next month. They never doubted that they could eat today from the work they did 'today', that they might not be able to do it again 'tomorrow'. When we make a fear-based living, our relationship with Money is also fear-based and not wholesome or healthy.

I am always checking my Heart to remain authentic for everything in life, and I keep questioning it for all the important decisions in my life. **I would like you also to cultivate this habit, to be honest to Self, and not do anything because you 'should', but rather because you 'want' to. That is how you will learn to be authentic. When you follow the path of authenticity, you can break all unwanted patterns in your life naturally.**

My journey to becoming authentic to myself first started when I was at school in India. In High School, I took up subjects which were wrong for me - i.e. Science and Mathematics. In the culture and environment in which I was living, there is pressure to pursue these subjects. Parents want their children to become Engineers or Doctors so that they get lucrative job opportunities. Arts subjects are looked down upon these days in India, which may not be the case in many western countries. The emphasis should be on good education according to the aptitude of the child, which unfortunately doesn't happen. Pursuing such studies just out of societal pressures is not being authentic. Society is also compromising with authenticity and true education for the wholesome development of a child when it shows such discrimination in importance and disproportionate emoluments in different fields of endeavour. So when I took the wrong subjects to study, I went into depression, as I just felt suffocated and unhappy. My parents couldn't understand what was going on with me and neither could I! My ego head had listened to peers and chosen the wrong subjects, but my heart and soul knew it was wrong and my whole being was in a state of inner conflict. I was depressed and my soul was literally bored and suffocated as though I was in prison. Being a teenager was a very tough period in my life. I remember many times I just wanted to be dead as I felt so unhappy. Education is taken very seriously where I grew up and children are put under a lot of pressure. I would often hear of students' suicides; if you don't score high enough, it's like the end of your career prospects. Pretty scary for young minds!

I was not authentic to myself at all then. And when that happens, for me, my voice stops coming out of my throat. I always feel my throat choking, even now, when I am not happy doing something. If I am not feeling true to myself, the signs show first of all physically in my body. Over the years, I usually react by feelings in my throat, knees, legs, back and feet. I literally don't want to move physically when I don't like something and if I did move, I would trip and fall all the time. Later, when I was in my 20s, I suffered a second knee dislocation: the first happened when I was 13. It had nothing to do with my fitness or health; I was always in sports and at one point was even the captain of my school basketball team. Even today when I am not listening to my heart, my knee will start to feel uncomfortable. And I use this discomfort as a compass to my inner feelings. I listen to my body, to all its aches and pains. It has always got a message for me, and usually, this helps me heal my physical issues indirectly. I just speak to my heart, as I explained to you earlier. The habit of keeping a regular journal helps you to stay in touch with the inner voice that you usually cannot easily hear.

During my teenage period, I also saw and felt how people told lies routinely, and I feel this is at the root of the corruption afflicting our societies. When you are not true to the people you work with, when you don't do your work properly and honestly, you have to lie and use money to gain influence. That's when you become unauthentic not just with Self and others but also with Money, so all your relationships are no longer about love and truth but about dishonesty and manipulation! I was seeing many people around me as not authentic to themselves and their relationships. I could see people I knew lying at my face, whilst deep down, the truth was very different. I could easily pick that up! It really made my teenage period extremely confusing. I was very intuitive, something which people around me could not understand and that I myself had no way of explaining! I was seeing people around me totally unauthentic and I couldn't digest it. Today I understand much better and know how to accept my sensitivity as a gift and to use it for greater good and power.

Later, in College, I took up the subjects for study that I liked, and totally recovered my Spirit! One of my teachers from school came to this College and happened to see me. I remember she said, she couldn't recognise me and was so happy to see me looking so well. I looked like a different person. I told her I was studying what I enjoyed. I even got "Best Outgoing Student Award" when I graduated from the College. I had briefly connected to my power at that point, but I lost it again when I tried to fit in jobs I wasn't supposed to be doing and then relationships! I was always following my ego head which was telling me what was right and acceptable on a CV or by society and people around, rather than listening to my heart, perhaps out of pressure to please or to be accepted! I realised the hard way that it is so very important to stay authentic in every single moment of our lives!

The question of authenticity also has a strong bearing to our commitment to improving our society and environment. How much are we really helping deserving causes, or are we merely talking about what's wrong and doing nothing about it? Why is it that when so much education is given to women in countries such as India, they still have no freedom to be really empowered, and rather, have to walk in fear of men who don't respect women, and then we hear horrific stories of rape. How authentic really is the society in offering equality to men and women right now? It starts from teaching young boys to respect and be kind to women, by parents and schools. Unfortunately, the awareness to do so, is missing in some environments still. It starts by changing simple old cultural patterns that do not serve this new age. For example, I have seen in India, that when there is a choice of man or woman to sit at a table for dinner at home, the man sits and the woman is standing. And I have experienced this myself and clearly remember an incident recently when a young boy I know, of about 18 years of age, takes my seat just when I was about to sit, and quite authoritatively too. This behaviour in the west would be shocking as the women are given seats first. Sometimes, we need to be conscious of little things as this, to bring change in a society as a whole, and that is the real education needed for such issues. But it is up to us how we stay authentic to offering our voice to such issues, and peacefully of course. I talk about how change needs to be peaceful and never dramatic in my later chapters. It starts from each home and it is really up to each one of us to begin being conscious of this.

YOUR WORK TODAY

Check with your heart by placing one hand on it and see how honest you are with the following topics. Write them down in your journal for today.

1. *Loving Youself?* - Your Body, Your Mind and Your Spirit? - How do you see yourself in looks, intelligence, confidence etc? Would you be able to say you love yourself unconditionally? Do you respect yourself in every way? Is any part of your body catching your attention through aches and pains? If that is so, question your Heart and that part of the body, why is it aching? Write it in your journal and see where it leads you.

2. *Loving all the important Relationships you have in life unconditionally?* - Do you need people around you for a reason such as gaining attention etc., other than just sharing love and joy? Are they there because you like pleasing people and can't say no, or are you expecting more from a relationship than you should, e.g., need a person to call you every other day to make you feel

secure? Check yourself honestly. Are your relationships based on conditional love rather than unconditional? Are you honest and equal in all your relationships?

3. *Loving your Career?* - If money wasn't the issue, would you be in your current job? If not, what would it be? What's stopping you? Perhaps you would like to do more in your current job, but have not realised it, or rather Intended for it. Or is it just the 'How' process that is scaring you, and stopping you from thinking about it? **To Intend, there is no rule to know the 'how'.** Our work should revolve around our passion for something that we love, and doing useful service, which is something satisfying and wonderful for us and others.

4. *Loving Money?* - You cannot feel safe in building anything new, if you don't feel supported enough for your basic needs. So it's crucial to get your relationship with money right. If money were an individual, would you love and trust it and feel comfortable? Or would you fear it? A relationship with Money is like any other relationship you have with people who are important and close to you. So it's a good idea to visualise Money as a person, someone whom you love.

There is an obvious need to create an authentic relationship with Money. What are you not asking or giving to Money in the relationship? What are your feelings about Money? Do you fear it, hate it, or are scared of it, or are you trying to please Money, manipulate Money for wrongdoings? Or is it that you feel guilty being connected to Money? If so, ask yourself 'why' and 'when' and 'where' did it begin first for you? You need to respect, value, love and have a good understanding with Money, and trust that all you ask from Money is received.

Speak to the presence of Money as a Friend, on a regular basis and literally make friends and feel the love in your heart. This relationship, like any other, requires clear understanding of your needs, as well as trust and honesty. Speak about your needs through your Heart, by placing your hand on it and feel the presence of Money. You can write the the messages you get from Money by writing or saying that Money says '...'. Just like human relationships, we have got to take care of the relationship with Money consciously. Today, you are beginning to think differently about Money. The topic of Money would be covered again, in greater detail in a later chapter, to take you to the next steps in your relationship with it.

***

Observe where your relationship is not right in all areas of your life. Ask yourself 'why' and 'when' and 'where' did it begin first for you? You can fix it by Intending to change the way you think, through forming your Intents, reading and speaking the same. Feel the love in your heart and focus on building a loyal and loving relationship with Self, Other People, Career and Money. Perhaps, you need to forgive the past incidents. So please use the DAY 3 Soul Clearing Technique on breathing out until you feel lighter about the issue, and by forming positive I AM Statements and focusing on them. And please read them often, so that you can bring about the change you need and desire. You may add important Intents in the 5 pages left empty at the beginning of your journal.

So if you see that you have been unauthentic about any aspects in life, be courageous enough to start seeing the truth and don't worry about 'how to change'. Keep looking for guidance on a regular basis through Soul Clearing Technique and take little steps to improve or change. Use the I AM Statements to bring about the change within you that you desire, and soon it will start reflecting outside into your reality.

If your relationship with any of the above aspects of Self, Others, Career and Money is not right, then it can affect anything else you want to bring into your life. It can create blocks to the goal you are working towards right now. So today, I should like you to become authentic about yourself and your life.

EXAMPLES OF SOME PARTICIPANTS OF WHAT THEY WROTE IN THEIR JOURNAL:

EXAMPLE 1 - Julie Wrote:
"About Me -
I fear that -
No one likes me
People are making fun of me
Feeling misunderstood, different, strange, weak and outcast and this comes from some experiences I had at school.

Relationships -
I am not being authentic at times in my relationship; I fear my partner is leaving me.

Career and Money -
I am not confident in my ability to have a business. Not organised yet. Everything seems a bit scattered. I need to get focused but it is difficult looking after my baby on my own and plus she is still breast feeding, really clinging to me. I barely have any energy to think about anything else or do anything. I want to get really focused. I know I need to let money go that I hold so tightly, to set up my business."

Briefly, my reply was: *"That's great Julie. Some of the I AM statements you need to work with are below. Please use Day 2 exercise to dig deeper into why you feel your partner is leaving or for other related fears you may feel the need to work on. Then please use Day 3 breathing exercise for these as well to release your blocks. And Intend the I AM statements mentioned below that are formed based on your blocks and fears discovered by yourself.*

Intent: I AM calling on the I AM Presence (Source/Universe/God) to direct my Higher Self that:
I AM accepting myself as I AM.
I AM accepted by people as I AM.

I AM easily understood by everyone.

I AM confident and strong within.

I AM loving myself unconditionally and others reciprocate the same.

I AM in unconditional love with my partner and focus only on sharing love and enjoying that.

I AM loved.

I AM connecting to people through heart and so I AM safe and strong as I give and receive love.

I AM connected to people around authentically from the heart. I AM who I AM.

I AM living in the moment.

I AM having the right focus on my work daily and prioritise each morning all the important things I need to do.

I AM having plenty of time and energy for all I need to do for my business.

I AM confident in getting my business running.

I AM having a beautiful relationship with Money. He/She loves me and takes care of me unconditionally. We have conversations and He's/She's always there with me. (Put one hand on heart and ask Money any questions and talk to it like you would do to a lover or a close trusted friend)."

I AM respecting Money.

I AM focusing only on service and joy in what I do.

I AM trusting Money.

I AM having an authentic relationship with Money where we are honest to each other about our needs.

EXAMPLE 2 - Lorita wrote:

"Loving me? Do I love myself?

I don't love my body and I am not confident with this body. I was hurt when I was a little girl. Children aren't kind to one another. I wasn't fat but just plump and already had some breast. It was really hard for me to accept this body and I failed to do so, facing others' looks and remarks. When I lost 5kgs, I felt much better but still wasn't confident and couldn't, up to now, be proud of my body, my feminine curves. But I love myself inside. I love the person I've become. My life has changed a lot since my first trip to Ladakh where I have found lots of answers about spirituality. Many people see me as always a peaceful person. That's a nice compliment but it's not the truth. The truth is I keep all my feelings inside so that on the outside all that appears is peace. Step by step, year by year, I've been working on myself. Since 2005, I do want my life to be the life I want, I do want to be free from my painful emotions. I know I'm on the right pathway to what I want in my life. I just need to be guided and be given some landmarks. This, I have found through my Buddhist friend's teachings as well as you, Robin, since 2008. You crossed my path for the benefit of my future life. What's inside me: good heart, fast brain, naivety sometimes, willing heart.

Loving relationship?
Relationships are always complicated for me. I can't find the right balance. My relationship with my dad has been very painful, hurting and I've only just started to be fine with him. Mum: I love her even though we have arguments sometimes. I always had a good relationship with my big brother. It was harder with my little brother with whom I've only got on well for the past 5 or 6 years. And boys! It's hard for me to be myself when I'm in love. I want to please the guy and forget who I am. I realised I was doing this recently, and I ended my relationship with a Tanzanian guy.

It's certain for me that being with someone means you deserve to be loved. Tenderness, warm hugs are so comfortable, they give so much peace when they come from the heart. It's always hard for me not to be dependent. I always feel like I don't give as much as I receive, or the opposite: I give too much of myself without anything in return. When you want to share your life with somebody, it can't work on a one-way relationship. But for the past few months, I have realised I need to be myself and not try to become like someone else. I need to keep my personality and be accepted for who I am.

The relationships I have now are family relationships and I'm happy with them. I have only one good friend, almost my mother's age, whom I like because we have lots of points in common and have nice conversations. Then comes my Tanzanian boyfriend. It's hard for me to say it's over. We split apart quite suddenly and violently. I'm still emotionally attached.

Loving your Career?

For this, I've promised myself to do the job I like and not the job that pays well. I can't imagine going to work without feeling happy. We spend too much of our life at work, if I don't like my job, that would be like dying slowly. That will be my first step in my working life.

Loving Money?

I'm scared of money! Money has often brought problems around me, as well as for me. I fear it. Money rules the world. If you don't have money, you're nothing in the Western world. When you have too much, you're not happier. I'm sometimes afraid to be without and think how would my life be then? I spend it but not easily, I need to think properly before I spend it."

Briefly, my reply was: *"That is wonderful Lorita, some of the I AM statements you need to work with are below. Please use Day 3 exercise for these as well to release anything you are still holding, as needed. And Intend regularly:*

Intent: I AM calling on the I AM Presence (Source/Universe/God) to direct my Higher Self that:

I AM loving my feminine body.

I AM forgiving myself for not being connected with my body and for not loving it. I AM now completely in love with my body.

I AM loving the way my body looks when I AM well fed and healthy.

I AM in unconditional love with self.

I AM always having easy and comfortable relationships with all and attracting wonderful new ones.

I AM looking to only share love.

I AM grateful I AM connected to my authentic self always and am comfortable being that with others.

I AM in unconditional love with others.

I AM at peace with my ex-boyfriend in letting him go unconditionally in return for peace.

I AM at peace with Money and its presence more in my life only makes me happier and I deserve that!

I AM respecting Money and friends with Money.

I AM living in the moment doing what I like and trust money is always with me.

I AM working in a job I like that pays me very well."

*****

Please keep using your new Intents to deepen the anchoring of your goal and all that you wish to change about you that came out of the work we did today. I will see you tomorrow!

Love,
Robin Bela

DAY 5
A PRACTICE TO REMAIN CENTRED, TO NOURISH THE INNER SELF AND TO STAY OPEN TO GUIDANCE : MEDITATION

Welcome to DAY 5 of the 30-Day Programme

Day 5 and Day 6 are chapters to help you find inner-peace and balance in this busy world, through some easy practices. They would require some quiet time. And for today's topic, you should ideally be doing it at home to be completely relaxed. Today's subject pertains to the importance of regular practice of Meditation. Meditation is a simple but powerful tool that can change your life, <u>if done every day</u>. It is a great way to start your day by bringing Meditation into your daily life and staying centred in your Mind, Body, Heart and Spirit. When you are centred within, you are naturally more peaceful, confident and happy in life. **Everything outside is a reflection of the inside.** With the deepening of your connection to your Inner Being through Meditation, you will reap benefits of desired manifestations in your life, as I will explain more in today's topic.

You will find that there is an increase in energy levels in your body as you meditate daily. Meditation brings clarity in mind, helps focus better, brings an empty space for you to receive what you need, including all support for you to receive abundance in life. Also physically, breathing during Meditation infuses more oxygen into the body, improves the way the brain functions, improves blood circulation, and most importantly, it is very good for the Heart as it relaxes and calms you and your entire body.

Meditation allows emotions to be processed and is a great stress buster. Meditation can help you to be peaceful, especially if you are very anxious about achieving your goal or about anything else. In the past, I had put on weight under stress. **I give major credit to Meditation for weight-loss.**

Just as our body needs to exercise, Inner Self needs nourishment too! Meditation attends to our Inner Self and impacts our entire being. For doing Meditation, all we need is some 'quiet time'. If we don't allow this, <u>on a regular basis,</u> there is no opening for creativity, ideas, or any new things to flow into our lives. Hearing your inner guidance gets even harder if the noise in the mind isn't quietened. During Meditation, you are not seeking any answers. You are just 'being' there, and allowing it to lead you. As you practise this, ideas and answers in your everyday life will flow more naturally as you go about your day, as it creates space for them to come. This process also clears all unnecessary energies draining you.

Regular practice of Meditation will develop your energy field, which includes your aura, and will build it wide and strong. At every breath, your aura is expanding naturally. Those of you sensitive to energies around you, will find Meditation a great tool in building a natural shield around yourself. It is not invoking any artificial shield around you, but the strength, your Power, is just built from within you outwards over a period of time naturally, as you meditate. When you are in full Power, you are always in positive and healthy energies. With this, things such as unnecessary emotions around you affect you less and you have more control of how you would like to navigate through your day, instead of being pushed around by the effects of certain circumstances, and even the energies of other people.

Meditation has helped me find energy to do more things in my practical day-to-day life, than I normally would do. I get smarter with more clarity in mind. I also feel joyful in the process as I feel so refreshed. I feel peaceful and find solutions to problems more naturally. It helps me to move confidently and quickly in times of uncertainty and emotional turmoil. **This ancient spiritual tool in my opinion is very essential in today's busy lifestyle.**

Initially, I had noticed that when I started meditating, it worked better after doing physical exercise, especially in the mornings, as it totally grounded me and brought me into my body as I used to find it hard to meditate straight away. Not any more though! I would recommend starting your day with

Meditation. Twenty minutes at a time is all that you need. This time frame fits perfectly with our day and age too. This is one way you can easily bring some simple practices to balance your Inner Self, into your daily practical life.

I will now explain to you the ancient Vedic form of Meditation, which is "mantra-based". A mantra for this form of Meditation is traditionally called 'Bija(Beej)' meaning 'Seed'. A mantra is a powerful word, sound or vibration which when repeated in mind, creates a deep state of relaxation and well-being. I would recommend you to learn this from a teacher directly as soon as you are able to, because you will then be initiated to a specific mantra that is best suited for you. But for the purpose of practicing now, we are going to use a commonly used Vedic mantra "OM" (or A-U-M). A mantra is a Sanskrit word. We are not focusing on any religious context of this mantra 'OM" (or A-U-M), or trying to find any meaning but simply allowing ourselves to experience the benefit of using it.

THE MEDITATION PRACTICE FOR NOW, AND YOUR WORK TODAY AND EVERYDAY:

1. *Sit comfortably, upright and close your eyes.* You can do this sitting in a chair. It is important to be seated upright and in the most relaxed, comfortable position for you. Do keep yourself warm as you may feel cold if you experience any kind of clearing. The environment should be as noiseless as possible.

2. After having thus assumed a very relaxed position, *gently start repeating the word "OM"(or A-U-M) in your mind.* Your sole intention is to repeat the mantra in your mind constantly at a comfortable pace. Please note, you should not say this mantra aloud during Meditation. In fact when you get your personal mantra, it's not to be shared with anyone. When the mantra is thus repeated inwardly, it connects us to the energy of silence and helps us reach the empty mind without thoughts. That is often called as a place of 'Gap', where all consciousness of every being is one, and connects us to

infinite possibilities. We do not carry any agenda before doing our daily Meditation. Our consciousness takes care of all our needs. The less you control it, the better!

3. *In the beginning, your mind may wander into thoughts and you may lose the mantra for a while.* This is normal, as thoughts will emerge in your consciousness, but as you gently persist with the inward repetition of the mantra, thoughts will gradually start disappearing.

4. *Don't force the length of the breath to be rhythmic.* You may notice some breaths are longer and some shorter, some denser and some lighter. Just breathe through all. You don't need to know the reasons, but in general it's a way of 'clearing' and expanding your energies in the physical and energy body and balancing your emotions too. You may sense these clearings as physical energy sensations or vibrations in body. Just allow them to pass and remain focused on saying the mantra in your mind. Those may be due to some stress or emotions being processed or physical body getting balanced. As you keep saying the mantra, you may drift away to an empty deep state or the Gap, where you can experience a deep relaxed state. If you come out of it, you can simply go back to repeating the mantra. In this process, you connect to a deeper self and the silence within you.

5. *After 20 minutes, stop the repetition of the mantra in your mind,* and remain in this blank state for a minute or two. End your Meditation by slowly opening your eyes, and sit still for some time, as it can take some time to adjust back to the normal environment. During Meditation, you may open your eyes slightly to check time. Avoid alarm clocks as abrupt ending of Meditation is not desirable.

You can do Meditation for <u>twenty minutes</u>, in the morning, before you begin your work routine. And it would be ideal if you can <u>meditate twice daily</u>, once in the morning and once in the evening, between about 4pm to 6pm. Avoid meditating a few hours before sleeping as it can keep you awake!

***

As you do Meditation every day, you will start seeing big shifts physically, emotionally and spiritually over a period of time, perhaps in just a month. However, you may start noticing benefits in overall well-being within a few days, as you feel yourself more receptive to inner and outer guidance. I noticed deep healing and clearing begin after I had been doing it daily for about a year. Meditation keeps offering me so much more in every area of my life. I don't miss my Meditation any day for anything!

I firmly believe that Meditation is not something spiritual gurus sitting in caves alone can do. It needs to be done by everyone including managers, businessmen, students, teachers, artists etc., to become more efficient at work, and most importantly, better human beings. Meditation offers us so much including physical and emotional healing, more energy as stress can tire us quickly, clarity to make clear decisions and to listen to our inner guidance, better focus, inner peace and relaxation to be able to cope with busy lifestyles, happiness with balance in our lives, solutions and ideas, to name only some of the benefits of practising this ancient Vedic form of Meditation.

This is it for today! Enjoy relaxing today and start receiving the benefits of a far more enriched life with Meditation. Please do try to get your unique mantra from a teacher who teaches mantra-based Meditation to fully reap the benefits of this form of Meditation. In the meantime, you can use the temporary mantra offered in this chapter. And don't forget to focus on your daily Intents. I look forward to connecting with you tomorrow!

Love,
Robin Bela

DAY 6

CONNECTING TO THE SACRED ALTAR WITHIN : A 10 SECONDS TECHNIQUE TO CONNECT AND REMAIN CENTRED WITHIN A PEACEFUL HEART

Welcome to DAY 6 of the 30-Day Programme

The technique taught here will help you learn to stay centred during any circumstance, say when you face a crisis, are stressed, fearful, confused, hypersensitive, lost, grieving, needing courage, or in any situation that has made you disconnected from your peaceful Heart Centre. And it takes just a few seconds to implement this technique. Many of my clients tell me that it has often been hard to stay connected to Heart, and listen to it. So, I would like to share a technique I connected to during my meditation. It's a simple and beautiful technique that I love using especially when I am in a situation where I have no time to meditate.

WHAT IS YOUR 'SACRED ALTAR WITHIN' AND HOW TO CONNECT TO YOUR SACRED ALTAR?

The 'Sacred Altar Within' that I am talking about, is your Heart. This is where your most profound Divine energies of 'love' reside. As mentioned earlier, staying connected to one's Heart is so crucial to being peaceful and happy. We do have sacred altars outside us, which we create to help us find peace. We can connect to this Source through our Hearts anytime we desire too. When we stay connected to our Heart, we do not feel afraid of new things in life, courage becomes easier, love is unconditional and solutions, healing and positive energies flow more naturally to us.

Below is a simple exercise to help you to stay connected to your loving, peaceful Heart at all times.

STEPS TO CONNECT TO THE SACRED ALTAR WITHIN:

1. To connect to this Sacred Altar Within, I would like you to simply do some breathing for a couple of minutes at least, and place your hand on your heart. As you do so, *close your eyes and ask your Heart to give you a geometric shape that you can easily and quickly draw to help you connect with the Heart.* For example, I have chosen for myself the symbol, 'Star', and it just came to me. This symbol should become sacred to you. You should choose it once and then stick to it always. In fact, if you are not sure what symbol you get when you close your eyes, just choose the 'star' or anything that comes to your mind first, say a circle, triangle or a square, the easier to draw, the better.

2. *Now, I would like you to imagine drawing this symbol repeatedly on your Heart with your middle finger,* which is really in the chest area. It will start connecting you deeply to your Heart Centre and away from your ever-thinking and worrying mind. It brings instant peace. You may start feeling more and more peaceful as you do, perhaps after having drawn the symbol about 10 times, which may just take about 10 seconds.

3. When you keep drawing the symbol on to your Heart again and again, in your imagination, you will probably feel your Heart becoming warmer, relaxed, peaceful or lighter. Just breathe with it, and you can close your eyes too, if possible in the environment you are in at that time. *You will know that you are connected to Heart, with the help of this symbol, when you start feeling peaceful.*

***

After selection of the symbol, the Steps 2 and 3 above would need to be carried out in normal day-to-day life when you are using this technique.

When we are connected to our Heart, we are peaceful, happy and confident in ourselves, and we listen to our heart to live life authentically. Our intention with this practice is to eventually not just remember to connect to our Heart during troubled times, but to live from that place of love as often as possible.

YOUR WORK TODAY

Find your Sacred Altar Symbol with the above steps, that you would use every day and especially whenever you are stressful, doubtful, unhappy, fearful or worrying. <u>All you have to do is to imagine, that you are drawing the symbol on your heart, again and again, with your middle finger.</u> You may have to draw, maybe <u>10-15 times,</u> before you actually start feeling peaceful. It just takes about 10 seconds to start feeling peaceful. That is when you are connected to your Heart, and your most Divine Authentic Self. Keep this tool safely in your pocket!

Please note, that the symbol you get unconsciously in mind, or select consciously, should not have any meaning, e.g., one participant received an image of an angel in a shell and said it represents safety for him, and I had to ask him to meditate further, or consciously choose something simple, without any meaning. If it's a circle, it's just a circle with no meaning. It is just a tool you use to connect to your Heart, your most divine place within you. And whatever you choose, it should take one second or so to draw it in your imagination. Don't take a complicated image that takes too long to draw.

EXAMPLES AND EXPERIENCES OF SOME PARTICIPANTS:

"The Sacred Altar is a nice idea, somewhere you can feel in touch with your spirit and Universe. I came up with the infinity symbol. It appeared and made me feel so calm and harmonious." [Nancy]

"I started to use the Sacred Altar technique on Thursday as I struggled to get a symbol into my mind before this to draw on my heart chakra. I asked spirit to give a symbol to me and I was given a white circle with a red cross in the middle. When I use this symbol now I see a visualisation of me "crossing myself" on my heart. When I do draw this symbol on my heart now I feel a sense of being very "centred" and it brings me back to my centre, my being, my body and grounds me too. It also feels quite powerful to be able to bring myself back to this core of myself as my mind wanders off regularly throughout the day and I get negative thoughts. It jogs me out of thinking too much! I have really enjoyed learning about the Sacred Altar work and will be using it from now onwards." [Sally]

"I have decided that my Sacred Altar Symbol is a turquoise love heart. A symbol which has always attracted me. It also always makes me feel happy when I see it. I feel at home when I see it, and for years I knew I would need it one day." [Rose]

"First I would like to share with you my experience with the Sacred Altar. I have used it only once till now, and till the moment I have used it, I was really not sure what it was. When I did the breathing very concentrated a red coloured heart appeared. It was hard for me to melt it in my heart. Then today (Friday) I had a stressful situation. I started breathing but noticed I cannot concentrate on meditating at all. Then I decided to use red heart to put it in my imagination on my own heart. After just few times drawing it on my heart I felt more peaceful. I drew about 10 times until I felt much more relaxed. Thanks for that. After that I continued my meditation and it was a lot deeper than at the beginning. Although after a while some of the concerns regarding my situation came back, but I was able to put it more easily on the side. That was really an amazing experience." [Alan]

Notice this week how often you use this technique, especially when you are stressed, doubtful, unhappy or worried, and then see whether you remembered to use it in those times. You may sometimes need to use it several times a day, to remain peaceful and centred. And when you did use, how did you feel? Write down any of your experiences in your journal, so that you don't forget. **It trains us to live from a peaceful, contented state of mind and heart.** So this is it for today. Stay connected to your Heart and have a lovely day!

Love,
Robin Bela

DAY 7
THE ALCHEMY OF MANIFESTING :
TAKE YOUR ACTION STEPS

Welcome to DAY 7 of the 30-Day Programme

I don't need to know how to reach the End, in order to Begin. When I begin telling Universe my needs, the answers and solutions just appear instantly or step-by-step! And I simply focus on the fuel of excitement and love for my desire.

You can't wait to be where you desire to be? The quicker you take those steps 1, 2, 3 and so on, the sooner you will be there, and many a times, the ticket to reaching somewhere, is to simply make a decision to start. Decision also begins by Asking for support for your needs to Universe or God, and let answers and opportunities appear to you. **The next step can become clearer as we take the first step.** I came across a quote by Michelangelo, *"If you knew how much went into it, you would not call it genius."* And yes I have burnt the midnight oil many a time, even writing this. This is exactly what today's topic is about, i.e., taking action to achieve your dreams and goals. Action can begin even by staying positive consciously about an outcome, Asking Universe/God for help etc., and of course, everything else that you need to do, e.g., hunt for a job. You need to follow your inner guidance, through keeping your journal, and keep Asking your Heart what Universe is inviting you to do, to reach your goal. Action requires a fair amount of discipline from our end.

Action also means making a decision clearly and quickly. Action begins by setting the Intent for goal/s. You can convert them into 'I AM statements' and start Intending every day. As you Intend, as if you have already achieved what you want, and keep 'Asking Universe/God's support', while 'feeling gratitude in heart to receive it', you are on your way to creating your reality. This simple way of living is the path to manifesting naturally.

We just assume that life needs to be hard and a struggle at times. If you spend too much time thinking, worrying, researching, or even wondering whether you will get it or manage it, you are not just procrastinating, but also increasing your fears of not achieving what you want. It's always a yes or a no, but so many people live their lives in the energy of 'may be', and you know what, these people are the ones who don't ever live their dreams. Their lives become stagnant, boring: you can literally see it in their body language, as they feel and look lethargic, as though they are dragging their bodies to a job they don't really relish, or simply being with friends they don't like, or being in a relationship that is actually a strain, all because they cannot say 'no' or 'yes' for their own happiness!

I had started putting on weight, and stopped caring about my appearance, simply because I was not able to face the decision, that I wanted to make about my marriage. And usually, your heart will know intuitively, sometimes almost instantly, what one should do in such a situation, but then you use your intellectual mind, and forget the first intuitive instinct you had about the choice. Why? Whom are we pleasing here? There is nothing moral about sacrificing your happiness like that, as you are being totally dishonest to others and, most importantly, to yourself. Doing anything without the element of joy, without truly wanting it in your heart, with dishonest or false motives such as 'looks good on CV, 'others are doing it', 'afraid of the new', 'what will others say', 'don't want to hurt others and hide the truth because it's painful', amounts to living a life for others, not self. It's not even living; it's like merely existing in a soulless life.

If you are unhappy about some situations in life, it's time to make a decision and take action. Just place your hand on your Heart, and Ask the question about what you want next, and see what answer you get immediately after you Asked. Say it aloud, and then take action! Do it! Move on with your life, and don't stay stuck! The longer you stay, the more the misery, fear and confusion. Bring on the excitement into your life! Decide now!

So, if you have made a decision that this is what you want, then the next step is to start taking the action steps for turning your goal into reality. I see many people with great ideas and passion, but they don't do anything about these. There is a kind of block in them. Just as you may have heard of writers having blocks while writing, so something like that may happen in taking steps to doing anything new. Would you call it fear? What is stopping you from losing weight, what is stopping you from becoming who you want to be? In my experience, when we just focus on our happiness, instead of listening to our ego, which may be saying 'you are not good enough', or 'you cannot do this', we can overcome this. It's like when we ignore the so-called eyes of the people who might be watching us, and instead, just act from the heart for pure joy, rather than to prove anything to anyone. Then we are truly living our life for self, and also for our purpose.

We feel awful if we don't do as we please. Once we start getting used to taking action from the Heart, for pure joy – it feels the right way to be - and I call that "living at our best". You can also call it 'self-care', or just learning 'to be authentic'. And there is no comparison with anyone: there can only be one you! When you realise that, there is no struggle in taking action. In fact, if you feel stuck, you will take every step to get those issues out of the way. For example, I couldn't afford to spend on marketing and advertising for my work in the beginning, so I found other ways to promote my work. I would teach programmes in different cities in the UK and also in India, but I always somehow managed to get students without having to do much marketing. I was just doing it for the passion, and was motivated by a desire to render useful service, and the need to do what I really wanted.

Once you start listening to the instincts, promptings and desires of your Heart, you will find that you are at peace with yourself, and Universe starts supporting you for all that you clearly Intend! That passion starts leading you towards your goals. Stay connected to the passion and reap the benefits, as you may have discovered in Day 1 chapter.

I should like you also to question yourself whether you are doing things for your own good or out of some obligation? Taking action is harder if you are doing it more out of fear of not doing the right things. Are you going to the gym just because you paid for it and now have to go, so you moan and groan as you make your way? Think of the message you are giving to Universe: I would like to be healthy, but what a pain! So Universe is not sure really, if you want to be healthy. If you are disciplined enough, gyms really are not necessary because you can do work-outs at home just for 20-30 minutes every day. Being authentic with self means being responsible for yourself. If you are, you will never let yourself get out of shape or be in fear of not being able to maintain your shape. You just do it because you are responsible and love yourself. One of my students once said that she would do the practices she was taught in the class, but she had no time otherwise. I interpreted that statement as: "I don't care about myself enough and it's ok to stay drowned in my ignorance." I told her, "If you are responsible about your well-being and happiness, you will never say that!" She just needed to decide and take action. You cannot moan about your life not moving forward if you are not doing anything about it.

Taking action on your desires may require you to look at different approaches. If you would like to start your own business but need money for day-to-day work, why not work part-time in a bookshop or somewhere else which is easy, and comfortable, and will provide a basis of financial support. You really don't need a high-flying job on the side if you want to focus on your business and start telling people who you really are now! It is important to start talking and saying to others that this is what you are now. I told everyone that I was a Writer even before I really got into serious writing. And similarly, I started telling everyone that I was a Coach and Teacher even while I used to work full-time elsewhere. You have to be able to experience being who you want to be so that you start feeling comfortable with it, and can allow things you are intending to flow naturally to you.

I know a person who was not able to take action because she was so dependent on receiving signs to move forward. As a result, she had stopped listening to her own true desires and inner guidance. She would say things like, "I saw a sign saying this city's name and so I should move there". And she got so dependent on signs that she would give reasons for every decision she made or did not make, based on the sign she saw. It was more like, at times, finding reasons for not doing what she should, out of fear of change. There is a big difference between an intuitive message received and trying to look for confirmation from outside you for all your decisions and yes, if you look, you might find things that will comfort you. But are they really your guidance then? I discuss more on intuitive signs later too, that when signs may be valid and when you need to listen and receive the guidance. They are usually sudden, repeated images, thoughts, feelings, incidents etc., and are received in response to a prayer or affirmed Intent. But I need to mention in this chapter that misguided dependency on signs can lead you to never moving towards your true desires. It is usually an excuse to stay where you are! It's important to get clear about what you want and what you don't want, and not leave things to chance or fate.

Now that you have hopefully decided and are ready for action, let me show you the steps to manifesting, where more than action, being in the receptive mode is crucial for creating ideas, opportunities, synchronicities etc.

YOUR WORK TODAY

(A) BEGIN TO TAKE THESE STEPS:

1. Let's start with what we have already talked about to begin taking steps for converting your goal into reality. Write down in your journal what are those decisions you still need to make and Ask for Universe/God's support for the same? Place your hand on your Heart, ask and listen to what it says. You may need to create more Intents or decide to give greater focus to your existing Intents.

2. Check with yourself and then write in your journal, if there is anything blocking you from taking action steps towards your goal? If so, take steps to clear these blocks using the Soul Clearing Technique.

3. What steps are you ready to take? Are you taking them today? If not, when? Maybe you will need to sit a few days with the Intents before you get this answer. Many a times, it's not something you will hear. You just start perhaps doing something suddenly, which you are meant to!

4. Also notice, whether it helps to start your day, by doing that action step straight away, first thing in the morning. For example, I get up early and do an hour of writing most of the days I am doing a writing project. So usually, by about 9 am I have already done my important task of the day. But try to do only the work that is creative, in the morning. I call early morning as sacred time for the soul. Ideally, try not to open your work emails or think about problems until you have meditated, and are ready for the day.

5. INTENTS FOR YOU TO FOCUS ON, FOR TAKING ACTION STEPS:

Herewith, I have some suggested Intents for you to focus on to help you take your action steps. You may include them in your daily Intents.

I AM calling on the I AM Presence to direct my Higher Self that:

I AM clear about my choices I make in life.

I AM quick to listen and understand my Heart and then make a decision.

I AM doing everything for joy and happiness for me, and as I do that, others receive it naturally. (You don't even have to try, e.g., if you are at peace, others feel it too).

I AM taking action steps towards my goal____ daily.

I AM taking the step of doing this _____ for myself today. (And check with yourself regularly).

I AM feeling passion and gratitude that all my Intents have already come true for me. (With eyes closed, feel the love and joy in heart for a minute or so).

I AM praying/Intending that I AM in service to do my best at work. (If your main focus is on work).

(B) LEARN THE ALCHEMY OF MANIFESTING!

Here is something more that we can practise in order to start attracting the best possibilities for us.

Ask Universe/God for support and say your 'I AM Intents' for your goal focusing on the 'feeling of joy, love, excitement and gratitude' in heart as if your Intents have already become a reality. I spend a few minutes daily just 'feeling love, excitement and gratitude' in heart, sometimes with eyes closed and visualising as if all my Intents have already become reality. And then, I just let go of any thought about it, and get into doing my daily routine, which is the key requirement for allowing any manifesting to happen. While so engaged in your routine, take small action steps towards the achievement of your goals/Intents. These small steps will trigger ideas and intuitive messages which will show what your next step should be. I will explain this more in detail below, but broadly, I consider these simple steps as the *'Alchemy for Manifesting'*.

The Love in the Heart is the fuel to any success. Universe will reflect back what you 'feel' and 'believe' within. So many a time, saying or thinking some **Intents alone can be meaningless, if they aren't said with vision, passion, and excitement**. You have to make it real with love and passion, your feelings and vision. The more we do this process, the focus and enjoyment for our work grows naturally. At times, for a new project, that is very much needed. **If you can visualise how it feels to reach the end, Universe then just fills the gap.**

What starts happening as a result is that ideas, opportunities, synchronicities and even motivation kick in you to take the baby steps required. Most of the time, I just get exactly what I Asked, like more clients, help when I needed, money etc. This process comes from a place of inner guidance and divine support, so that you will feel safe in taking those steps as you start this process. I also realised that sometimes **when I Asked under the pressure of fear, I created nothing! That is why the 'letting go or surrender, and going about my daily routine' step is very important to reinforce the faith, follow the process of gratitude, trust and focused Intent.** Trying it regularly, will increase your speed of manifesting and trust in Universe, that you are provided for everything you need. Just Ask! You start becoming a part of the natural flow of Universe, and all wonderful synchronicities start becoming a normal feature in your life, but only when we let go of the 'control' and place our 'trust' in Universe, that we receive what we have Asked.

SALIENT STEPS TO THE ALCHEMY OF MANIFESTING:

1. MAKE A DECISION: Be clear on what you want and make your decision. The Intention should be crystal clear, because Universe reflects back your focused Intent or your half-baked wish.

2. CREATE INTENT: Create an Intent regarding the decision made about what you want, and simply say the I AM Intents you need to focus on for whatever you need today.

3. ASK FOR SUPPORT AND BE OPEN TO RECEPTIVITY: Sit with eyes closed if you like, and Ask for Universe/God's support with love in Heart. Do not spell out the process of 'how' you would like to receive what you are Asking. Simply Ask and Intend that you have received, and just feel grateful. One sentence can be enough.

4. FOCUS ON IGNITING THE FEELING OF LOVE AND EXCITEMENT FOR WHAT YOU ARE INTENDING TO RECEIVE: Feel the gratitude, passion and love for a few minutes in your heart of what you have Asked as having already been granted to you by Universe and express thanks, e.g., 'Thank you Universe for bringing

me ....' You can dream and visualise how it would be to have the energy of the completion within you. For example, being in love and how it makes you happier, or how money offers you all material conveniences, peace of mind, fun, excitement etc., or your creative project of how you enjoy being in that process, and feel satisfied completing it. Focus on how what you want makes you excited about what you are creating through the Intents/goals. **The secret to having anything in life is that you radiate excitement as if you are already abundant and content in life. You don't wait for situations and circumstances outside of you to complete you.** That is why, when you achieve something in your physical reality that you wanted, you usually feel worthy to receive it.

5. LET GO AND RELAX, ALLOWING STILLNESS AND PEACE WITHIN - THE STILLNESS PRACTICE: Now just go about doing your daily work and 'not thinking or worrying about what you have Asked' and you may choose to remind yourself instead of how grateful you are for having received that in your life. Remember, worrying is not going to create anything you want! So if you are in the habit of worrying, you will have to remind yourself of the above process a number of times till you get better and quicker in getting what you want in life. I would also like to remind you of the concept of *'pushing'* and *'pulling'* or in other words forcing or overstraining to get something, that was talked about in the Prologue of the book. **Our aim is to see us stand upright as everything comes to us naturally when we are in that energy of relaxed and content state where we trust that all we Asked for is taken care of by Universe.** Therefore, *'letting go' is a very important step to allow manifesting to take place.*

Naturally, in the state of Stillness, our intentions are clear, without any confusion or worry in mind, and Universe picks up the clear message of what we are wanting. With no resistance, it simply mirrors back what we Ask.

You can *practise moments of stillness* by **sitting with your <u>eyes</u> <u>open</u> for a few minutes or as long as you like, and just being Still, when you are not 'thinking', 'observing' or 'feeling' anything.** Just find the empty place within you where you are just still. We remove ourselves from being on 'push' or 'pull' mode to get anything, and allow ourselves to receive naturally. Universe always gives us what we want. It is only our desperation, fears, neediness and worrying that cause the road blocks to success. In this space of Stillness, just be, and start connecting to your complete self that you are already, by removing all control to be something. There in that moment, you connect to all infinite possibilities. This can be repeated several times a day or whenever you like. This helps us get aligned to the 'Now' and our 'complete Self', and allows us to let go of unnecessary control over life, and accept joy in this moment.

6. LET YOUR ACTION STEPS BE TAKEN: And then take small action steps towards your goal according to the ideas, opportunities and intuitive messages you receive.

7. CANDLE FLAME EXERCISE TO DEEPEN THE FOCUS ON YOUR GOALS: This last step you may do whenever you can, if not everyday. Light a candle and look at it for a few minutes feeling the spark of joy in your heart and feeling the peace within you for being that you want as already accomplished. Simply Intend as you watch the flame: 'I AM at peace and content knowing that I AM what I feel myself now to be.' Just breathe into that. This exercise would help you to get a deeper focus on your dreams or goals.

As you keep Intending and Asking for support from Universe over a period of time, you will see that the speed of receiving gets quicker.

EXAMPLE 1 - Pamela wrote:

"I am pretty good at taking actions but I am not good at doing things for me.

For instance, I have wanted to learn to do proper dancing all my life (ballroom and modern paired dancing) and I haven't done anything about it simply because my husband doesn't want to and I am nervous about dancing with another partner. I need to take action and sign up for dance lessons even though it will be hard for me to maintain them (there is nothing locally where I live and I would have to travel regularly for several days to attend lessons). I have never asked Universe for anything as I have thought this selfish until now but I am asking now and it seems to be liberating as I am acknowledging that I am worthy of asking for what I want and need. I have wasted years waiting for others to join me to do things I want to do. I need to just go and do my own things myself and not wait for their approval or consent. I AM grateful for all that I am learning to help me to have more power in my life."

To that, I replied:
This is beautiful! You can just have these Intents to support you:
I AM led to dancing classes that are perfect for me and easily accessible.
I AM finding things to do for myself.
I AM enjoying dancing, and opening myself up to new skills within me. I AM excited!

Focus on how it makes you excited!

EXAMPLE 2 - Moira wrote to me:

"Q. What would I be doing if money was no object?

A. I would be running a social enterprise that is 1:1 counselling, therapeutic youth group and workshops/courses for children and teenagers. It would focus upon respecting and valuing our children as I really do believe they are our future and until we nurture them as a society we run the risk of creating more problems for ourselves. I have qualifications and experience in this area but am not confident it is enough. I looked more deeply at this and I found I know this is what I am here to do, as this work uses my natural abilities, however I am scared of the responsibility that comes with it and fear I would let people down. Thought of it as a nice dream but you won't pull it off. Who do you think you are? And where do I start? Fears that I am not creative enough. All these thoughts are present, also the size of the work load and commitment makes me feel resistant to it."

My response to that was:

Questions I would ask you to ask yourself and dig deeper:

Why are you afraid of responsibility? Once you receive the answer using Day 2 work, clear with breath work in Day 3 and instead hold this Intent: I love what I do, so am good at being responsible about it.

About Where do I start: I would like you to sit every day in the morning after focusing on your Intent and doing Meditation, and write on a page your ideas for business, and see whether anything comes to you for taking action steps daily.

Start and focus on steps that can be taken in a day at a time. You are thinking too far ahead. Instead, focus on enjoying every day and how much you did today only. Also, you can have the following Intents:

I AM enjoying working in the field of counselling, social enterprise, with youth.

I AM getting all ideas for creating programmes for children.

I AM following my heart in what I want to do, and that's all I need to do for converting my dream/goal into reality.

I would like you to focus on how achieving this makes you feel excited!

***

I know some people, who have the required skills for the positions they want to reach, but somehow just cannot take that crucial step to help themselves to go to that level. I see them as not committed, and simply not taking daily action steps. There is really no escape from being responsible to yourself for your true desires. Most of the time, they are thinking too far ahead instead of just focusing on taking the required step 'today'. If you are passionate, and what you like to do excites you, makes you feel good, then you need to have the attitude of being unstoppable and of a go-getter. And just start enjoying doing it. **Your focus should not be on 'how' but on 'doing' and in the joy of 'creating' it**. If you are still hesitating to take action, ask yourself where your focus is? If your focus is on fears, you need to learn to put your attention on passion , excitement and service. And then clear the fears through Day 2 and Day 3 work.

Many a time, I am planning to do things that I have no idea how, e.g., planning a trip to some other country and then soon, the money to cover the cost appears, or the plan on how to go about it just becomes clear, or Universe would send me something for free too as explained below:

I have many more stories to share of instant manifestations, but a few manifestations to share from my practice of "Intent work" are, for example, a couple of times I received free seats at some expensive events that I could not then afford. I would just allow Universe to take care of the request I made. And it would just happen, at times as gift from someone who could not make it there! I would even forget I had made the request to Universe when it would appear in ways I couldn't have imagined. I was not leaning on or pushing energetically for the outcome, so it would happen. To tell you another interesting example, once I had a full row of seats empty next to me in a busy flight, which I had in fact Intended in my mind, as I was then feeling unwell, and wished to lie down. And in another travel story, my automated suitcase lock had got stuck before checking in my suitcase for the flight and I Intended some solution to come as I didn't want to bother breaking it physically when I reached home. On arrival, by the time I picked my baggage at the airport, I found the lock gone and my bag sealed with some wire. When I opened my suitcase at home, I found the broken lock inside with a note saying that my suitcase was picked for automated check at the airport, and they had to break the lock! Such instant manifestations can become a part of life quite at an unconscious level, but when we start taking steps to working consciously first as outlined in this chapter, that can be the beginning for you.

You never get clarity or solutions unless you focus on getting them. The process is almost like I am telling Universe what I want by putting my Intention of good feelings and thoughts about it and focus on it with excitement, and soon Universe starts responding to me by offering me options and solutions. So take the step forward today, and trust that God created you to be self-sufficient, to provide yourself all you need. You can do it!

Remember, you don't need to know how to reach the end result before you take the first step. As you start taking steps towards your goal, the end will gradually start getting clearer. Thanks for joining me today again. See you tomorrow!

Love,
Robin Bela

DAY 8
PRAY OR ASK FOR A SMOOTH TRANSITION

Those who are not inclined to "Pray" for whatever reason, may use the word "Ask" in the context of this Chapter. Universe/Source has been an essential support for me always when fear was high, or when I felt I had no clue where to go, and how to go about things in life next. But one thing I have realised, that if I Intend that I like the answers to come to me peacefully and easily, they do! But you have to remember to 'Ask' that to Universe consciously. The changes, which you are seeking to create in life right now, don't have to come the hard way! You Pray/Ask, and Intend, that it's going to be easy and effortless. Prayer in itself is a form of 'Asking', and thanking for your needs to be met, whether you address it to God or simply, in a non-spiritual way to an Energy Form as 'Universe' or 'Source'. 'Intending' that we have been doing in this Book, is also a way of Asking for more in our lives.

Before I separated from my ex-husband, I prayed and Intended for a while that it would take place 'easily, effortlessly, peacefully, and organically'. Please note the words I have used here. How you 'Intend/Ask' and 'believe', is what takes place. I also prayed that my ex would talk about it and do the decision-making. When it took place, it felt so normal and it happened exactly the way I had asked. It went so peacefully that people around me couldn't understand, why I was so peaceful and why I wasn't shattered and miserable with all the changes. For me, the whole process was peaceful because I intended it to be so, and I had prayed the same for my ex. And he too moved easily to a place he liked and settled quickly. All changes took place smoothly. Our first conversation was for 10 minutes, and the next day we were looking at bills. Yes there was pain in the separation from what we were used to, but more than that, we were happy that we had taken the courage to be true to ourselves and to each other.

Change doesn't have to come with harsh words or blame. It can also be peaceful, if we keep our egos out of it, and keep the focus on how to keep the transition period as peaceful as possible. So, the key thing to remember always is : How you Intend your experience to be and you may also call on the extra support from God or Universe. In my experience, there is more power in the Asking and receiving as you call upon for extra support from God or Universe, as I had also explained in Day 3 relating to the Soul Clearing Technique.

You don't have to be scared of the 'New'. Simply Pray/Ask and Intend in advance for it to be the way you want. Talk about the experience of change, how it should 'feel' like, e.g., I repeatedly used words such as 'smooth', 'peaceful', 'organically' and 'effortlessly' in my prayers before separating from my ex. You can also use them for the changes you are going through to achieve your goals. You may be bringing in an exciting change for yourself, e.g., having a baby. Think of the 9 months of pregnancy as exciting and joyful, and Intend that it goes easy, effortlessly, relaxed and with great joy.

You only receive if you Ask! Praying/Asking along with Intending is a doorway to receiving an unlimited supply of support from Universe. It's like opening the door of receptivity even wider, because when you Ask, you have signalled to Universe that you are expecting and ready, which is a very important requirement to bring in smooth and quick manifesting of all that you want.

I know of many people who have worked with me as clients, who simply have no clue about what 'Asking' means as they have just been givers all their lives! Or some just forget to Ask! That is why, reading "I AM Statements" regularly, helps. It's like asking Universe to support you. You can even invoke any of the Gods you normally pray to, when you read your Intents daily. "I AM" also means the God within you, so you do invoke your highest Divine state too in that process. You just need to have the Intent that you Ask Universe/God to support you and all your Intents, and thank God/Universe. Simply feel the gratitude. This also amounts to a Prayer or a form of Asking and being receptive to the new. Those who are non-spiritual, can simply focus on the 'Asking' through Intents, which is really the main requirement to receive anything that we specifically want in our lives.

If you focus on what you want, opportunities and support start coming through. But you really don't need to settle for less or to know the 'How' before you Pray and Ask for what you want, because all that is needed is the earnest, focused desire to have what your Heart would like, and feel grateful, and most importantly, trust that you already have it once you have Asked. Just like anyone else, you deserve to get the best. Check with yourself what is blocking you from simply Asking and trusting that you will receive? You can clear it by breathing it out and just Intending the positive.

I know from my own experience of setting up my business, that MBA and marketing skills were not enough, and I had many a humbling experience of simply praying for the right people to be brought to me. Today, my biggest marketing tool is my faith in 'Asking' Source/Universe, for support.

Religious prayer was never ingrained in my upbringing, but I used to pray as a child in my own words, saying what I wanted God to take care of and help me with. I used to look at the moon and pray, almost as if I was seeing some Divine energy. And I loved knowing about all faiths or religions. Over the years, I have understood that the words you use in a prayer are not important. What is important is how open your Heart is, when you Ask, how you feel peaceful and grateful in the process of Asking, even before you receive what you are Asking for, and most importantly, feeling the presence of Universal support for you already there. Many say that they feel better after praying, as they start feeling the support of Universe.

When you Ask, you simply do so as if you have already received, otherwise you are not trusting God/Universe! Deep down, it even reflects that you don't trust yourself to receive. Simply give thanks for all things you want and ask Universe/God to show you the best way to get what you want. You may have noticed that I have added thanks to God/Universe at the end of examples of 'Intents' in the chapter on Intents. It's simply in order to show trust in Universe for what you are achieving.

YOUR WORK TODAY

1. *At least once a day, in the morning or before you go to sleep, address your thoughts, concerns or worries to God/Universe/Source and express gratitude for taking care of these.* Simply send love from heart to whom you are Praying/Asking to, and feel the peace. How much time you spend is not important. It could be for 30 minutes or just 2 minutes. The quality of the experience is more important than the time spent. You may also recall the 'Alchemy of Manifesting' process we did in the previous chapter to enrich the experience. Or just do it separately as and when you like.

2. Remember to Ask in your prayer as to *how you would like the experience of change and transition to be.* Transition in life doesn't have to be hard. It should be fun, peaceful and easy, especially when you are creating such exciting things for yourself. And Ask for whatever you need in this process, e.g., patience, self-care, excitement, confidence etc. You can say that, **'I AM patient, taking care of myself, excited and confident as I create this change in life. Thank you God/Universe/Source for making it take place easily, effortlessly, peacefully and organically.'** If you were anxious, you should feel better with this. If you still don't, it means you haven't really allowed God/Universe to take over your worries and are still holding on to them. Trust and let them go! Connect to the feeling of the outcome you would like to experience. You have to stop controlling, and have to allow the space for things to flow to you. Allow the creativity and synchronicities to start flowing through to support what you need. Breathe!

3. When you Pray/Ask, it is important that you honour yourself by believing that you deserve what you are Asking for. This means that the language you sometimes hear people using in prayer - 'God I am begging you to give me..' is actually simply saying to God/Universe that I don't deserve it really but can I have it? Well, Universe only beams back to you what you beam out. If

you trust instead, and forget about the 'How', and simply 'Ask' with peace and gratitude, you will most likely receive what you want. When you have peace and gratitude in your heart, rather than fear or worry, you can attract anything quickly into your life. So your constant effort should always be to get to the positive mind-set that all is well. Also, any healing, forgiveness and clarity you need, I believe, will truly start with a Prayer/Asking. With time, the power of Prayer/Asking increases and just becomes profound, as does the speed at which healing, manifesting etc. all take place.

4. *Intents suggested for you today:*

∞ I AM connected to Love, which is a Higher Source, through my Heart. When I am connected to my Heart, I am able to feel love, and peace coming back from God/Universe. And that's when I trust that my prayers/requests are answered.

∞ I AM open to Asking for all I want, and I trust I have received once I have Asked . I AM at peace.

∞ I AM bringing the change in my life that I want easily, effortlessly, peacefully and organically.

∞ I AM focusing on what I want as already present. In seeing and feeling that, I feel gratitude, and love for Universe/God/Divine Energy present within me.

5. *Also, please feel free to explore saying prayers from religious texts of your own, or of others, if you are open to trying.* Many ancient words used in such prayers carry powerful energies, which have an uplifting effect. The more positive words you say, the more positive things you attract in life! I love reading different forms of prayers and visiting holy places of all religions. I find them all equally loving, peaceful and healing to visit. And I am grateful that I was brought up that way by parents who were quite liberal. I remember that as a child, I would put all different Deities' pictures together on my chain, and

loved any Movement, which promoted peace, love and universal well-being. This view has helped me stay open to all wisdom of different religions, and has given me a lot of freedom and power to be responsible for my choices and thoughts.

SOME EXAMPLES FROM MY PARTICIPANTS WHO WROTE TO ME:

EXAMPLE 1

Doreen says:

"I'm not really sure what I should be praying for right now! I do now each night ask for Archangel Michael to protect us in our sleep as we have had a few 'disturbances' of the spiritual kind at night - although not when I pray for protection, so I feel this is important. I do ask Archangel Raphael to help heal my horse and our dog who has some allergy to something - but I cannot tell how effective this is or not. I have wondered whether to ask for help in training my horse and for the business to be more prosperous, but don't know who or how to ask."

And my response was:

"Asking is still new to you. And as you tried, you were still wondering if it was ok to ask in a prayer, for help for abundance and the training that you need and deserve. Yes of course you can Ask for help through prayer! Whatever is crucial to you, you simply Ask in your own words by saying, "God/Universe I AM Abundant and supported always. I AM doing extremely well in the training with my horse and it is amazing. Thank you God/Universe" and so on.

The way you Ask can never be wrong, what is important is that you Ask! And it is so important to feel gratitude, excitement and love in heart as that is a sign of you really trusting and receiving what you have asked for. Focus on being peaceful about whatever you have asked as already achieved. So you would see your horse and dog as healed, and feeling the energies of peace along, as an indication that you have been heard by Universe/God."

EXAMPLE 2: I Love this sharing, I hope you too will!

Lynnette says:

"Praying isn't something I was brought up doing and as I don't practice or believe in a particular religion it seemed a slightly alien concept. But I do ask Universe for help sometimes (when I remember to!) so I thought it would be nice to try praying to Universe as well. So I did! Today I've been feeling slightly disheartened that the event I'm planning has not yet had the response I was hoping for, but after ten minutes of breathing deeply and praying, I feel more at ease that the right thing will happen.

I remembered an old song or hymn we used to sing at primary school. As I went to a Church of England primary school the 'you' in these lyrics was obviously referring to the Christian God. But I realised 'you' can easily also refer to 'Heart', 'Spirit' or 'my Higher Self', and looked at this way, this song is really wonderful for me!

"One More Step Along
The World I Go
One more step along the world I go,
One more step along the world I go.
From the old things to the new
Keep me travelling along with you.
[Chorus]

And it's from the old I travel to the new,
Keep me travelling along with you.
Round the corners of the world I turn,
More and more about the world I learn.
All the new things that I see
You'll be looking at along with me.
[Chorus]

As I travel through the bad and good
Keep me travelling the way I should.
Where I see no way to go
You'll be telling me the way, I know.
[Chorus]

Give me courage when the world is rough,
Keep me loving though the world is tough.
Leap and sing in all I do,
Keep me travelling along with you.
[Chorus]

You are older than the world can be,
You are younger than the life in me.
Ever old and ever new,
Keep me travelling along with you.
[Chorus]"

***

I can use so many prayers from all religions as examples, but I think that all of you will know how to find your own. I just want to explain the simple things about Prayer and Asking that we don't usually find in textbooks. For those on the Internet, there is always Google. I should like you to find what suits you. Everyone is different.

I will be there tomorrow with your next topic!

Love and Many Blessings!
Robin Bela

DAY 9
GET HOLD OF YOUR 'RELAXATION FIRST AID KIT' : THROUGH PLAY

Welcome to DAY 9 of the 30-Day Programme

You can never create anything under a stressful and fearful state. So it's important to learn to relax and enjoy the process of achieving our goals with ease. Learning to relax is also a process which is helpful during the period one is waiting for an outcome, in order to let go of any anxiety, so that one is able to simply trust. Some people, who believe in working extra hours as a way of life, may find the 'simple way of being', as explained in this chapter, quite alien! Truly, you cannot be successful in having good health and happy relationships while overworking and overstressing, or while simply having the habit of worrying 24 hours. You will also find that such a lifestyle will drain you, lead to stress, and will in the end, affect your work and all spheres of your life.

How many times have you gifted yourself the extra time to take care of yourself, or given yourself the well-needed time off, and just done something for yourself, without any reason or feeling of guilt? We are born on this Earth not just to 'do' but also to 'receive' equally. Are you allowing yourself to receive for yourself lately, or are you just doing things for others, or are always entangled in completing the list of things to do? By allowing yourself to receive simple pleasures of life, you start inviting more abundance by the law of attraction! I hope that I have now caught your attention on this topic. It is a very important tool I use when I feel stuck in life, when I am getting no ideas and especially when I am feeling fearful. Usually in that situation, I realise that I have not been giving myself time off regularly, ideally on a daily basis, when I am not thinking, watching or listening to anything work-related, or that is emotionally draining. It's exactly then that I know I need to connect to my inner child, to bring more joy into my life.

Are you one of those who can work 10 to 14 hours a day or more, just because you love your work so much, or are really enjoying the approval from the work place, and end up overdoing it? I know someone who was going through a similar situation, and would try to recover her drained spirits by simply over-shopping, to the extent that her friends would say that she needed to de-clutter her house. She was in fact indulging in over-shopping to compensate for the time she was missing to enjoy life in general, with people or even by herself. Really, money cannot buy happiness, and overworking cannot either! It will just burn you out in time and cause adrenal fatigue. Yes, I too have been in that phase when I first started my business. Now I like to have a healthy balance.

Recently, we have been doing a lot of intense work in this Programme, so today's lesson falls perfectly in place now to bring things into balance and allow you to relax. It is important to include 'Play' in our lives for our mental health just as we ensure daily vitamin intakes for our bodily health. It's what opens your Heart and relaxes you to 'receive' the good things in life. You then connect to positive energies immediately because you are most likely doing something you love and it opens your Heart naturally to 'Give' and to 'Receive'. You need an open Heart to allow any 'giving' and 'receiving'. This allows the things you want to come easily to you so that wonderful synchronicities of opportunities and meeting the right people in life can begin! 'Play' is a great tool to help in manifesting goals! Play simply creates the fertile ground of 'love' to sow your seeds of Intents and keeps you away from 'fearful' energies.

Bringing 'play' into your life is such an easy tool to make you more receptive to the good things in life! It puts you out of the 'trying to control everything in life' mode, and instead gets you in touch with your intuitive side where things just start flowing naturally to you. Also, when you get back to work, you will find that you are much more efficient too. You will feel your heart much lighter, you will have the energy to do more, and you will find that you are naturally more generous to others too! And your 'Giving' doesn't tire you any more! But instead, you give much more and also receive much more.

To allow new things in life, you have to let your inner child play so that ideas and solutions come to you easily.

Now what exactly do I mean by Play? Yes it can be being silly and laughing with your children for no reason, doing some art, listening to music, dancing, enjoying walking, watching a movie, travelling, cooking, getting a massage, going swimming, playing tennis, watching sports, reading, enjoying sunshine, gardening, spending loving time with friends and family etc. Don't include your work as fun, e.g., my mother is an artist, so when she paints, it is her work and she needs to find other things to take a break.

YOUR WORK TODAY

1. *Write down at least 10 things you love doing.* I have noticed that some people don't even choose their holidays according to what they want. They go by what their friends think is cool. For all you know, a cruise is not what will relax you, but perhaps a quiet time in the hills may be the answer! I really want you to question everything in life, to be authentic with yourself and find out what you really love! If you are one of those people, you are only trying to please people to make them like you. It's coming from your own insecurities. Instead, you need to fill your own well of self-love. It means really caring and loving your life in everything you do. Today, I would like you to recall and to write down at least 10 things you love doing.

2. *Pick one of the things that you haven't done for a while and do it.* Just immerse your Spirit in the activity and have fun! If you are one of those who just doesn't know how to have fun because you have been a workaholic or only know how to give to others, or simply feel guilty taking time off for yourself, I can tell you then that today's task may not be easy for you to keep doing in the long run. I should really like you to consider this lesson as the most important one for you to remember in this Programme.

You must let yourself loose and allow your heart to open and ensure that it stays open, by bringing play into your daily life! Make sure that out of the list of 10 things you love, you are doing one a day! Yes, it can be something for just 10 minutes such as listening to some music to lift up your Spirits! Recognise that time for self as a gift which you are giving to yourself. But today give yourself more than just 10 minutes; go for at least an hour!

3. *Do question yourself if you feel guilty about giving time to self and for self-care.* Are you overworking? And what can you do to bring a good balance between work and play? I have learnt with my own experience that even though I love my work, not taking care of myself only burns me out physically: most importantly my heart, and I am definitely not giving much to others then! My Heart then feels heavy: sometimes in such situations, you can feel emotional too, for no reason. It's just that you are tired. I experienced that when I was new to this field of therapy and coaching.

With my own experience, I try and remind my students of this same tendency. I know one of my students who is such a giver and gets into the burn-out stage quite often, and then her doctor says she's going through 'depression'. Of course, she is depressed because her inner child is not having any fun in life. It may be difficult to find a scientific answer to her depression but it is obvious that she has to first learn to love and care for herself before she can attend to others; otherwise she is just like an empty bucket trying to give to others. If you are in the field of helping and caring for others, you really need to practice extra self-care, which can be deemed to be a skill that you have to learn.

4. Each of the 10 things you love to do, as listed out by you, should be done regularly. **Instead of doing things at a stretch, introduce play in between the day, and you will find yourself performing at work much better in the long run.** Also, you would most likely enjoy what you do more. So your only job today is to remember what things you love doing and to do them. Have fun and get yourself full of positive vibes by the end of the day! And make sure the list of 10 things or more you write is kept somewhere within reach, or just remember them as your 'Relaxation First Aid Kit'.

99

I had some people actually say that they could only think of 4 or 5 things at the most which they loved doing. I have to be honest, I was the same when I started. I remember I was so stuck in my work at that time that I could not think of anything beyond it, which had led to my burn-out. So I insist that you remind yourself of what you liked doing as a child or even what you fancied doing but never really got around to doing. And take it seriously. I had many participants send me work for all days of this Programme but did not bother sending 10 things they loved doing. The things which sound simple to do are sometimes the most important things. If you cannot even remember the things that you love, your life is without any joy at the moment, and really you cannot expect any joy in the future if you don't want to start inviting it into your life now. **The things you love are your natural vitamins, therapy and antidepressants, which ensure your natural wellbeing.** So, safely keep your list of delights, and use it!

You can Intend today: I AM connected to all things I love doing.

Examples from participants who sent their 10 things they loved doing:

EXAMPLE 1

Brenda's 'Relaxation First Aid Kit' includes:

1. Having a long soak in a hot bubble bath
2. Playing Scrabble!
3. Playing games with children
4. My pets
5. Drawing / Art
6. Writing (I love putting pen to paper!)
7. Using Aromatherapy Oils for my self and in the house
8. Spending time on self development (Spiritually)
9. Driving
10. Being in peace and quiet

EXAMPLE 2

Aisha's 'Relaxation First Aid Kit' includes:

1. Walking in the countryside
2. Watching sports
3. Swimming
4. Baking (and eating!) cakes and bread
5. Yoga
6. Gardening
7. Sewing/being creative
8. Spending time with friends
9. Watching films
10. Reading a good book

***

Relaxation creates a sense of well-being, which paves the way to happiness. So, let us not wait for our happiness to show up, but dive in now! When you are happy, you attract more joy into your life. The wonderful author Robert Holden has described it in similar words: "You can manifest things only if you are truly reflecting them as already present in your life." He goes on to say that, 'there was a study done where the people who were happily married were already very happy before they met their partners.' In other words, the people were very content with their lives and were not focusing on the lack of a partner. **While focusing on enjoying our lives, we naturally attract more joy as a result!** The love energy we talked about in the manifestation chapter 7, is all about this. When we are happy, good things come to us.

Have fun today and see you tomorrow feeling lighter, open hearted and with more good positive energies within you and around you!

Love,
Robin Bela

DAY 10
TAKE RISKS AND TRY SOMETHING NEW

If you are one of those who found the DAY 7 lesson on 'taking action' very hard, then this lesson is very important, as it will show you how to become a person who always takes action on any idea, and is ready to take risks and be adventurous. Most of the time, our intuition gives us amazing ideas, and we just miss them in the blink of an eye, because we think it's just wild imagination. But your imagination is the key to all that you can create. Only if you allow those ideas, that wild imagination, to linger a little longer in your thoughts, in your feelings, will you find the real gem. It is not wild imagination any more, it starts feeling quite real and possible. And when we take risks, our imagination is given an opportunity to open up, and we find ourselves working with the synchronicities of nature.

Taking action doesn't mean that you need to know the whole route, from A to Z. But the important thing is to keep the focus on the end result, and the 'in-between' starts filling in. I have to be honest that when I was writing this Programme as an e-course initially, I had no clear picture of what I was going to write and had no idea of turning it into a book later. But I knew what I wanted my participants to achieve, and so the required steps to help them attain that, just started pouring out in my writing. I literally wrote the complete e-course in 30 days. Yes, I was breathing and living every moment of this experience, and I allowed my my inner guidance to show me the way.

Years ago, I worked in a Company in the field of marketing, and left it to become an Energy Therapist and Coach. I did not have the full picture then either, of what exactly lay ahead of me. I had no experience in this field, and had no one to guide me. There was no one to offer me a job, as it is a self-employment path; neither was there anyone queuing-up outside to get therapy from me. I had no real proof that I could do it, or even make a living out of it, but I left all the lucrative perks of my job, and started working in a place that allowed me 2 free days in a week to start my practice. That one year was really busy and hectic, but I did manage, and soon, I left the job completely to work full-time in my chosen field, which was dear to my heart. Had I not taken the leap of faith in my wild imagination then, I think I would have had a completely different identity today.

There are some remarkable stories of how some people tried something new and took the risk in believing in their passion, like of J.K.Rowling, of how she wrote her book after her divorce, when she was penniless and raising her child and was rejected by 12 publishers before her first Harry Potter book was published. Later, at a graduating class at Harvard in June 2008, she said some wonderful things and pointed out how taking risks is really essential to our living:

"You might never fail on the scale I did", Rowling had told that privileged audience. "But it is impossible to live without failing at something, unless you live so cautiously that you might as well not have lived at all - in which case, you fail by default."

Colonel Sanders, the founder of KFC, had started his dream project when he was 65 years old! He had got a social security cheque of only $105 and was mad about it. Instead of complaining, he did something about it. He thought that restaurant owners would love his fried chicken recipe, use it, their sales would increase, and he'd get a percentage of it. He decided to drive around the country knocking at doors of restaurant owners and sleeping in his car. Do you know how many times people said no till he got one yes? 1,009 times!

And there is this unbelievable man who lived his life on taking risks, Thomas Edison. No list of successes without taking risks would be complete without the man who gave us many inventions including the light bulb. He'd said:

"If I find 10,000 ways something won't work, I haven't failed. I am not discouraged, because every wrong attempt discarded is another step forward."

103

A good way to develop the capacity for taking risks is to make a commitment to yourself to try something new every day. It could be to take a different route to work, go out for a walk on impulse, watch a different TV channel, read a different kind of magazine or join a new dance class. I had joined a belly dancing class a while ago, and later I signed up for pole dancing. I also went for some Spanish cooking classes that I so enjoyed! You may wonder whether you can do it, but somehow just go with the flow. Pole dancing, I later realised, was a good experience to try, but I did not continue. I guess that not all things you learn, you love. But you would know what you really love in life, only if you keep trying new things.

Start with little things, and then you will find that taking risks in bigger things such as a change of job, developing new ideas at work, change in relationships, improving health etc, will become easier, more natural and assured. You get a sense of natural confidence that you can do it. Try new cooking classes or simply a new recipe, read a different kind of book than you would normally, try wearing something you usually wouldn't think of, take a trip to somewhere out of the ordinary, meet new people, and make new friends through social gatherings etc. Just say yes to trying something new. As you do so, you are in sync with life. You are not resisting anything, and the actual wonderful synchronicities of life that can happen - happiness, friendships, opportunities and more - just start appearing in life magically. Today, as I was sitting at a place other than my usual haunt where I like to sit and write, I bumped into an old friend, and that meeting was so nice and helped us to get back in touch.

Please remember that the things I am asking you to do today, are different from the list you prepared in Day 9 lesson, of things you love doing. These things are completely new to you, and can seem challenging, but at the same time exciting, just like how you might have felt, when as a child, you were anxious to ride a bike for the first time, when there was an excitement in the air, in anticipation. I would like you to connect to the same feeling as you try new things in your life. You are discovering more of yourself and you are learning to be more open in your heart. It is time to come out of your shell if

104

you have been one of those who just do things in one set way. If you are, I am really excited for the new things about to come into your life!

YOUR WORK TODAY

1. Write a list of the new things you would like to try in your life. What would you like to do today?

2. *Are you resisting allowing the new to come in to your life because you are afraid to take risks?* Check with yourself now and regularly, especially when you feel stuck. If so, then it's time to infuse "Chi", as the Chinese would call it, which is simply "energy", into your energy-field by making yourself move out of that stagnant state. **If you move towards doing something new, you will start discovering that you can't wait to see what more you can do!** Surprise yourself and experience your magnificent powerful self! Life will become an adventure and you will feel you are living in the moment, rather than waiting for the future, or remaining stuck in the past.

3. *You can also Intend today:*

I AM calling on the I AM Presence to direct my Higher self that:

I AM open and comfortable to trying new things in life!

I AM open to taking risks and being adventurous.

I AM doing things I always wanted to.

I AM trying new routes to places.

I AM meeting new people.

I AM travelling to new places I like - think where?

I AM trying new vocations – think what?

I AM trying new ways of dressing-up.

The list goes on...what would you like to do but never did, that's not on this list? Please add them, and say the Intents along with your daily work, to invite all this into your life.

3. I would like you to now think, of what risk you are ready to take, to find your happiness in life, and achieve the goal that you are aspiring to, in these 30-Days. Are you ready to do what it takes? Perhaps it can be a humbling experience because you aren't sure if you will be good at it. But that is when you have to take the plunge, and it is a risk worth taking. You follow your gut instincts which are our natural God-given compass. For a moment, think of all ideas that come, and not worry about the 'how', as long as the end result excites you. So set your new brave Intent/s with what comes to you.

EXAMPLE: Rosalind went for real adventure as you will see below what she wrote for today's work!

"On impulse, I suddenly decided to put my coat on and go for a long walk through the woods. I wasn't sure if this was a safe thing to do but I survived (my heart beat faster and my senses were all hyper alert) and I was amongst nature in all its glory. Standing beside waterfalls roaring with power and intensity (making me feel humble), overlooking beautiful scenery and setting, soaking up peace and quiet with not a soul around (even the birds were quiet). This was a lovely place to practice my meditation and state my Intentions. I also had another chance to play as I caught up with a bunch of children who were playing and asked me to join them in their dens (trees that provided shelter and protection with imaginary furnishings and monsters lurking outside with only a stick or a branch to fend them off). I ripped my leggings climbing over the tree stumps and I was splattered in mud from top to bottom but I had so much fun.

I hobbled home and had to call the cavalry (my husband) for a lift as my heels were blistered and sore and I could hardly walk another step. He was amused by the state I was in and responded well to me having fun in the woods."

Have an exciting and adventurous day!
Love,
Robin Bela

DAY 11
LET THE BELIEF BE STRONG AS A ROCK : "ROCK" YOUR DREAMS

Welcome to DAY 11 of the 30-Day Programme

To bring about any change is not always easy. To allow change to happen, it is important to build your inner strength and focus intensely on why you are wanting change in the first place. Understanding that will connect you to how important this change is for you and why you must believe in your dreams. Today, you are going to let your belief in your dreams grow stronger. **The only separation between you and your goal is whether you 'believe' in it.** Or are you still casually wishing it or wondering if you can achieve it? Once you decide with conviction that this is what you want, and stay firm as a rock from within, you have created a laser-beam focus on what you want. By the law of attraction, you are simply going to get what you want, believe in, feel and visualise, through constant reminders to yourself.

The sharper the focus on your Intent is, the stronger is your Belief in Self. To increase your belief in self, you are not focusing on the process of 'how' to reach your goal, but instead, on the joy and excitement of creating it. And slowly, the steps you should take, one by one, start becoming clear. As you do so, you will notice that you begin to feel as though you are already living the lifestyle of the different person you want to become: for example, you may start dressing up or talking like a confident counsellor that you wish to become. I, for a long time, Intended that I AM a Therapist and Teacher even before I became one in reality. If you cannot take the courage to feel your goal and believe in it, you simply cannot create it.

Usually, when you achieve something, you feel it to be quite natural and well-deserved, and you do not wonder as to how and why you got it. It is natural for thoughts to manifest in reality as you focus on them. Be sure to stay away from sceptics during this process. In the beginning, share your dreams only with those you are comfortable with, as you need people who support you rather than those who break your belief in your dreams.

In the initial stages, it may seem that you are faking your belief. This is because your mind hasn't experienced the other way of being, as suggested here. So, you have to first train your mind to think and feel that way. And slowly, it sinks in. That is why, repeatedly 'feeling', 'believing' and 'imagining' your dream, consciously for a few minutes every day, is crucial. Remember again to avoid contact with fearful, doubting minds and stay positive by using your daily Meditation, by staying connected to your Sacred Altar Within, following the Steps to Manifesting as explained in chapter 7, feeling and visualising your dream and praying that you 'easily', 'effortlessly' and 'joyfully' reach your goal as mentioned in the earlier chapter, while releasing all your anxieties. And if fears still linger, you might want to check in with Soul Clearing Technique, to clear them. Remember to focus on the excitement of what you are doing and becoming.

Achieving a goal should not be seen as a test but rather as an enriching experience about enjoying doing something you want and love. Keep reminding yourself of how much this means to you, and stay focused on enjoying the process of achieving your goal. Imagine how a social carer would focus on the service and joy of doing his or her wonderful work; or a dancer would perform for sheer joy and love for the art. Find your reasons!

I would like to ask you, how confident are you about achieving your goal quickly? I was once dealing with a health issue that wasn't serious, but I of course wanted it to be healed completely. It first occurred to me that if I thought of it as healed and healthy every day, it will start getting better. But then I instantly realised that by so thinking, I was making an assumption and an Intent that the healing would take several days and that I no longer believed in swift healing. I then worked with the following Intent, which yielded quick results:

I AM healed. I believe I AM healed. I AM healthy. I AM.

You can use the words 'I believe I AM' or 'I AM believing' along with your I AM statements' and make them more effective. Do this especially when you are still not able to visualise yourself achieving your goal.

I believe that the underlying firm belief in the real possibility of swift healing and speedy achievement of goals can work wonders for everybody, including my clients, who see me personally. I would rather see 100 people than 20 regular ones. I don't work like a massage therapist who likes clients to come back regularly, as my focus is on healing and creating quick and lasting solutions. If I already assume that they are coming back, how do you think I will create complete healing or provide help for that person? Yes, they may need to see me again, but that's a decision to be made after the session I do with them, either in person or through distance.

I also ask my clients to believe in the real possibility of swift healing because I sometimes find that a client's belief in their healing too can be a problem. I once had a client, who was healed physically in the movement of her legs, in just one session. Before the session began, she actually told me, "I don't believe things are going to improve." Now my belief was probably stronger, and so she was walking well after the session: she was shocked, and perhaps strangely, a bit annoyed that she was fine now, and didn't want to hear how it was her thinking itself which had created that problem. I never saw her again, but if she still remained stuck in her beliefs, those physical problems could reappear! She was stuck on the need to receive pity and sympathy to balance the need of self-love, and also used her walking difficulty as a mental block and an excuse for not taking the required steps to move forward in life.

I had another client, whose issues with people, which she felt affected her life, were all cleared. But she kept insisting that something was still there, due to which, her back was not feeling right. So in the end, I had to say, "Let go of the feeling of being a victim", and that helped her to open up her block. She had been finding it hard to believe that all her issues with people had been cleared. This was because she was stuck in the belief that others had taken charge of her life and she was a victim of their actions towards her. But now she realised that she could take charge of her life and interestingly, her back got better. So check yourself honestly to see if your own beliefs are blocking your healing in any way. Has it started affecting you physically? Check with your body and talk to it.

Today, in order to deepen your focus on your Intents, I would also like you to do some 'visualisation' and 'feeling' work towards achieving your goal, with some music. Yes, I would like to see you 'rock' in your own life, as in a movie! Listen to any music that inspires you; see yourself enjoy the process of attaining the goal peacefully, in a relaxed manner. It really doesn't have to be a struggle. You decide how you would like it to be. I have a few inspiring songs below for you that you may perhaps like to listen to on the Internet. It's a varied collection, so I hope you can find something suitable here, or you can think of one yourself, perhaps in your own language. Feel free to close your eyes if you like, and create your own real movie!

Build your zeal and zest for your dream stronger today. Build a strong belief in your dream. Smile as you move with it in heart, body and mind. Feel it in every cell of your body. Here is a quote I love, which says it perfectly:

'What matters is not the idea a man holds, but the depth at which he holds it.'
~ Ezra Pound.

And as you dream, ask yourself, what action steps am I to take today towards my goal. See what ideas come to you as you enjoy listening to some music today to inspire yourself. **When you let your imagination run wild, great ideas can simply drop in!**

Albert Einstein once said that he discovered the law of relativity when he was listening to music! He said, "It occurred to me by intuition, and music was the driving force behind that intuition. My discovery was the result of musical perception." And I love what Plato, one of my favourite philosophers, said about Music: "Music is a moral law. It gives soul to universe, wings to the mind, flight to the imagination, and charm and gaiety to life and to everything."

110

Next, I would also like you to express your vision on paper! You will see what I mean, as I explain this a bit later.

YOUR WORK TODAY

Check with yourself honestly to see if your own negative beliefs are blocking full belief in your healing or achievement of your goal in any way. If they are blocking healing, check with your body and Heart, and talk to it and write in your journal for better clarity. You may need to work with Day 2 and Day 3 Soul Clearing Technique, if you discover your beliefs are hard to clear. The negative beliefs, when removed, facilitate rapid healing. Speedy achievement of goals is similarly possible. And then write your new Intents for this purpose. To replace the old patterns of functioning, you have then to repeatedly focus on the new patterns embodied in your Intents and goals.

It is easier to dream about goals when there are no negative beliefs blocking your way. And let me remind you again, that **to increase your belief in self, you are not focusing on the process of 'how' to reach your goal, but instead, on the joy and excitement of creating it.** And below are some ways to strengthen your belief in your goals by growing passion and excitement:

PART I: WITH MUSIC

1. *Find your reasons for excitement in your goal.* How does it make you feel now? Your work today, is to dream and develop a strong 'Belief' within yourself, of that goal of yours being achieved. Feel the inner strength grow like a 'rock' or 'flame' in your heart, daily, by breathing it in, with eyes closed. Remind yourself why you are doing this and how important it is for you! Feel the fire within for your passion of taking those steps towards your goal. The belief doesn't appear from outside but is grown consciously from within. So if you are lacking in conviction, you simply focus regularly on an Intent to achieve your goal. You should feel the strength in your conviction just within a week, and it just keeps growing, as you start taking the steps. Focus on the joy of creating and achieving it.

2. *Take a step further in your dream process, by spending some time day-dreaming about your goal, as if you were watching a movie in your mind:* of course it's all about the new exciting you, that you have already become! Feel the excitement in your heart and body, with a feeling of gratitude of already receiving it! You probably do that already for things you think you will never get, but I would like you to dream as if it's real and you have achieved it. I recommend using music to inspire you.

3. *Below are some suggestions of songs that you can also listen to,* that uplift the heart to some good vibes and get you excited further towards your goal. And of course, you would have your own list of songs you like.

And as you dream, ask yourself: *'what action steps am I to take today towards giving reality to my dream.'* And see what ideas come to you as you enjoy listening to some music today to inspire you:

Bobby McFerrin - Don't worry, Be happy
Vangelis - Chariots of Fire
Pharrell Williams - Happy
Michael Buble - Feeling Good
R. Kelly - I Believe I Can Fly
Celine Dion - The Power of the Dream
Michael Jackson - Man In The Mirror
Bob Marley - Lively Up Yourself
Ace Of Base - It's a Beautiful Life
Bob Sinclar - World, Hold On
Bob Sinclar - Love Generation
La Valse d'Amelie (Orchestre)
Bon Jovi - It's My Life
Yves LaRock - Rise Up
Gwen Stefani - What You Waiting For?

There are so many songs I'm sure that can inspire you. I just mentioned some that came to my mind now. If you know some nice, crazy, amazing ones that lift your spirits, do listen to them and get plugged into your dream as real!

4. Were you able to dream and see yourself as you want yourself to be when listening to some music? What action steps did you see that you need to take for yourself? You can write them down in your journal.

I now do this quick 'mental picture of having achieved what I want, with gratitude in heart', sometimes in just a minute, to keep my fuel of passion burning, as a part of my daily Intent work, or just as I pray. You can now do as well.

Use the words 'I AM believing' in your I AM statements. For example, I AM believing that I have succeeded in achieving my goal.

EXAMPLE 1

The response of Mary, one of the participants of my course, to today's lesson was:

"Over the past week or so, since starting this course I have realised how deep my insecurities and fears are and why I am finding it very hard to visualise my dreams and Intentions. It has been so many years of feeling the way I do and now I am being asked to think positively! And when I say positive things, people often agree with me and intend what I have said. If I say negative things, people usually correct me or say things like "yes but think of it positively" or "don't be so negative".

I have also found that if someone talks negatively a lot (like my Mum), you want to shake them or find yourself making a positive statement to make them and yourself feel better. Which means that I could say positive things all the time if I wanted to!"

The Intents we formed which she needs to read regularly are:
Intent: I AM calling on the I AM Presence to direct my Higher Self that:

I AM believing I AM easily able to stay, feel, think and imagine positive things all the time as it makes me happy and joyful. I AM enjoying seeing my dreams come true!

I AM patient and compassionate with my mother and sister and just breathe with them peacefully.

Mary is now visualising herself as a positive person, and imagining how she looks and behaves as this positive person, perhaps through images in mind and gets further motivated through listening to some inspirational songs.

EXAMPLE 2

Below are some more statements used by another participant Diana on the course who was stuck with the belief of what others think about her ideas. You may use these if you feel you need that support too:

Intent: I AM calling on the I AM Presence to direct my Higher Self that:

I AM believing that others are accepting my guidance as it comes through my Heart, the pure state of divine.

I AM believing that My Belief in myself is the most important thing for me to be happy and successful in life.

Diana now listens to music focusing on the Intent of feeling the peace and love in her heart. The more she connects to her authentic self, with love in her heart, she will feel confident of how she comes across to others and most likely stop bothering about it. It is her lack of self-worth that is making her think that way. She may even sing her Intents and feel the passion get even stronger.

PART II: DRAW AND CRAFT YOUR VISION TO REALITY

This is the second part of today's visualising process. We are going to put all that we have been envisioning about, in our mind and heart, onto paper now, and express, create our dreams on the physical plane, and make them more real in our lives. I would like you to draw or cut and paste images from magazines that represent your dream. Now you can stick to the main goal, but feel free to add anything else you desire, e.g., your main goal is to lose weight but you can also add pictures for money or anything else you desire. You can even do it on a word document by finding images online. I actually cut pictures of people and put my face on their bodies, for goals on weight, for example.

Just try to reflect the feelings of your dreams on the paper. You can cut and paste pictures from magazines, perhaps some inspirational messages from newspapers etc. Just get creative and have fun! *If you had trouble dreaming in your mind's eye, you might find this much easier.*

After you have converted your dream/vision into a painting/collage, put it somewhere you can see it daily. It can be a clip-board, or keep it on the table where you work, or anywhere where you can be reminded regularly about your dream.

As you see it so often daily, what happens is that you simply get used to the idea. It feels quite normal and not so new to you anymore. It allows your belief to strengthen within, naturally.

****

During the visualisation exercises done today, you may get various ideas about the action steps that you need to take for the achievement of your goal. Do write them in your journal before you forget. Note all your feelings, thoughts, visions etc. Then take at least one action step daily. It's then that your belief starts becoming a reality. You can do it. You are doing it! I AM rooting for all of you on an energetic level.

I shall see you tomorrow! Have a day full of excitement about the NEW YOU!

Much Love,
Robin Bela

DAY 12
GETTING AUTHENTIC WITH MONEY :
CREATING A LOVING RELATIONSHIP WITH IT

Welcome to DAY 12 of the 30-Day Programme

Understanding your relationship with Money is so important because it determines how much money you will have in life. As we really cannot live without money, it is best to learn to create the right relationship with it. Long before money came into existence, the process of obtaining goods pertaining to one's daily requirements was called sharing, love, understanding each other's needs, which later developed into the barter system whereby people exchanged commodities that they required. Soon, the exchange went on with people over distances, who had never met each other before. As trade grew and people wanted to keep a record of all such transactions, it led to the use of numbers and Money. But let us not forget that the origin of Money was in sharing, love and understanding each other's needs.

The reason why Money exchange exists is also to offer a process by which one can offer something that the other needs and when it's not always possible to offer back something equally valuable. So, money exchange is quite useful but it's all best done with love in heart, and sometimes, it is just love that you are offering through money as in India where I grew up, where there is a custom of offering money to children as a gift by the elderly when they visit them. So in the past, the energy of love for exchange was given a physical form, let's say, a face or a body in paper, a form we call as Money.

Now, when we stop focusing on the 'sharing love aspect' of Money and look at survival needs only, there is no such exchange of love. Imagine a friendship where one is needy and is friends with somebody only to get something out of that person. You may know the person all your life but how meaningful or blissful would the relationship be? Then that is the quality of your relationship with Money. Would that relationship be blissful and would it last? Do you think you could expect any love or abundance back? Maintaining a relationship like this gets very tiring.

Don't you think then that it's time to change and open your heart to offering love through all you do, and enjoy such a relationship so that you naturally receive abundance and love from Universe? You too would be happier doing what you love. Else, it is survival of the fittest kind of fight, when really, Universe is there to provide you with everything. **When we stop believing that Universe supports us for everything we Ask, we live in constant fear and forget our passions and what we like, and become slaves to fears.** It is then that the struggle begins because you receive abundance only if you put love and passion into what you do, and not just do something merely to get money. That becomes such a soul-less life!

What has happened over the years is that people, out of their own mistaken notions of their wrongdoings, have created fake relationships with others through Money, and given Money a bad name! Such an image of Money in your psyche or even in your ancestral family memory, can impact the way you see Money and how much you have of it. What you fear and don't like or what disturbs you, you just cannot have more of it! So, it is important to correct one's relationship with Money and restore harmony and love with it.

I find that some of my students who become therapists and coaches have a tough time asking for money for the hard work they put in, or to increase their rates by even £5 for the services rendered, when they should and most importantly, want to receive adequate remuneration. I know that those who have been regular clients for someone, are not there for what they are charged, but for what service they are receiving, and in my experience, in service industry specially, I would be happy to pay more if I am getting what I need. So, why are these students of mine, offering so much love and healing for their clients' well-being, afraid to ask for sufficient remuneration when on the other hand, they might demand more money if they were not paid adequately or not on time in office or at a restaurant or in a strawberry field where they worked; and a work probably they didn't like at all?

Usually, you would think that you deserve more in a job, where you put your heart and soul. It is a misconception that Money is not connected to love. And anything we can offer with love, some of my students would say, "why should money come in the picture?" Well, it's fine unless you are getting an hour of love and healing back from your client! Or your client is your friend or a member of family perhaps? Else, you are neither loving yourself enough, nor valuing and respecting your time and energy. Also, if you want to offer better service or do more of whatever your business is all about, you would like to charge reasonably, justifying your living expenses, unless you are a pensioner, or someone not bothered perhaps about making much profit. These people, including me, in the past, have been such people who had practically no relationship with Money, were reluctant to ask for our fee, and rather could be taken for granted. And when I got underpaid and was over-worked, the quality of my work wasn't the best too!

My relationship with Money started, as far as I can remember, at the age of 5. I remember my mother used to put all the money for the month in one shelf of a cupboard. I had no idea then that money was just not available freely to take away like all fruits or things to eat lying around in the house and that it was something wrong if you took some money from the cupboard, as after all, mum also did so. So every day, I would take the exact amount out for my ice cream lolly after school, and after a few weeks passed, my mother of course found out and was quite angry. I had no idea why though, back then! But I certainly stopped doing it because she told me that God would write, 'I am a thief' on my forehead, if I did so. I at least learnt that what I was doing, needed permission, else it's called stealing, and that Money doesn't grow on trees!

I certainly got that phrase over and over again all my life from the society and saw people clinging to sometimes unhappy jobs for the safety of a salary every month. It's almost like giving power away that you cannot be happy without Money. So I did get the feeling always that it takes a lot to own Money, that it requires hard work and a lot of proving and justifying to have it. Especially with my Dad working in senior positions in Police, I learnt about a lot of people acquiring money through corrupt means. I was discouraged from going to friends' houses whose parents were in business, if my Dad wasn't sure what kind of business it was as he didn't want to be connected to anyone who might be engaged in some illegal work. So I grew up thinking that it is perhaps wrong to make money from business, and that if you do, most likely, it is out of wrongdoings. That's the impression I had about Money, which was at the back of all issues with Money I may have had. The first thing I needed to Intend was, 'I AM deserving to receive Money easily and effortlessly through the things I love doing.'

Later I realised that I always had Money that was just enough for me for each month, which resulted in a lot of stress, as I wouldn't have any savings. Later, as I did the process of digging out my fears as explained in Day 2, I discovered that I just didn't think it was good to have more money than I needed to pay my bills. So I would manifest through my work the exact amount I needed every month. When I asked 'Money' why was I going through that, 'Money' answered what I have written below in my journal. I also discovered my blockage that was affecting me not only with regard to money but also my relationships in life too. You will see how I work through the Day 2 process to discovering the core beliefs I had with respect to Money. Now this is what I had written in my journal:

"As I am imagining Money as a person who is there in my life like anyone else is, it is easy for me to see clearly what kind of relationship I have with Money. Also, I was able to have loving feelings for it as I was looking at it as more than just a piece of paper. As I started focusing on connecting and understanding the relationship with it, I realised it's been always that I have just enough money, never too much as if things will go wrong if I do and interestingly, this has been the case with me with guys too, feel that if things are going too good, something will go wrong. Why do I believe that? Why do I not allow real love and abundance to flow through my life constantly? My answer to that was: I am blocking the flow because I feel I don't deserve it, I feel like I am drugged with happiness and would lose control of life or do something wrong. I realised that when I think of the perfect guy or perfect lifestyle and money, I keep saying 'not now', as if my life would disrupt. It's all on an

unconscious level. I feel that too much money will remove focus off my work. And really that is part of me that's not trusting that I'm responsible to take care of my business and myself.

So why do I feel I cannot take care of myself? As I ask this question to myself, I feel a sudden rush of energy in my legs. It is like I have triggered the real issue that blocks me from literally moving forward. In the past 20 years almost, I have had physical problems around legs on two occasions when I had knee dislocations, the last one being about ten years ago. But recently, as I had posed this question to myself, I had a few trips and falls reminding me of my soul searching that I had been doing. Now I know that in energy healing terms, the lower part of the body is connected to earthly matters such as money and safety. I also remember that in school, I was into sports but kept getting injured on feet and knees regularly and used to be sent home, so much so that the Principal of the school often called me 'Delicate darling'. And this pattern continued in my early twenties with my knee dislocation and foot sprains. It's like I cannot stand on my feet! And therefore, I also had the sense that I didn't know what I wanted more and whether it would be 'safe in my hands', so it's best to do what others say is safe to do and receive just what's required and not take more at hand. But the real problem or blessing in disguise began when I started to listen to my Heart and heard what I really wanted to do in life. I know I was scared to step out and grab the happiness and say I deserve it and am safe to have more money and love. There was a part of me that said I might harm myself or even others by taking more things to take care of. So I began answering the question, why am I earning just enough money to sustain myself? Why is it that I just get overwhelmed with extra money or even love? The answer I received from my Heart was, 'I would do something wrong with extra money or waste it or cause harm'.

Recently, when I was questioning all these things and understanding these things within, the smoke alarm suddenly started ringing for no reason and became faulty. I had just completed a meditation and was focusing on my inner dialogue about money. I quickly pulled a ladder and stopped the alarm but at the same time, the ladder just collapsed and I bruised myself on my foot. I realised that me stepping out of my comfort zone about Money was ringing a fire alarm within me that it's not safe to step out and I had literally manifested it in my reality showing me that my core block was even stronger than what I had realised in my journaling notes. Money is such a teacher and here I am awakened and more ready to receive Money into my life now. I AM responsible to receive more love, happiness and Money and I deserve to receive. I AM safe to receive more Money! Since then, Money and me have been friends and I hear Money, it cares for me! All I do is Ask and Intend for more. It is by the law of attraction we know that what you love, think and feel is what you get; and also that what you fear, hate and are worried about, you attract. So I realised that it was up to me to focus on what kind of relationship and feelings I wanted to create consciously with Money. With my new relationship with Money after I had cleared my issues with it, I was more comfortable and trusting to hear loving words from 'Money' that it's there for me."

When I ask people who have blocks related to Money, the common issues I have noticed are that 'they never had any kind of loving relationship with Money', 'felt it was wrong to have Money', 'felt guilty of having money', 'they can have it only if they are lucky' or 'don't feel they deserve it'. I also found that all the aforesaid issues with Money arose from lack of self-love. Also, many a time, such people didn't know how to take care of 'self", which had even been the case with me earlier, as in the case of my story above.

There are others who just mistreat their relationship with Money by borrowing when they clearly cannot afford it. It's like getting happiness and love on credit from the future. We create an unauthentic relationship here with Money. It's not honest and trusting as we don't believe that Money can be with us now. When the key to 'life' really is in the 'Present', we need to learn to believe and understand that we have all the tools in the moment to take care of ourselves. When I realised that and noticed how I was buried in debt with credit cards and store cards, I just couldn't breathe any more. I focused constantly for 2 weeks on how to clear it. In the end, I found the money and cleared most of it at one go. I know if I hadn't focused on it, the solutions wouldn't have appeared. I felt so free to let go of the monthly payments and also have extra cash in the month. I was more concerned with the process to be honest in my relationship with 'Money'.

The next step for me was to ensure that I had the Money always with me, beside me, and that it's not going to run away. I stopped thinking of the 'how' question completely. I simply started Asking and deciding what I wanted and soon the options and ideas started to appear. **So the key to doing anything in life is not decided upon by how much Money you have for doing something but rather by what you like to do first and then the Money appears. You have got to Intend for it.** Speak to the energy with love and be excited how Money makes your life amazing and happy. Morgana Rae, a teacher about Money concept, really takes it a step further and says that we should think of Money as a lover and talk to it. And I can see the connection as our relationships with ourselves, friends, lover, money - all are dependent on how you perceive 'giving and receiving love', in general. If our heart's not open fully to love in general, it will reflect in the way you give and receive love to all other aspects of life.

Sometimes, solutions for receiving more Money might come to you in different ways. And may be, instead of more Money, sometimes luck appears as a gift from Universe! For example, I loved the house where I was staying and didn't want to share it with anyone. So I decided to tell the landlords that I would be moving to a smaller house where I won't need to share. But to my surprise and delight, they asked how much I was going to pay for the smaller house, and reduced the rentals accordingly and let me stay on my own. The landlords trusted that I maintained the house well, so they got what they wanted and I got what I liked. Sometimes, it's not just about making more Money but also saving. I remember that just a few days earlier, I had 'told' my House that I loved it, and loved taking care of it and at the same time was wondering what was the best way to save Money. So, I was thinking of moving out to a smaller place, but Universe helped me find a better deal and solution that I couldn't have imagined. And remember in the end, Money and love are all the same. Whatever exchange is of equal value, takes place quite effortlessly.

I believe that some people who have worked in salaried jobs, find it extremely hard to receive Money from a person for a work done outside a salaried job or if they are starting a new business for the first time. They are the people who never had a direct relationship with Money, and perhaps feel that Money was wrong to have, and that it was safe to receive money through the employers they may have been working with. But the day they have to go and sell something directly, they just cannot receive the Money as if it's a new issue of asking for Money, and the question of deserving etc. comes to their mind as it's about their value and not of their employers' anymore. They were receiving Money earlier too but it was under the guise of salary and they didn't have to ask for it every month. It just comes into the bank account. So they would escape the process of dealing with it every month. So these people focused only on the relationship with their employers and not on Money. They won't be aware that they needed to correct their relationship with Money right away and not wait till they needed a raise and asked for it. Or perhaps, they really wanted deep down to get out of the job and do something new and perhaps start a business.

In the long run, our relationship with Money also reflects our relationship with our self, our self-worth and feeling of deserving happiness. So even if you may feel you are in the right job and happy, and don't want to bother about the relationship with Money, I would really encourage you to address your relationship with Money so that you can identify and resolve core issues which may perhaps be affecting your self-confidence. This will also give you confidence to not be so dependent on the job you are in, especially in these days and age when people are losing their jobs so often. It's the age where people need to find their own direction and self-worth and not just be a part of the crowd. Everyone is unique and deserves to find that unique self, their full worth. It would foster their growth whether they are employed or self-employed. And also, this will help them recognise that they are not just their job! They are much more. You bring the special you to the job and everything else in life. It might open you to so much more as you discover confidence perhaps to pursue some hobby or ideas that would make your life even more fulfilling. Accepting Money as normal is also a process of 'accepting' and 'respecting' yourself that you deserve all happiness and abundance like everyone does.

It's a two-way relationship with Money like any other relationship. Overspending and getting into heavy debts is not a two-way relationship. That's you taking Money for granted, not respecting it or valuing it. It also stems from not respecting and taking care of self, otherwise you wouldn't lead yourself to a situation where you are covered in debt. Every relationship in life is a reflection of ourselves in the end.

In my view, looking at our past ancestral history hundreds of years ago, we are not a society which is used to being in debt to the extent we are now, and so handling debts is perhaps not in our genes. It's almost as though Banks have abused money and offered people excessive amounts of Money to borrow, and also notice how they make it hard to pay back with high interest rates. I don't think any bank should give loans unless they have also placed a system for them to pay back easily. If you ask the bank, they are not bothered about you paying back the full amount as they are benefiting really long term with the interests. So we can perhaps call these banks as the villains in our love story with Money! Now society, being heavily in debt, has no clue as to what to do. To get out of the situation, all Prime Minsters and Presidents of countries are having a tough problem with the debts. All they have to do is ensure that their governments don't overspend and teach people to learn to be self-reliant and not teach wrong habits of borrowing excessively! In the end, the banks are not benefiting too! As you can see, the relationship is not balanced, people are unable to pay, and banks are going through a crisis. All relationships that are abused or are unauthentic, would go wrong in the end, whether these are with a person or with Money.

YOUR WORK TODAY

We understand that opening our heart to Money is crucial, whatever it takes: forgiving yourself and letting go of any issues you may have had with Money in the past and starting a new relationship of love, trust and honesty. A good way to start examining your relationship with Money is simply by visualising how it appears to you as a human being. What kind of feelings do you have for Money? Notice and clear the problems in your relationship.

Speak to it heart-to-heart and ask how you can love more money, and it might answer you saying it's always been there for you but you never looked at it lovingly. Whenever you are in doubt as to where to find Money, that is a sign that your relationship with Money is not there or needs attention. So write to it, speak to it with hand on Heart, and bring back the feeling that Money is always with you, taking care of you. Then focus on taking your next steps.

1. *Check with yourself:* What kind of relationship do you have with Money? Think of it as a person and then you will know what you need to focus on to improve your relationship. Intend to look at Money as a Friend.

2. *Does money come and go or stay with you?* Check if there is anything wrong with your relationship with Money? Is it a struggle to have money in life? Question yourself why?

3. *Think of all your fears with regard to Money* in the same way as I explained the process of finding the root cause of your fears and blocks under Day 2 topic. Keep digging the reasons until you find your core issue behind whatever you can find as a block for Money. Then change the wordings of your Intent as to what you would like to have, and write your new Intent on which you want to focus. And if you have any blocks to be cleared, then just breathe them out once as explained in Day 3.

4. **Some common Intents for Money that can support you:**
I AM calling on the I AM Presence to direct my Higher Self that:
I AM always connected to my love for Money and I feel its love for me constantly. Life is so good with it.
I AM deserving to receive Money because I respect myself. Offering and receiving Money is an act of love.
I AM responsible with Money.
I AM honest with Money.
I AM loving unconditionally and need nothing to prove to receive love back from Money.

I AM trusting Money.

I AM taken care of by Money.

I AM taking care of myself. And I AM taking care of Money too.

I give love to Money easily and receive love from Money easily.

I AM deserving to receive more love, happiness and Money.

I AM safe to receive more Money.

Once your old issues with Money have cleared, it is important to ensure that a loving relationship with Money is created as explained below:

5. Some points to remain in a loving relationship with Money:

* *Ask for help from Universe.* Ask often 'What would it take to create the __sum of money? Show me the way Universe.'

* *Stop blaming Money* for all things you can't have. Instead, Intend that it is what you want and ask Money's help and look out constantly for all answers and solutions. Universe brings to you anything you focus your attention on. Make sure that you Ask without fear, and with love, trust and excitement of having reached the goal.

Know that Money is with you always, and cares and loves you. If you feel it is missing, speak to it right away and clear the misunderstanding in your heart just like you would do with any relationship. This also relates to self-worth issues. When we are in the best of spirit and are kind and loving to self, we are more open to receiving effortlessly.

* *Keep finding constant love for Money.* Let Money know you love it and it excites you. Feel the love in your heart. Speak to it. Develop your relationship like any relationship would grow over a period of time. I usually find that when I feel the warm, loving, fuzzy feeling for Money, and whatever issue I may be having with regard to Money gets solved or starts to get better. It's just like any relationship, you've got to keep the friendship and love going.

* *Find excitement of what Money can bring to you.* When we focus on 'joy' of how abundant and happy our lives are and imagine more Money can offer, then we naturally attract more of good things. But if we focus on constant worry, we are then focusing on 'lack' rather than on 'abundance' and attract likewise into our lives. For me, this is the most important point to remember.

EXAMPLE

Lauren called me when she wanted to expand her therapy business and as we dug deeper into what was blocking her, she came up with her issue of not starting now because she wanted to be perfect first. This is a perfect example of self-worth issues affecting flow of abundance in business. Since childhood, her parents always made her feel that she was not good enough and needed to work harder to be perfect. So due to fear of being not good enough, she kept procrastinating the process of beginning. Even when I would lay out the steps that she needed to take, by the next call, I noticed she was still not taking any action steps and was happy to be in the planning and researching side of things. As I asked her to feel in her body where she felt the block, she felt 'butterflies' in her stomach. She informed that she felt fear there as and when she thought of moving forward. Stomach (above the navel) which is referred to "solar plexus chakra" in energy healing work.

Lauren also felt that she would lose freedom if she committed herself to more work. I realised that she wasn't aware deep down that she always had the choice to control the amount of work she did, like saying 'No' to a client when she was busy and booking another time that was convenient to her. So I had to help her clear the blocks about 'being perfect and worthy' to receive more Money. And the truth is that, 'we begin' and then become 'near perfect' with practice. Also, I had to explain to her that she needed to know that she could take care of herself and feel safe to have more work and Money and that she could handle it easily because she had the freedom to do it her way! She wouldn't lose any power or control over her life by trying something new and she also needed nothing from outside to give her permission or to prove that she was good enough to start! She was already 'ready'!

127

The Intents formed for her were:

I AM committed to my path of helping others and showing them the direction.

I AM having all the freedom as I commit to my work.

I AM free to work as per my needs and I voice it easily when needed.

I AM taking good care of myself always.

I AM choosing to do all through my heart and so everything is perfect. And I don't need to focus on perfectionism.

I AM already there and ready to start and expand my work.

I AM worthy of all my desires.

I AM compassionate to the understanding of my family sometimes.

I AM perfect at this moment.

I AM only doing what I want to do.

I AM doing everything at a relaxed pace and never pushing, and I take good care of myself as a priority.

I AM doing things for love and out of passion for helping people.

I AM enjoying this process.

I AM open to receiving.

I AM truly worthy because it comes from a place of heart, all that I do.

I AM worthy of receiving all the abundance.

I AM there already where I want to be!

I AM courageous to move forward in my career.

I AM easily able to say No when needed.

I hope you have fallen in love with Money today? Or at least, have started to feel closer to it. Grow and nourish this relationship for your entire life, and ensure that it becomes your best friend. Then, you will find your feet firmly on the ground and you will know that the Mother Earth is taking care of your material and physical needs as you do what you love!

You just need to decide what you want and ask Universe to help you. And keep doing your bit as you focus on reaching where you want to be, and soon, you are guided intuitively and receive opportunities. You don't have to have evidence of possessing Money to start doing what you want because if it is the first time you have Asked and have put your focus on something new that you want, you may naturally not have all resources right away. You have to simply allow time and options to appear and your job is to look for them, work for them and have fun creating new things in life. Sometimes, I wanted to do things for which I had no money right away. But that doesn't mean I just say I cannot have it because I have no money! That is just blaming Money. Remember this is one of the things you don't say or your loving relationship with Money gets affected. Instead, what I do is, simply my usual Prayer/Asking, and then have a conversation with Money and feel the love in my heart for Money and say that I like to have this new thing in life which would make me immensely happy, and I just feel my heart calm and peaceful as I feel the love in my heart. It is then I know that All is Well! Answers do start appearing soon and also Money in my bank! Simply trusting Universe alone can be enough.

Money really wants to do its job of offering us all abundance and prosperity, as it loves us. You just need to see that loving side of Money and allow it to offer you its support by keeping the faith.

See you tomorrow dear 'Abundant Reader'.

Much Love,
Robin Bela

DAY 13
BE GENEROUS TO YOURSELF AND LIFE IS GENEROUS TO YOU : PRIORTISE YOUR NEEDS DAILY AND ASK UNIVERSE

Welcome to DAY 13 of the 30-Day Programme

If you are one of those who work only for perfection, then it's time to dismantle that aspect of your make-up, and not be so hard on yourself! Be generous to yourself, by appreciating how much you are doing. Open your heart to yourself, even if it might mean being slightly late on this 30-Day Programme with me, or may be achieving just a little part of your goal today, which could be simply feeling more confident about yourself. That's an achievement too. You cannot reach where you want to be without passing through these mini achievements, and constantly staying positive for yourself. Give yourself the time.

Being generous to yourself also means loving yourself unconditionally, which of course doesn't mean being a couch potato and loving yourself for it! But whatever action steps you are taking, be appreciative of what you are doing. The important thing is that you are taking action steps every day towards your goal, even if it is just for 15-20 minutes for a start. You are doing your best at this moment, and that is all that you should need to find contentment and peace with. It's not a battle, but a process for building and living your dream. **The real life is in the journey and not merely in the result; and our goal is to enjoy the process. People are always waiting to start their perfect life, but in truth, you can be there now by embracing this moment as perfect, as you are taking those steps towards your goal.**

While you are doing so much thinking, planning and working on your goal, it is essential that you take good care of yourself, and prioritise what's important to you each day. Being generous to yourself is also giving enough time for achieving what you need. That's a very important quality of a grounded person. Every day in the morning, take time to decide what it is that you want to focus on for today, and that you really need to get done. It could be between 1 to 3 things, and the rest of your daily work is built around these few things. You can put one hand on your Heart and decide what it is that you want to focus upon today, and as you get the answer, set the Intention and see how Universe starts responding to you with ideas, perhaps bringing you the information you need to help you get your work done more quickly. You can simply Ask Universe to help you with your Intentions. Only if you 'Ask', can you 'receive'! In my case, I find that I often get a call or email from the very people, with whom I wanted to get in touch with.

You will see how, by being generous to yourself, life is generous to you. It's simply the law of attraction. What you feel and give yourself, you will receive back from those around you. Usually, people who take care of themselves, are much more relaxed and present in the moment. They also are able to give others more in life, as they are filled with energy and self-love. You really cannot offer others much, when you are tired and empty in energy and love within. Self-care is crucial to creating abundance in life.

Being generous to yourself means being mindful of all you do. Allow yourself to enjoy the little daily chores too, by simply being present in the moment. Enjoy the bubbles of the foam as you wash the dishes! As you sink into the moment, you are comfortable with not rushing anywhere, and you just know in your heart that you are taking your daily steps, and enjoying this new freedom to choose exactly how to feel at each moment in your life. The focus is more on enjoying everything you do and staying in the moment, in the 'now'. **As you start being generous in taking care of yourself in every way, you attract generous opportunities, people etc. But you have to first feel the abundance of everything in yourself, whether it is love, money or health.**

Being generous also means that you should neither over-do, nor under-do. It means taking care of your needs, for instance, rest, exercise, eat well, allowing enough time to enjoy doing the things you like etc. I should also like to add another tool to the above list today: the importance of stepping into nature and fresh air. It clears all your fears and instantly connects you to the natural healthy state of 'You'. Now doing that, is being generous to yourself. Notice when you are feeling tired or overwhelmed, and take responsibility for changing your frequency to positive right away. It takes you out of the mental state which may be causing your fears, and brings you back into your body with your feet planted firmly on the ground. That's why it's often expressed in holistic terms as being 'grounded.' So if you find things around you are overwhelming, and you no longer feel grounded, just walk it off outside, get centred and then try your visualisation, Meditation, Stillness practice for a few minutes, forming Intentions etc., taught earlier in the book.

Connecting to nature, hugging a tree, is all part of the process of grounding and fully connecting your body to Earth. It allows you to be fully present in the moment, rather than being lost in thoughts, or feeling scattered in all you are doing. Being grounded brings clarity of mind too. Remember another great way to centre yourself quickly is by connecting to your Sacred Altar Within (Day 6 work). By drawing the symbol on your Heart a number of times for a few minutes in your imagination, you can bring yourself consciously and easily from a fearful head to a loving Heart straight away! And breathe!

I learnt the need for Self-Care, which I call 'Self-Love' sometimes, the hard way. When I started working as an Energy Healer in the Therapy Centre and Fayres, I ended up over-doing the work. The result was extreme fatigue, and I fell ill. I remember my right arm was literally not in a fit state to move or do anything for months. I just had to take a break from giving so much to others. It was then that I realised, that in order to follow my passion for helping people more, I needed to take even greater care of myself more than I do of others. It's only then that I can joyfully give to others, otherwise I am really sacrificing my energy, and it becomes more of a duty and a grind, than pure joy. At that point, I ensured that I didn't miss things like Yoga/exercise, drinking plenty of water, Meditation and also doing things that I enjoyed other than my work. It took me a while to get my head around to this way of thinking, as my mind was occupied 24/7 with how to develop my work, since I had to survive being self-employed. But I can tell you, by bringing those things into my life, I was much more efficient at work, and ultimately, also had more energy to focus on my work. Being generous to yourself makes life more generous to you. Everything around becomes easy, relaxed and manageable as you have more energy for everything.

You know that lifestyle shown in Hollywood films of actors and actresses doing 10 things at one go and looking cool! Some people may get tempted to try to follow in their steps. In reality, it is not cool at all. Usually, it's the lifestyle of a chaotic, disorganised, unfocused person! Prioritising what's important to you, really brings clarity, and also makes things manageable. Focusing on one thing at a time rather makes you move swiftly towards your goals, and it also makes your daily life enjoyable, relaxed and productive at the end, as you have greater energy to do more!

In fact, we all often try to do many things at one time, and my body, in my early twenties, could feel the effect of it. Now, I prize myself on having a relaxed lifestyle: the secret to high productivity comes not from running around too much, but rather from living joyfully. Universe recognises a happy 'you' and gives you more happiness, or simply sees you in your stressful state, and keeps giving you more of the same. So my focus has always been on how I can enjoy my day today. It is just as Deepak Chopra would say under Law of Least Effort chapter in his book on The Seven Spiritual Laws of Success. I remember when I used to tell my family that it was my favourite chapter, they would joke that I was just lazy! But I was, and am, serious; it was the most important chapter to me and still is!

I studied in a Catholic college and I remember a nun had once shared with me her shock at how the Head Girl of the college always sat reading books, relaxing under a tree. She'd told that she went up to her and said, "You should be running about and doing some work." "Do you know what she said," the nun had quizzed me. "What?" I'd replied, waiting for her reply.

"She told me that she had all the work being done while she was sitting under that tree; she had delegated all the work to people around her!" I was quite impressed. Hidden under the 'law of least effort' lies a good manager and also joy! I know I had to learn that in my younger days in College, so I needed to hear that then. I used to believe no one can do a better job than me, so I would really overwork and take on everything myself. As a result, I got myself into sticky situations, when people around could have helped me! Learning to delegate, and let go of control, was an important lesson for me.

YOUR WORK TODAY

a) Ask yourself, *"How can I be generous to myself today?"* Write them down to remind yourself always to do those things.

b) *Prioritise the daily mini goals* you would like to focus on. Do it in the morning as suggested above, by placing your hand on Heart, to see what your Heart says you should focus on today (1 to 3 things), e.g., those focusing on losing weight may get a message that they should focus on diet today and shop for certain food; those wanting to increase trust within self may be getting a message to ensure that all words spoken today are truly positive; those wanting to start a new business can receive a message to put some ads around, or it can be as mundane as speaking to a friend and trusting what you get. Be intuitive and creative and don't look for logic. Simply thank God and Universe for help after you have set the Intention. I want you to see what you get daily, and remember to be generous to yourself if you haven't managed to do it all!

Also, if you are overwhelmed at work, try this process where you choose to prioritise *the* 3 must-dos for the day at work too. Through this process, as you keep trying, you will find yourself much more focused and content within yourself. Things will feel manageable and you will feel much more in control as you really fine-tune your focus everyday. You will get into the habit of sending clear messages to Universe from the grounded peaceful state you have achieved.

c) Intend aloud to anchor the Intents of this lesson today:

I call on the I AM Presence to direct my Higher Self that:

I AM generous to myself and I ensure good care of myself with positive thoughts, self-care and taking action for all my needs.

I AM open to receiving self-love unconditionally.

I AM prioritising all I need to do easily everyday by setting daily goals.

I AM tuned into my inner guidance daily.

And breathe into those Intents, allowing them to sink into you by repeating them a couple of times. You may add them to your daily Intents if you feel the need to anchor them further within yourself.

d) Notice this week, whether you are feeling that as you become more generous to yourself, life feels smoother, happier and more comfortable? If not, focus on the above Intents even more. You are probably new to this concept of self-love.

EXAMPLES FROM SOME PARTICIPANTS:

EXAMPLE 1

Sebastian told me about this day's work:
"Although prioritising is still not "in my blood" (not doing it regularly but getting there) - but I have started prioritising stuff for the next day the previous night before I sleep and that helps - So I think it is just to get myself in the rhythm of doing that, and the pattern will be consciously built up."

EXAMPLE 2

Maybe you don't need a very action-oriented goal for the day. It may be about dealing with your emotions. And this example is about that:

Rosaline told me about this day's work:

"My goals:

I have placed my hand on my heart and the messages I have received so far are:

1. Focus on yourself and your needs and don't feel guilty.

2. Enjoy having the right holistic treatments to help you get pregnant again. e.g. shiatsu, reflexology, acupuncture. (I am having shiatsu on a regular basis).

3. Make peace with your past so you can move on to the new stage in your life".

EXAMPLE 3

Josephine told me about this day's work:

"Yes, prioritising is important in order to not feel overwhelmed.

1. Write down all the different forms of meditation I know and research more.

2. Draft an ad for therapy training course for the local community notice boards.

3. Sort through my healing Mantras and categorise.

I did all three and kept developing on them all week. Great way of motivating myself. I am not putting the TV on at night!! Which I waste so much time watching. I have tried to do this for a couple of months, so I feel like I am moving forwards and getting into the mindset of having my business. I feel great."

***

Thanks for all the work you are doing! I just want to give a virtual hug to you today for reaching so far!

Much Love,
Robin Bela

DAY 14
CREATE YOUR SACRED TIME AND MANAGE TIME RESPONSIBLY

Today, we are going deeper into the topic of managing time, which we discussed briefly in yesterday's subject on being generous, as this deserves greater attention. One of my teachers from Stella Maris College in India, Mrs. Kamala Arvind, once said something, which I loved. She was addressing her remarks to those who were bunking classes or leaving college on the excuse of going to the Library. She said, 'The freedom offered for free time goes hand in hand with responsibility.' I agree with her. It's when we responsibly balance important tasks in life with pleasure, that we are really in a state of freedom with time. This is how we can learn to manage time.

It is empowering when I schedule my day's work, complete what I wanted to do work-wise, and also find time to relax. It does not make me feel that I am losing freedom, but in fact gives me control or rather authority over freedom of time. Also, it's sometimes hard to keep up with time, if what you are doing is done half-heartedly. It's more likely you are doing it out of the need that you 'should', rather than 'you wanting to do it'. **When you do things from the starting point of 'wanting to do it', you love being committed to time rather than chasing time.** If you feel you are in that state of chasing time, it's time to prioritise and remove things not important for you in your heart. It does help to understand what you would like to do today, in order to manage your time well, as we discussed yesterday.

Time management means making sure in advance that you are doing what is important. I like to, as I said, do my writing work first thing in the morning most of the days when I am working on a writing project. Now this does not mean I am rigid about it. If I don't follow that pattern on any day, it's a choice made responsibly.

I call the usual morning routine with Meditation, exercise, creative writing, Prayer and Intent work as having sacred time for self, knowing that certain things are irreplaceable in life as they make my life so much happier and productive. Scheduling 'Sacred Time', or quality time for self, regularly within your daily life will keep you naturally grounded. **For me, scheduling 'Sacred Time' in the morning is the single most important requirement to finding the complete balance during the day, and also a platform for creating new things from a place of an empowered, calm state rather than from a tired, weary and rushed state.**

When you start working on your Sacred Time for self, which may be the time just after you get up in the morning, you may find it tiring to keep this up for a week or so, but soon you will get used to it. It is like when you started brushing your teeth as a child, it seemed like a big chore, but now it's natural. But as you continue with your Sacred Time schedule, you will feel a natural sense of freedom and power and also control, over your life. It is a very grounding experience, or in other words, you feel very centred, in control, and focused with everything in life. The peace, happiness and confidence you feel 'within' starts reflecting 'outside' naturally. And Sacred Time allows that connection to our Inner Self.

Ensure that you have a daily routine for everything, allowing time for the body and mind; for professional and household work, as well as time for socialising/relaxing/spending time with family. This will come naturally and easily as you will have plenty of time when you are used to being centred and organised. If you say you don't have time, then I can give you an example of how, with Intent, you can slowly change and finish jobs on time. I used to work in an ad agency in India. There would be several ads going into the newspapers every week, and my job was to make sure that it was all done and coordinated amongst clients, creative people and media. Now at times, I would be sitting in office till 9 pm and mostly, was not leaving office until 7 pm. Then I got better at organising my work. I would send out work to the creative department well in advance and ensure the ads were done well in time with clients' approval. I then started leaving for home every day at 5 pm sharp! I remember that after a few days, some people started raising eyebrows as to whether I was really doing my work. I think there is sometimes a work-culture belief in some places that if you are not sitting beyond office hours at your work-place, then you really are not doing enough work. But I have never been the kind of person to do things in order to please others. I would sit longer to work at something from my own choice rather than to impress others. I remember my very young and lovely Manager Anitha, who then told me that I was very efficient. All I was doing was to set my Intention to get all my work done before 5 pm. This in itself made me very organised. Then all ideas or ways of making that happen, would start appearing to me. But if we already assume that things will take a lot of time, then that is exactly how it will be. Remember, you really don't need to know the 'How' to start. Rather, you need to start asking Universe for time to do the things you want to and simply feel your desire, even just once in an Intent Statement in the morning.

Being organised also means that when we are going for appointments, we are well on time. If you are one of those who is always late for appointments, then it's time to feel responsible and ensure that you give yourself plenty of time, so that you are relaxed and enjoy your day, rather than always carry the stress of being late. This is being generous to self and others, and it allows you always to be in the state of mindfulness. I have had problems with keeping appointments, and did things at the last minute, but I have changed that to a great extent, for my own peace, and to experience a more relaxed state of mind, and be stress-free. **As you work with time, you will notice that you are truly having freedom and joy in life. You will feel you are not running against life, but with life.**

I have seen people who are always late for things, and as a result, get extremely ungrounded and lose their sense of what's needed at that moment. So their communication becomes full of anxiety, and ambigous too, as they are not able to focus on listening and being receptive. Because of that state of mind, they sometimes forget some very important tasks, or make wrong decisions. One of my friends has always been late for everything, and often becomes very confused and mis-communicates on phone during that time. She loses her presence of mind and does things in a rush out of a sense of duty, tinged with guilt, rather than for pleasure, or because it is what she wants to do. This is not a good habit to form as it can increase stress, and lead to other health problems.

Also, when you start functioning out of a sense of guilt, your actions and relationships in life become unauthentic, and are not exactly giving you any happiness. I have noticed that the friend I mentioned above, also tended to withdraw into her own world to balance and recover her state of peace. But all she needs is to pay some attention to organising her time.

Dalai Lama was once asked as to what was the secret to his peaceful nature. He replied that the secret was to give himself plenty of time for doing everything in life, including arriving on time for appointments. I know he talks a lot about mindfulness, and I believe this is truly the secret to being generous to yourself in life, to leading a peaceful, happy, and abundant life and also to being a greater reservoir of energy, time and love for others. This really stuck with me, and I constantly imbibe this into my life, more and more.

YOUR WORK TODAY

1. Check with yourself if you are always running against time? If so, what can you remove from the things you do daily? Or, do you need to make peace and allow yourself to enjoy what you do? Connect with your Heart and see what you get.

2. Are you taking care to be on time?

3. What is your daily routine from the time you get up in the morning? What are the things you really want to ensure you do daily during your Sacred Time, e.g., Meditate, exercise, focus on your Intents etc.? What's your morning schedule like? Are you able to stick to it? If not, may be you need to

take another look at what suits you. I had to change my morning routine a number of times to find out what suited me best. Each person is different: take the time to find out what suits you. Also, no one is the same all the time. Your routine may need to be adjusted according to the situation or circumstances you are in. Create some routines and make them your personal rituals that you do every day. It will help you feel more centred and grounded within yourself throughout the day. **I'd say that if you have seized the morning, you have pretty much seized the day!**

3. Some things you can Intend:
Intent: I AM calling on the I AM Presence to direct my Higher Self that:
I AM having plenty of time to do all I want.
I AM listening to my heart to see what I need to do everyday.

I AM generous with myself with time.

I AM enjoying freedom as I work with time.

I AM finding daily sacred time in the morning for myself with Meditation, exercise, prayer and doing my Intent and anything else I need and it makes me truly balanced in every way.

Feel free to add the above to your daily list of I AM statements.

EXAMPLE:

Pam says:
"I am really enjoying planning my day to enjoy my sacred time. I have even learned to turn the phone off when I meditate and breathe out old fears (previously I would stop and answer!!!!)."
***

I wish you a day where you are totally in control of your life, in power from within, and feel the joy of freedom!

Love,
Robin Bela

DAY 15
WHAT KIND OF BOUNDARIES HAVE YOU CREATED OR ARE STUCK IN?

Welcome to DAY 15 of the 30-DAY Programme

You are half way through the Programme! Great going!

Talking about today's topic, it is very important to understand what kind of boundaries you have created with the people around you. It can totally affect your power within, in what you say, do, and feel every day.

When I talk about maintaining boundaries, what I really mean is to stay within your own energies and not allow others' emotions, Intentions and moods to affect yours, or look for others' energies to support you or feed your insecurities. It is about strengthening your energetic boundaries. So many times, we feel upset for no reason, or are carrying the burden of others' guilt and opinions on ourselves, resulting in our feelings becoming muddled. It's really time to get clarity, so that you can see as to which of the emotions and feelings within you are really your own, and which, you are picking up from around you, that you don't need to carry. Once you are able to differentiate, half your burdens are simply going to disappear like magic. It's a simple matter of asking your Heart at that moment and you will know the answer. A good way to get that clarity is also to keep a daily record in your journal, which will keep you more closely in touch with your feelings. I know people who carry not only their own guilt and emotions, but also those of others. For them, getting in touch with their emotions through keeping a journal is crucial.

So, why do you pick up these unwanted emotions? Perhaps, you care about the people around you, in which case you should remember that you can be there to support others, but this must not be at the cost of imbalance within yourself. It may be helpful to talk less about those issues, and to refrain from

142

too much repeating and arguing. Instead, just give them a message in one statement and Pray/Intend that the same thoughts will soon also resonate with them. Stay compassionate of their understanding of what you believe in, and be kind. "We cannot really carry people, we can only care" as Sonia Choquette, a well known author, says. So make sure you know where to draw your boundaries.

Also, it's not important to interfere too much in the lives and opinions of others, however close your relationship might be, as this will only create more imbalance in your energies, while they might just not be ready to accept your intervention, howsoever hard you may try. It's really helpful to accept people as they are. Everyone is on a different soul journey, and you are not here to change people, but rather to accept them as they are and learn to share and live with them joyfully. You can pray and/or use Intents about that. I have seen the quality of relationships change, as I did so.

Once I had a student, who came across as rude to everyone in the class, including me, but she never really realised that, because she was simply *'defending'* and creating her boundaries from a position of fear. But as we progressed over a couple of programmes, she developed into a completely different person, whose company, I now really enjoy. I had really prayed and Intended for that change, because I wanted all my classes with her to be peaceful, and in this way, I learned to understand her more. So eventually, I was able to subtly show her the way to bring about a change in her behaviour, and luckily, she accepted this. But had she not accepted, I would still have prayed to be of support to her, and for our relationship to be harmonious and peaceful. In acceptance, your energies remain intact and you just allow people to be as they are. Your energies are not drained or leaked in any way in this neutral state. In fact, people may change by lowering their defences and grow close to you, but that can happen only through unconditional love and not through force. So our job is always to stay within our own boundaries, through acceptance, with love, and not by forcing people to change, but by just praying, Intending, and subtly or indirectly suggesting it to them.

If you are like my student above, and are over-protecting yourself, because you feel unsafe, you need to let go of your guard. Also, question why you have put up this guard or shield. Most likely, you may have experienced an incident in the past where you were hurt, and simply didn't allow people to come close to you and were always on your guard. Simply recognise and breathe out these limitations, and Intend the other way round, as explained in Days 2 and 3 under Soul Clearing Technique.

I have another story of someone I know well. She has created a *'strong shield'* around herself, because she is so sensitive to emotional hurt that she actually comes across as someone not sensitive to others' feelings at all, and highly rude, which is her defence mechanism. She has problems with the concept of 'sharing', or being there for a friend. Also, this defence doesn't allow her to be intimate with any of her boyfriends and her relationships don't last too long, although deep inside, like anyone else, she longs for a long-term relationship. It is highly important for her to learn to stay within her energies, and know that it is not important to 'feel' and get entangled with everything that comes her way. As a teenager I was like that, but over the years, I have learnt to see others' emotions as they are: others' and not mine. All I did was to listen to others' emotions without getting caught up in their drama, but with the Intent of being there for the person, and also, if possible, allowing the person to resolve his or own issues, and most importantly, help both myself and that person to see and reach the positive outcome. So, you are not living their lives, but just being there in their life story. Being in that state, you are more likely to have the clarity to think clearly for the other person.

You can make an empowered decision, and not be an empath, a sponge, for all the emotions and lower energies of pain that come your way. You could Intend if you need to work on this - 'I AM there as a support for others easily and effortlessly, as I see their situation resolved. I AM seeing the positive that's there and to come.' And most importantly - 'I AM observing others' problems (and not absorbing! - it's for your information but we will not emphasise what we don't want in the Intent) and notice others' problems from above'. Breathe during this time, as you may be feeling overwhelmed with other people's problems, so you can consciously stay present for them and not become ungrounded along with them. You can do Day 3 breathing work, saying the Intentions with it to clear this, if it is one of your own core patterns. I of course had to learn this a long time before I myself became an Energy Therapist and Teacher. It's like noticing problems from above, in a detached way, rather than letting them pass through you. You can also say that it is learning to not being empathetic to unnecessary situations. This can really help you to be present and grounded during any difficult situations.

Having healthy boundaries is also important in ensuring that people don't take advantage of your time and energy. Are you one of those people who just doesn't know how to say 'no', or feel guilty in saying 'no'? It's OK, we have all been there. But if it's a habit, then it's a problem. You have no control then over your energies, and your life, and really have no boundaries for yourself. This means that people in your life may be too dependent on your energies to keep them happy; they suck up the life out of you although they usually don't realise that. Ask yourself if you aren't able to say no because you are a *'people-pleaser'*? Now here is where your relationships become really unauthentic with the people around you. I have made mistakes in the past, when I couldn't say no to some relationships simply to avoid causing hurt. Later, those relationships became a liability for me, instead of providing happiness. At this point, it becomes harder to get away from such relationships.

Now some people-pleasers just need a lot of attention which can also be draining. I once met an acquaintance at a party, and even though I hardly spoke to her at the dinner table, each time I turned to her, I just felt as though I had a headache coming on. I could energetically sense her so wanting my attention. As an Energy Healer, I am quite sensitive to picking up such vibrations very quickly. But you can train yourself to sense vibrations by noticing how you feel with each person. If you feel good, it's fine, if not, keep your distance, and perhaps check with your Heart later to find out why. It can save you so much headache later! This person also turned out to be quite a big liar, again in an effort to please those around her. I always felt that all she wanted was love and acceptance from the people around her, but she would say anything without thinking. I now see that it all stemmed from her finding it hard to be accepted by the family she has married into, and also the new culture she was embracing, so the need to please arose in order to feed her insecurities.

Here's a different example of someone with *'too open energies'*, whom I call 'An Apologising painter'. This painter, in a span of 10 minutes, apologised to me about 5 times quite unnecessarily! It's almost as if it has become a habit with him! He somehow believes he's always wrong, and deep down, is hurt perhaps by rejection, and has ended up blaming himself. When I was connecting with him, he was in Spirit apologising to me too! I am usually able to hear and sense the real person within. He obviously is not able to appreciate himself. He would need self-love and appreciating Intents. I really wanted to tell him that! But there is always a time and place for such things, and that certainly wasn't when he was about to paint my room ceiling! This is the kind of person who has no boundaries, and is too open because he wants to be accepted and please those around him. He's the kind of person of whom someone might easily take advantage of.

I know someone who offered his opinions when they were not needed, and also embarrassed people through personal remarks, thinking he was actually helping them, when really, he was being nosy. He was pushing the boundaries and forcing himself upon others. This person would impose himself on others by going uninvited into their homes, or by trying to bond with them by sending yearly birthday cards. He was trying his best to get attention from outside, when he really doesn't have to impose himself upon others in order to be liked! That just drove people away from him. If he would respect others' boundaries, then in turn, others would respect his too.

Check yourself to see whether you are *too dependent on other people, and are a* **'Boundary Pusher'**, so that there is no separation between your energies and theirs. Usually, it's acceptable between little children and parents, but otherwise it's not so healthy. Yes, you may be sharing your life with them, but don't be the one to suck up their energies. So be honest. Have you been wanting to fill your empty bucket of love by demanding others' attention more than you should? I must admit I had this trait within me, and this was one of the factors that created a very unauthentic relationship between my ex and me. Once I learnt to fill my void of self-love myself, I found that the things changed. Had the relationship started simply on the basis of unconditional love and sharing and not to fill my insecurities, things might have been different today.

YOUR WORK TODAY

(a) Your work today is to see if you fit into any of the aforesaid examples of unhealthy boundaries, and whether you are willing to change?

(b) **A quick review again to see where you might be stuck with regard to boundaries:**

1. Are there people you are unable to accept and so you try to change them? And if they are not ready to change, do you become defensive?

2. Are you such an empath, who absorbs others' problems?

3. Are you over-protective with too many shields around? I once found a person who was completely blocking herself from allowing her business to grow because, in general, she had blocks to receiving and had put shields around her in order to feel safe. I had to make her realise that she was safe and had strong boundaries and that she should know when to step back, if needed, by simply saying 'no'. But she needed to drop her defences to allow people to connect with her even in business.

4. Are you a boundary pusher?

5. Do you feel guilty in saying 'no'?

6. Are you scared to say 'yes' and remain closed within? Or are you accepting things less than you deserve?

7. Are you a people-pleaser?

8. Are your energies 'too open' for anyone to push and drain you around?

9. Are you too dependent on other people feeding your happiness or in other words do you look to others for your happiness and cannot find it within at all?

10. And lastly, are you able to stay strong within your energy field by simply Intending and breathing when the moment comes to claim your boundaries? Are you able to differentiate your energies from others' when you feel moody or emotional? Most likely, you are feeling low because you are picking up on others' unwanted energies, and it's important then to recognise this and disconnect.

Sometimes, these insecurities can also be picked up from family. Whatever you realise about yourself from the situations described above, write them down in your journal. You can Intend to release your emotions through breath-work just as you cleared your fears, and create Intents, as explained in Soul Clearing Technique under Day 2 and Day 3 work.

(c) *Intents you can focus on:*

I call on the I AM Presence to direct my Higher Self that:

I AM conscious of the good and bad energies and learn to say no to those I am uncomfortable with. I am claiming my boundaries.

I AM letting my defences down to saying yes to new things and people in life.

I AM bringing like-minded wonderful people into my life unconditionally.

I AM accepting people around me as they are.

EXAMPLE

Lorraine, who recently separated from her partner, wrote for today's exercise:

"Oh Dear! When I read this I can identify with all aspects and see that I am a bit messed up here. I have used a 'barbed wire barrier' as what I have thought of as a coping strategy – as a defence against further hurt. In one case, although I didn't call it imbalance, I knew I was no longer comfortable and needed to pull back, but wasn't able to say outright, just made excuses and withdrew, causing obvious hurt to the person concerned.

I can't say no easily. I usually weigh up the negatives to me versus the positives for my friends, and usually end up saying yes to something I might prefer not to do. Most times, once I have agreed, I am happy to get on with it. I have learned over the last few months to say no to new people I've got to know rather than agree to something I don't want to do – they don't know me as my former self in the same way as old friends, and I find it easier to please myself. Once I have made a commitment to do something I always stick to it, and I do it with good grace.

I interfere in as much as I ask Tom, my ex what he has been doing with himself, or is planning to do, so that I know – I ask in a casual way so as not to be obviously prying, but do it from a need I feel to know about his life. I have tried/hoped to change/influence his behaviour towards me to fill my 'empty bucket of love'. I recognise traits in me which can be seen as 'people-pleaser'. I often do things because I feel the need for their approval. I do get genuine pleasure from giving though, so it's not all to please them, it's to please me too.

I recognise I am too dependent on Tom and find it so hard to separate – I'm happy if he is happy spending time with me, but struggle not to resent when he appears to be happy without me. I do try not to be bitter, but have the feeling that his happiness without me seems to devalue the lifetime we spent together – does that make any sense? That was a hard task to do; my honesty with myself and seeing these thoughts and feelings written down has not been comfortable!"

Her I AM statements formed were:

I AM facing all problems easily and effortlessly.

I AM speaking, seeing and accepting the truth easily.

I AM saying No easily when I need to and staying true to my feelings.

I AM comfortable with separation of my life from Tom.

I AM clear as to why I want to be separate.

I AM at peace that I still love Tom and it is natural but I respect my needs and boundaries.

I AM at peace that new and more wonderful experiences have replaced what I miss as it's important to be true to my feelings about my past relationship and how I really felt being in that.

I AM at peace that I know what I want and I truly want happiness and peace for both of us as we are now single.

I AM healed in heart with regard to my relationship. I simply breathe in love and breathe out peace (Do this for sometime till you feel peaceful).

I AM accepting my existence.

I AM accepted within me by myself.

I AM filled with love in my heart and am at peace. Everything I want is within me.

I AM only open for unconditional love (This is just for your knowledge that this statement is a reminder that it's not to feed any insecurities).

EXAMPLE 2

Rosaline wrote to me for today's lesson:

"I feel like I do get my power "sucked" quite often and I do try not to spend time with people who I know "drain me". There is a woman at work who totally drains me and I try to avoid being in her presence. I can't put my finger on what it is, but she just annoys me intensely as she demands a lot of attention and wants things done for her every day, which she could do herself. I think she reminds me of what I used to be like! I like helping people but only to a certain extent and I feel have no time for people that take advantage of my good nature.

I have tried to get into a daily routine of closing down my chakras before I get into work so that I am not too "open" to the energies around me but sometimes if I have forgotten to close them down properly, I get all sorts of strange energies coming in. I get headaches or thoughts, which don't seem to belong to me.

I have wondered if I am 'too closed' sometimes though as people seem to drift around me as if I am not there! I know that I need to be very protected on a daily basis as I am too open to what is around me and I often feel other people's pain or sadness. I also take things home with me and turn over conversations in my head before I go to sleep as well as worrying what others think of me and whether they like me or not.

Answering your questions on - "Do you spend a lot of energy trying to change people around who are not ready to listen to you and get defensive? If so, notice where you can stop and save your energies":

My Mum and Sister snap at me a lot and they seem to get irritated by me. This is something I look for in other people now too and I feel that people do snap at me a lot, My Mum calls me a "walking dream"! I hate it when people give me advice without me asking for it or if they tell me things I already know and they haven't bothered to find out if I know or not. I also hate being patronised or someone trying to change me so I consciously do not do it to others.

Answering your question - "Do you have a tendency to say 'Yes' too often, or 'No' too often? I do over-commit to things and I know I am too busy. Quite often I haven't got one night free in the week and I feel exhausted just looking at my diary! Recently when friends asked me when they could meet up with me, I realised the extent of how busy I am and how I had not one single evening free. I also don't give my Mum enough time and she often says that I am too busy to see her. I am usually exhausted when I do see her which is not productive and I get cranky and emotional for no reason on a regular basis. I have come to realise that this is maybe because I don't have any time to myself!

I have not found a solution to this yet. I have tried to clear my diary but I do evening classes and meditation classes and also offer massages and see my partner and this has been going on for months. As it is a new relationship I have been trying to give time to my partner and cram everything else in. Any tips Robin please?"

My reply to Rosaline:
You are focusing too much on other people's negative energies, and the fear of having it on you is bringing it around you. When you focus on the negative, or fear of the negative, you are by law of attraction bringing those energies within you. I would suggest to stop closing your chakras or doing anything at all. At the most, just imagine a white shield around you. But I should like you to get the power from within. The thoughts and actions you are producing out of fear are artificial, and they are just not necessary. Just stop focusing on the things you don't like about others, and as you breathe, you will find your aura is expanding and healthy through Meditation. You are born safe and protected. Just choose to focus only on the positive. When we give in to fear is when we lose power. So think and feel positive by continually reminding yourself.

With regard to time, do you really need to do so many classes? Once you learn, can you not do it yourself from home? Perhaps you do need all the classes. Check within. Question: What are the things you are doing just to please others and do you really want to do those things? Do only things out of love. I myself went to some classes, but when I got busy I just continued the same routine myself from home. Place your hand on heart and ask your Heart.

If you keep writing these thoughts in your journal, you will be able to keep a check over anything you are overdoing before it gets too much to handle.

I have first of all offered her some additional Intents to keep working on from now on:

I call on the I AM Presence to direct my Higher Self that:

I AM focusing only on me as it keeps me naturally within my own energies.

I AM praying whatever it is about this woman in the office that irritated me and that I see trigger emotions within me, I AM Praying/Intending it is healed within me and I AM at peace.

I AM focusing only on my thoughts.

I AM patient and compassionate with my mother and sister and just breathe with them peacefully. (You will see that they will notice that and will change in time as you keep Intending this).

I AM having enough time for myself.

I AM able to prioritise easily what's important for me and what's not.

I AM safe in my skin.

***

See you tomorrow for another empowering step towards your goal! Do remember to keep your Meditation and Intents in your daily routine

Love,
Robin Bela

DAY 16
ACCEPTANCE OF CHANGES THROUGH GRATITUDE, STAYING POSITIVE AND FLEXIBLE

Welcome to DAY 16 of the 30-Day Programme

When you are making changes in your life, be sure to realise that these may not be easily acceptable to the people around you. If you get into the futile process of persuading people around you to like the new you, then you are dragging your energies down. We can never compel anyone to accept our ideas. It is up to them to accept what they like. Your job is to stay in unconditional love and accept that the changes you are making are important for you. The people who really care for you, will always be there for you in the end. Sometimes, it just means that people around us, haven't changed with us and so, we may perhaps experience loss of friends. But it will feel natural as the friend liked the old you, and you are becoming a new person. I don't say you will lose all your friends, but you may lose some of them and you have to be ready for such things when making really big decisions in life. You may find that there are some difficult decisions you have to make, so you will need strength and the inner belief that what you are doing is the right thing for you.

When I separated from my ex-husband, my own very close friend found it very hard to digest it as she was close to both of us. As I write this today, until now she still hasn't accepted it, and is pained about it. I can understand that, and pray that she heals, and maybe, even accepts the new me and recognises that this was not easy for me either. It was like enduring another loss whilst dealing with the separation from my ex-husband. Ideally, I would have liked to have her there for emotional support whilst I went through my own difficult period.

I would like to share a quote or affirmation by *Louise Hay*, author, which helped me a lot once I realised that I cannot change the people around me:

"I cannot change another person. I let others be who they are, and I simply love who I am".

Similarly, when I left my job to do what I wanted, very few people really supported me. In fact, my ex was truly supportive of my work. I am grateful to have had that support and I often called him an Angel for that. So for a long time, many people probably thought I was crazy to leave my career where I was doing well. They would talk to me strangely and I would pick up their vibes that they probably thought I was a failure. They would ask questions like "Can you make money out of this?" Too many people just live in the world of 'safe careers' and I had dared to step outside: the thought made people uncomfortable. It is natural. But I was so much in love with what I was doing and so passionate about it, that I hardly cared for all this. Rather, I stayed away from the sceptical people, or those who would change the conversation as soon as people started talking about it, because I really didn't care to persuade people to believe in me. I believed in what made me happy anyway. It also saved my energies and it made it easier for me to stay positive, which is so important in the delicate stage of change. Years later, I now see that the funny part is, most people love everything I do now without me having to try to be accepted. My own parents who were earlier so concerned about what I was doing, later attended my programmes, love what I do and are the biggest promoters of my work now.

You do require a lot of patience with the people around you, and have to allow time for them to digest the changes you are going through. I know how worried my ex-husband was when I was leaving my salaried job, about whether we would manage financially with me being self-employed; so, not only was I giving assurance to myself, but also to him. I highly recommend Praying/Intending, for the right words to come out, if you want your loved ones to understand and accept more of what you are wanting to do. It has taken so much time for you to reach where you are today, through your own inner journey, and similarly, you have to allow time for others to comprehend this change in you too.

One of my clients felt she was taken for granted at her work. After doing a session with her, I made her realise how it stemmed from not valuing herself. I told her to respect herself before others could do so, and guard her self-respect by saying 'no' whenever required, without any feeling of guilt. She was afraid that people at work would not accept her new Self. This change need not be sudden, but slow and easy. And I would like to remind you of the Day 8 Intent that 'the change within and around you takes place easily, effortlessly, peacefully and smoothly.' People love and respect you naturally, if you do so to yourself unconditionally.

As you change, you may feel that your life is becoming exciting, but at the same time, fears may even creep in. It can feel like a rollercoaster ride of ups and downs in emotions, as you are experiencing not just others' emotions, but your own too. It's really important to stay positive and keep the focus on the end result. Just observe yourself by being conscious that all doubts are just fears of the unknown and not real. You create what you start 'feeling', 'believing' and 'thinking' all the time. So why believe in fear of something that may not happen? Instead, choose to make sure that you change frequency or nature of your thoughts to positive, through positive Intents.

A great way to shift the frequency of your thoughts to positive is to be grateful for all the wonderful things in your life. Just sit for a moment and count your blessings. If you can't think of anything, notice the beautiful sun, sky, birds, trees, the bed you sleep in, the smile of a baby, the breath you are taking and so on. As you do so, it will lift you from lower, negative frequencies to positive straight away. **Try being thankful for those things you don't yet have as though they are already yours.** I have seen some amazing things happen when I do that. Often I find myself singing a gratitude song as I wash the dishes! That is how you not only accept your changes but also manage to stay in the positive frequencies. It's a question of practice. You get better at it as you keep reminding yourself of this simple exercise. **And remember you cannot fool Universe; a genuine appreciation is needed, not just mechanical reading or saying some Intent statement. You require to feel it genuinely in an open Heart.**

The other way to change your frequency of thought to positive of course is by being in nature; just go for a walk and the fresh air just cleanses your energies. Breathe consciously as you are out. Physical movement is crucial too in lifting up your energies, so really don't sit around if you are low in spirits. Simply doing something at home that needs getting up, moving or exercising can help too!

During the phase of change and transition, you need to stay flexible, and be open to allowing yourself to experience life in a different way. It will mean that you are being dared to do the things you perhaps feared. The less you resist, the easier it becomes. I have always been protected and taken care of from a young age by my family, and then later by my ex. This was not so good for me because when I became single, I experienced problems in becoming truly independent and more responsible for myself. I actually, however, enjoyed that process. It made me feel, I can do it too! As a child, even if I needed a chocolate, I just had to tell a servant or guy working under my Dad, who would be standing outside the house, and he would get it for me! That was a part of my upbringing with my father's perks of being a senior police officer in India, when I didn't need to lift a finger in the house and even outside. I always had a chauffeur-driven car to take me wherever I needed to go, and I led a very protected life. Let's say that when I came to the UK, I really had to learn to live a normal life. Even carrying grocery bags was a new experience for me! You can imagine the state of my true power at that time! No college degrees could have helped here.

As a child, I was always shy and looked for outside approval to feel confident, but I have changed a lot since then. When you do the things that you like and believe in, your power comes from within. You don't need approval from the people around you. You don't have to look for anything outside to gain confidence and to be open to change. So if you feel fearful, do the things that you like and believe in, and you will find the fear goes because you start connecting to the real you in the process of doing what you desire.

YOUR WORK TODAY

1. Check with yourself and write in your journal, have you changed recently?

2. Are you afraid to change?

3. Are you noticing the people around acting differently to you due to your changes or your new way of thinking about yourself? It is important to acknowledge what is going on around you, just breathe with it and don't ignore it. You are powerful enough to face it all.

Create your Intentions if you come across any blocks within while going through the above. Breathe them out till you feel cleared.

4. *The following Intents may help you further.*

You may add this too to the daily list of I AM Statements you are reading.

I AM calling on the I AM Presence to direct my Higher Self that:

I AM accepting the changes within me and around me as I choose new things in life easily, effortlessly, smoothly and organically.

I AM staying focused and centred within heart through Meditation, Sacred Altar Within and other tools I know.

I AM staying flexible to where I need to go.

I AM staying non-judgemental towards people's reactions to my changes.

I AM always surrounded by people who are positive about my changes.

I AM believing in myself.

I AM seeing the fears but as I see them with love in my heart, they just disappear. I keep moving to where I AM to go.

I AM staying positive by counting at least 10 things I AM grateful for when I need to shift my frequency!

I AM accepting people around me as they are and I love myself for who I AM.

EXAMPLE 1

Nicole wrote:

"Yes I have changed and can feel much more lightness inside. My thoughts are becoming more positive, however my words can be quite negative and there is a discrepancy between thoughts and words. This is because I was finding that I was becoming silent with friends as it is seen as big headed if you speak positively about yourself. With my friends the rule is generally that we put ourselves down jokingly and I haven't properly succeeded in doing this differently yet."

Her Intents formed are:

I AM calling on the I AM Presence to direct my Higher Self that:

I AM proud to see the positive aspects about me and simply do without the need to prove myself to others.

EXAMPLE 2

Tanya wrote:

"I discovered in the course that subconsciously I am afraid to start working because when I was nursing I went on call 24/7 for work for many years and stopped having fun and seeing friends. Also put myself in compromising positions to get nursing work. Since the summer I have become empowered, however I am afraid I will end up putting the clients first in order to get work and not make time for fun."

Her Intents formed are:

I AM calling on the I AM Presence to direct my Higher Self that:

I AM very good at caring for myself.

I AM loving taking care of my needs.

I AM loving myself and taking care of self more than others.

I AM free and safe to live my life in line with my soul's desire.

***

I hope you are enjoying the changes within you. See you tomorrow.

Love,

Robin Bela

DAY 17
AFTER A CLEAR DECISION, SURRENDER TO THE MOMENT : THROUGH STILLNESS

> *"Once you make a decision, the universe conspires to make it happen"* - *so said Ralph Waldo Emerson. And that is exactly what happens if you decide clearly and stay focused on what you wish to create.*

The theme of today's chapter is in continuation of DAY 7 on the Alchemy of Manifesting, i.e., making decision and taking action. By now, you would know how your progress is with regard to your decisions made earlier. How focused are you with your decision to pursue your goal? Is it something, you go back and forth on, still? When I connect to my strength or power within to create it, I have full faith in achieving what I want. If I don't, I know I am unsure somewhere, and it's time to make a firm decision, or even to reinforce the Intent through Prayer and I AM Statements, and even better, with an action step towards the goal. Making a decision is really the process of accepting the truth within, and to stop looking outside for answers. We sometimes do not like accepting this, because it requires making some changes in our mode of functioning or beliefs. Once a decision is made, one doesn't have to make much effort after that for the process to begin. **Simply state the Intents about your goals/desires to Universe, and let go of any doubt of whether these will materialise, how they will materialise and, most importantly, when they will materialise. This is the process of making a firm decision and surrendering!**

It was often very hard for me to learn to surrender the thought of, or attachment to result. **Surrendering doesn't mean letting go of the result but to not think about it all the time, worrying whether it will happen.** Once you affirm your daily Intent, you should not need to fear that it will happen. That's when it's really important to call upon God's/Universe's grace.

There were times when anxiety, doubts and fears gripped me so strongly that I wasn't able to focus on the joy of what I was creating and wanting. They started blocking what I wanted. Things started clearing only when I Intended and prayed to surrender for grace, and soon I would know clearly in my heart as to what it was that I wanted under all those fears and confusion. I really faced my fears and accepted their presence and Asked God/Universe for support to help me let go. The next day I recall I was so peaceful, and the whole need to feel what I was missing suddenly disappeared. I felt that a part of my power had returned. I was no longer dependent on the factors outside of me to keep me happy. I was able to create happiness, peace and strength from within through my internal focus. And also strangely, the attachment to the result of what I was wanting, in fact, disappeared for my highest good because the attachment was in my fearful ego, not really in my Heart. When we connect to our Heart, we start getting a clear message of what exactly we want, and are able to make the right decisions. The Prayer/Intent below is what I used to connect to my Heart which you can also use and write in your journal as a reminder:

"I Pray/Intend to God/ Universe that I am Praying/Asking for grace and mercy to take away this internal fight within me that is keeping me out of sight of my goal. I Pray/Ask that I have clarity and know exactly what my Heart wants and make a clear decision."

Acceptance of your own mistakes is such a healing experience, which also helps you move forward and to make the decision to move on. It also can resolve so many inner conflicts. I know many people who understand this but are afraid to be seen as having made a mistake. I myself found it very hard to see that I made a mistake in choosing my life-partner. My ego, guilt and pride had a tough clash with the truth. But once we accept the truth, letting go is easy, as such acceptance also amounts to having made a decision, which really sets you free to make the change. This may also require self-forgiveness. I came to understand that the quicker I accepted the mistake, the faster I would heal and be able to move forward.

If you are unclear about what you want or don't fully believe in it, you stay out of the positive flow from where you can manifest anything new you want. And in this process, you remain in a state of anxiety, unable to let go of the fear of not reaching where you want to be. At times, we are still talking in the language of 'ifs', 'buts' and 'maybe', and that is the main reason we are usually nowhere near reaching our goals. I recently spoke to client who wants to make more money in her life and is working on it through Intents. When I asked her as to how she was, she replied casually that the money situation was 'down as usual!' Now, no Intent you use would work, if you were to continue to use negative language, in your daily conversation. If you continue to use that language you are reflecting and reinforcing your inner belief that it is normal to see money at a low level in your life; whereas, if she had said, 'I am working on improving the money situation in life', or even better 'I am Intending that my money situation is improving', it would mean she has really decided to go for it! But talking in the language of 'not have', 'if' or 'maybe', is when you are stagnant in your life and there is literally no life-force or determination in your resolve.

Making a crystal clear and firm decision, which is talked under the first step of 'Alchemy of Manifesting' in Day 7, is such an important process that you need to consciously allow it to reflect in your actions, thoughts and words, in order to allow anything new to start coming into your life. In the beginning, you just have to match your thought frequency to that of what you want, by becoming, through behaving and feeling, that which you aspire to be. Catch yourself consciously when you don't and change your language of thoughts and speech to the positive. So in other words, **once we surrender the worry of the 'how', the decision is made!** And may I also say that once we take an action step towards the decision made, we have surrendered how it is going to happen, and are already on our way towards our goal! For example, writing a page for the book you want to write, is a positive step forward.

When we learn to get our 'present' right by staying positive and talking in the right positive language, everything else falls in place and we attain the peace of mind that we are searching for, everything starts happening, we suddenly become 'content' with our lives now and the future is taken care of, as a part of that natural process. It was a journey for me to learn this. In fact, every time I used to think about achieving what I wanted in a relationship, I would see an image of me getting hit by a bus or a car, or me falling from the window sill or falling down the stairs. This happened not once but repeatedly for several months. When I delved deep down and questioned myself, I found that I had doubts about everything I was wanting - asking myself, can I really have that happiness? - And I wasn't letting go of the fear that it might not happen. This meant that indirectly, I didn't allow myself to be clear about what I wanted and hence remained undecided, as **I was giving Universe mixed signals. One moment I want it and then the next moment I am fearful of it happening! So Universe really cannot get a clear message of whether I want it or not.** I have to state my Intent clearly as if I already have it and believe in it! But I had a core belief that I cannot have happiness forever, and so before I could imagine what I wanted, I would see myself being hit by a car or something. In order to clear this recurring pattern, I had to do the Soul Clearing, as explained in Days 2 and 3. It took me a while to let go of completely the fear of accepting my power at that time. This not only kept me unsettled, ungrounded, undecided, but also gave me less focus to take practical action or achieve anything on that path.

If you are harbouring any fears of achieving your goal, then your shaky decision to achieve the goal is really not a clear message offered to Universe. Everything, whether it is a career or a new relationship or a new self-image, can come to you, only if you firstly, face your fears and accept your truth of what it is that you really feel and want; keeping your journal can help you reflect on that regularly; secondly, decide and start taking daily action with positive words and action steps etc; thirdly, let go of the result and surrender to the moment by keeping the faith through Prayer/Asking, 'Stillness practice' and other ways explained in this book.

We talked about "Stillness" under Day 7 relating to Alchemy of Manifesting. It is crucial to find our stillness within to help us surrender to the present and to stop worrying about past or the future. Think of mercury, the chemical element, in a small bowl. If you keep hitting it with a finger, it keeps breaking into pieces and when you stop, it all settles and comes into its true state of being. This is exactly what happens to us when we worry, we get scattered in our being emotionally and physically. **We are born to be perfect; if we stop fighting, finding faults and searching outside us, we connect to our complete self-sufficient being to receive all we want through the Source. A great way to find that complete alignment to our self is through the Stillness practice.** You may do it for a few minutes or more as you find it relaxing. You are not 'thinking', 'observing' or 'feeling' anything there but just 'being', staying still and relaxing. It can become a very joyful process and leads to a 'mindful' way of living. We are simply content and perfect in our feeling, just the way we are. Only when we bring imperfect thoughts of worry, do we create the disturbance within us. Else, Universe is happy to offer all we Ask. We just need to get used to feeling content naturally, in Asking and receiving.

Staying in the Moment is the key to stop 'trying to control' situations and people, and to Surrendering. I am so conscious of this 'trying to control' energy that I know I can feel a tug or pull on my abdomen outwards. I literally feel as though I have a pot-belly. Also, when I am experiencing this I really feel as though there is no energy left in my body. I feel drained. That's when my power is leaking from me and I am forcing my life force or happiness to come from others or through situations beyond my control. But what if others don't comply with what you need? You are then totally off-balanced. This is when you really need to surrender, Pray/Intend and stay in the present moment. **You don't want to be controlling your present with past resentments and also future expectations that are not in your hands, and certainly not people.** I like to remind myself by saying the Affirmation by *Louise Hay* - "I cannot change another person. I let others be who they are, and I simply love who I am." Saying that a number of times would really help you when you are not able to let go of the need to control others.

I believe 'acceptance of truth or decision' and 'surrendering', go hand in hand. For example, are you one of those whom a man or woman has rejected or hasn't as yet taken up your offers, and are you still sitting wondering how it can work out? If so, I have to give you the hard news that you are going nowhere and are stuck in a state of ego, trying to control things which are not within your power. You really have to let go through acceptance of reality. Otherwise, sitting in the 'ifs' and the 'could be' situations is playing silly, and that is when we really give away our power for our happiness to someone else or to an ideal situation, e.g., I'll be happy when I get that job. Yes you can say your Intents and pray that it works for the best, but you cannot sit and try to control outcomes, someone's reaction or attitude etc. Even if it works, it will be forced and not natural, and usually creates an unauthentic relationship where one side is manipulated through emotions such as guilt.

Sometimes, acceptance of the hard truth and facing it is really important in order to move on. In fact, in my experience, once you let go, often the situations you are hoping for, come your way more naturally and organically. Saying the the aforesaid Prayer/Intent and *Louise Hay's* Affirmation can help you. Believe me I have been there too! Really, Praying/Intending regularly for 'mercy' and 'grace' to allow you to move on would help. I would say again and again the words 'mercy' and 'grace' whenever I feel anxiety rising up within me.

One very important aspect about surrendering is that you stop thinking about something all the time and wishing that you could control it! It is such a relief to your body and mind when you let go of a situation you've been holding onto for a long time because it takes up so much energy. When I went through holding onto such a situation for a long time, I remember that after letting it go of, there was such a relief that I simply needed to take rest in bed for some time. **When we let go, it doesn't mean we don't believe it will come true, but rather that we trust and stop humanly trying to control what we cannot.** It actually frees up energy to allow things to happen. Usually, we literally hold our breath in this state of anxiety, which prevents all "chi" from flowing towards anything good. It is when you free up the energy that your belief gets stronger rather than when you are worrying about it. The need to control everything is now so deeply embedded in our human nature that we have lost the true essence of living life with faith, and actually in the process, have also lost our true power while in search of it outside us!

My Own Examples of Acceptance of Decision and Surrender:

I had a pattern of trying to control outcomes of situations but have reduced it to quite an extent in all spheres of my life, especially work. I really had to learn to switch off. I remember when I left my job and changed to self-employment, I couldn't sleep for nights. In fact, I would get ill due to worrying. It took me almost a year to let go of that fear and start being in a place where I can naturally attract success and even money. From the place of fear, you cannot attract any money, love, success etc. It is important to understand that you do have to decide what you want, i.e., state your Intent in prayer/I AM Statements, take your daily steps towards your goal and just stay in the moment by enjoying and focusing on your daily experiences and expecting the best. I would recommend doing these exercises: Meditation, Sacred Altar Within, Stillness practice, gratitude and being out in nature to help you to stop focusing on the problems and help you to release anxious energies. I would also like to remind you of the list of things you can do in your 'Relaxation First Aid Kit' to help let go!

I have seen disputes clear between my friend and me once I accepted how the situation was, prayed for the best and surrendered. I just projected my Intents specifically out to Universe through Intent statements that we would be happy and peaceful. This requires being non-judgemental. Sure enough, within one week I was already feeling good about my friend and I started to understand her better, and then things between us returned to normal. My daily action here was just staying positive, non-judgemental and saying my Intent that my friend and I are happy and at peace with each other. When I say the Intent, it's just during that 'second' I pay attention to it, but otherwise I don't think about it the whole day. If you are trying to make something happen by waiting and literally holding your breath to make it happen, you are not allowing the outcome to emerge. If you keep mulling over your progress to your request, you are delaying it! You have to surrender.

YOUR WORK TODAY

1. Check with yourself if your goals are clear and you have clearly decided what you want without any 'ifs' and 'buts'. Give this message clearly to Universe through Intent. And face any fears you may have to committing to it without worrying about the end result.

2. If you have anxieties or need clarity to help you focus on your goal and surrender anxiety, simply Pray/Intend. Below is a Prayer/Intent I have used which is really just my own words. You can use it or adapt it to your own words. (And let me explain again for clarity, when you say the 'Intent' by also invoking God, it becomes a Prayer. The Reader is welcome to work with Intents by also calling upon Divine energies.)

You can say aloud or in mind:
"I Pray/Intend to God/ Universe that I am Praying/Asking for grace and mercy to take away this internal fight within me that is keeping my goal out of sight. I Pray/Ask that I have clarity and know exactly what my Heart wants and make a clear decision."

3. Intend today - I am in full faith that I am led to the right outcome in___.

4. Write down if there are there any situations in your life that you have still not accepted? Are there any unresolved issues with people or your own past mistakes? Are you trying to control people and situations? If so, it's time to face the truth, stay compassionate, non-judgemental and simply Pray/Intend for peace and happiness for all, and surrender your worries to Universe. You can put it into your daily I AM Statements. The daily statement which I used at that time about my friend was: 'I AM having a happy and good relationship with my friend'. It kept me peaceful through that period.

Think of any people you want to change, and affirm:
"I cannot change another person. I let others be who they are, and I simply love who I am." *[Louise Hay].*

167

5. Intend to Surrender the need to control - Every time you worry, recognise that you have to allow this time of exploration, growing and knowing more deeply what you are going to achieve. You just cannot rush it. Surrender the need to control. Not knowing the proof of what your future holds does not mean you can't start living the life you want. You start now by taking some action steps towards it. Every day starts becoming clearer and better than yesterday. And that's a good achievement and inspiration to stick to!

7. You can practice moments of stillness by sitting with your eyes open for a few minutes or as long as you like, and just being Still, when you are not 'thinking', 'observing' or 'feeling' anything. You are simply staying aware in those moments.

EXAMPLE 1

Rani says,
"Your email with today's lesson came just in time! I was having a problem detaching/surrendering from an intention when I got this email. I usually pray to detach and try some other ways! But I think some things are ingrained very deeply and need a lot of releasing, breathing and praying to detach from."

My reply to that was:
"Don't assume it will take long, what you Intend, is what it will be. When I said the prayer above, in a day the whole feeling of me needing something disappeared. It's literally asking God to have Mercy to help in letting go. And when we become humble, let go, miracles happen. Stay sincere in your asking."

EXAMPLE 2

Lucy wrote to me,
"I may confess your prayer went right to my heart and I found it was the perfect way to step toward faith. I Pray to God/ Universe that I am praying for grace and mercy to take away this internal fight within me that is keeping

me out of sight of my goal. I pray I have clarity and know exactly what my heart wants." I do repeat it before going to sleep and add some thoughts, words, depending on the mood of the day."

EXAMPLE 3

Julie used the Prayer above for clarity in her relationship:

"I said the prayer over and over at bedtime and when I woke in the night. Felt I am faking it a bit but trying hard to completely let go. Not even sure why I can't because I want to so much. Later I was drawn towards a book on my shelf by an Arabic poet called Daoud Tahboub – This poem is called For You, but I have read it as if I have written it 'For ME'

"What won't I do to turn your days into a constant joy and your world into a wonderful place,
To fill your heart with deep delight.
For your eyes I'd do the things I never dared to dream about.
What won't I do to draw a smile of happiness on your sullen face,
To make your worries a matter of the past.
To let my eyes have the pleasure of always seeing you O Dear.
Just tell me what you want me to do
Name a wish or whisper a word.
That's all I'm asking you to say
Please do, please do, please do.'
It seemed to confirm for me that I must pray for clarity for what it is I really want and learn to be open to receive it."

***

Thank you for allowing me to share this with you today! Have a great day ahead. And I shall speak again with you tomorrow.

Love,
Robin Bela

DAY 18
GET AUTHENTIC WITH YOUR BODY

Welcome to DAY 18 of the 30-Day Programme

Today, we are going to work on a very important subject, and that is to look after your body. Your body is the house where your beautiful Soul or Inner Self lives. We have been looking after our Inner Self all these days in this Programme, but now, to have our needs best met in the outer world, we need to focus on having a strong body too. This is utterly important, as those who forget the importance of a healthy, strong body, and develop physical ailments and issues, will find it extremely difficult to connect to the power within. This holds true for all, whether they are spiritually inclined or not. To fulfill our dreams, a healthy body is a basic requirement.

I can tell you that I connect to my spiritual being and the power within better when I am in the best of health, and am taking good care of my body. It's then that I also attract more good things in life. I can handle higher intense energies to go through me as an energy healer when I am physically strong enough, and also have more energy to endure any difficult situation in life.

One of my own students had a tough time understanding the dire need of physical fitness and good health, even for doing healing and therapy work. She would eat pot noodles to save money. She's already lost half her skills as a healer by being under-nourished. I could tell that she never exercised, and so would find it very hard to stand long enough and would tire herself very quickly. Also, she never did any work on self, i.e., energy work, meditation etc. So really, what she offered others was really without any happiness, but rather with pain. What do you think the receiver's experience would be? She would turn up at events with me like this, where we had to deal with many people. For me, this was totally unacceptable: I was rather unhappy about it and had to tell her. Today, a couple of years after that incident, she has taken my advice and is doing better. I have seen some of my students go into depression when they overdo working on others and forget to learn to take care of themselves, most importantly their physical and mental health, which includes good diet, exercise and Meditation. You need to know how much you can handle, and should never overdo work.

Many a time, very intuitive and psychic students of mine, simply cannot handle the level of spirituality and inner power they start connecting to, because they have weak bodies, with literally no capacity to take in what's coming. They become totally ungrounded, and often feel they are in their own world, floating in their heads and not living an earthly experience. You might hear these people often say that they feel they don't belong to the planet! They are usually so ungrounded that they don't know how to live practically, be on time for things or even make money, as that requires them to have their feet firmly planted on the ground and to be practical. They often believe that they are only meant to be on mountains, away from the civilisation! Only if you can get the perfect blend of mental health and physical health, can you really have a successful existence on Earth.

Of course, you might be looking after your body to lose weight for the sake of appearance, and no doubt that also boosts your self-esteem. It doesn't mean that you will get the perfect body and weight straight away, but I can tell you that once you simply enjoy taking care of your body, improving its strength and appearance on a day-to-day basis, it makes reaching your target much easier. But it requires consistency, pretty much throughout your life. It's not something you do for a month just for the sake of a better appearance. It also, in a way, tests the love and respect you have for yourself. So start getting into the idea of allowing exercise as a normal part of your life. There is more than one benefit to be gained. I have seen myself improve in mood, looks and feel-good factor, and become grounded, which means that I am not easily overwhelmed with situations: I have more energy, my confidence is boosted. You should think of physical fitness as a gift to yourself.

On many occasions, when I had fearful thoughts about something going on in my life, I would simply exercise to bring myself back into my body and out of my over-thinking, fearful mind. It's such a great balancing technique.

171

It helps me stay more joyful and focused on all I want to achieve. Also at times, when I feel drained, or my auric field feels heavy when stressed, or perhaps after arguments, just exercising lifts it up and brings in new energies within me. I also find after I exercise that great ideas come to me for my work, or the solutions I am searching for some problems, come through. And if you are not able to focus on Meditation, try exercising beforehand, and you will find that you will be able to meditate better.

When you are exercising, it is very important that you do it with zest, from the heart, and not from a fear base of 'oh my God, I have to lose weight', otherwise you will hate the experience, and not get any results. If you are too focused on forcing yourself to get somewhere, it won't work. When I exercise, I love it. My body usually craves for it if I haven't done it for a while, as I can see how dull or lacking in energy it feels without it. **Observe how your body 'feels' when you exercise and don't try any thinking whilst doing it. When you are starting, you have to listen to your body and find out what kind of exercise and how much of it you should do, and then the strength within your body will gradually grow. I would say that each individual's body needs different forms of exercise.** Hold your hand on your Heart and ask the question as to what kind of exercise you should do every day, and then do it. Do this questioning every day of this week and then see where it leads you.

You can Intend/Pray for the right forms of exercises, teachers etc. to come to you. I always do this. I have sometimes been led intuitively to doing exercises by myself that I have never done or seen anyone do. My body has the knowledge to tell me what I need. All power and answers are within, which may also include guidance to learn something from someone else. I don't need a gym because I really want it to be tailor-made to my needs, and as I start asking and praying for the right exercises, e.g., for arms or thighs, I am led to doing some particular exercises. I do one that I believe is done in ballet class but I didn't know it previously. I am self-disciplined simply because I love myself; so I don't feel the need for a gym. I may go to gym if I feel the need to use any of the equipment or feel the need to learn some new form of exercise. Normally, I can do all the required exercises at home, and sometimes do these for just 20 minutes if I don't have more time. This way, I can't blame lack of exercise on not going to the gym! And I lost 3 stones which is about 20 kilos, in less than a year without going to any gym and without doing any dieting. **I just Intended/Prayed and listened to my inner guidance on the exercises I should do, and the food I should eat.** I stayed positive and focussed on visualising how I wanted every part of my body to look. I really dug out my power from within to create my reality to the extent that people say I look almost 10 years younger. Earlier, I probably looked a few years older than what I was!

I remember that when I started exercising seriously as a routine, for the first 2 months I hardly lost any weight, but I started feeling much better about my life. I felt and looked happier, and to my surprise, people would remark that I had lost weight! **To achieve anything in the physical realm, you first have to start feeling and acting as per the desired result. It comes from feeling good and excited about what you are creating.** Then I started measuring my weight regularly to stay motivated and also to see if my inner guidance, that I was following, was creating the result. Make sure that you don't fear your weighing scales, as you want to get to the bottom of this in every way, and not leave any stone unturned, especially if the scales are not showing good results!

I also joined a belly dancing class for a short time, which by the way, is a totally fun way to exercise, and I love the part where we actually work with our power centre, the solar plexus chakra in our energy body, which is the abdominal area. When we learn to keep the abdomen strong, and learn to start feeling our strength physically and not just in our heart and mind, we can feel the confidence and power not just within, but outwards too. Start feeling that your belly is strong and firm, whenever you exercise, and also when you are walking. I have found Pilates system of exercises extremely powerful to connect to the strength of my body and losing weight. I just followed a DVD on Pilates! You will see the difference in your self-esteem, in the way you deal with people and situations, with increasing confidence!

173

So, you should form your own exercise routine, according to your requirements and suitability. I do a mix of weights, yoga, pilates, belly dancing, aerobics, cardio and just regular dancing sometimes! I just pick and choose intuitively what my body tells me to do every day. It's important to listen to your body. I know my father is a big fan of Yoga and has been doing it regularly since I was a baby. I also know one of my friends lost a lot of weight through balancing her diet to a more healthy routine and simply using the cycle machine in a gym. Everyone is different. I know that cycling, at the time I lost weight, wasn't suited to me.

Once I did a marathon of a week of intense exercise whilst, at the same time, I was working extremely hard at my job. I know the next week I was just craving for some light work-out like Yoga and also some Tai Chi, with whatever little I knew, or rather my intuitive body was teaching me! I can also tell you that during the week of extreme exercise and hard work, I lost no weight. But the weeks that followed when I was relaxing, including some days with no exercise as I needed that break, I ended up losing a few kilos! **It is no secret, that to lose weight, you not only need to keep a check on exercise and food, but also on your stress levels and sleep.** If you are one of those who find yourself always stressed, I would recommend trying 'Rescue Remedy' made from flower essences that helps you to stay calm in stressful periods of life. You just need to take 4 drops on your tongue 4 times a day. You should be able to get it from any local store.

So to lose weight, while you are watching your food, let's not forget the water intake, ideally about 8-10 glasses a day, which is good to keep the bodily processes going and in balance. There is also a need to watch sleep patterns which could be distorted due to anxiety levels. Adequate sleep and rest is very important to keep a check on weight as well. **Another very important tool to losing weight, believe it or not, is Meditation! It naturally reduces your anxiety levels and relaxes your body.** I have found, Meditation is the most powerful thing I can do for myself. It is truly a gift. I hope you are continuing to do Meditation as taught in Day 5. If not, just get back to it through constant gentle reminders to self. I give major credit to losing weight to Meditation, as my weight was a lot due to stress, and being sensitive to other people's energies.

Initially, I used to exercise once or twice a week for long hours in response to my stamina and motivation at that time. But with experience, I have learnt that 20 to 40 minutes daily exercise brings better results for me. In the 12 months from when I started, I lost about 20 kilos, which is about 3 stones. There was no particular change in diet as I was eating healthy in any case, but if you aren't, you have to listen to your body and notice when you are really not being authentic to your body's needs by eating the wrong things. **Ask your body to guide you by making you feel good when you eat the right things, and when you are not eating the right things, just ask your body to make you feel uncomfortable and make sure to pick up on those signs.** Also check on portion size of the food you eat. I prefer to eat 4 times and eat a smaller quantity but that suits my body and metabolism. Yours could be different. Experiment and see what suits you. Start tuning into your body. And yes it may take a while. You can even have a conversation with your Heart and ask 'What steps would you like me to focus on for looking after my body?' This is a process that is always ongoing for me.

I used to eat meat, but I had given up eating it over the past 4 years. But just recently, I started eating it again. It's not for any moral reasons, as I do believe everyone has different needs. For instance, I imagine athletes could benefit from that kind of food. When I had stopped, I think it was God who had made me do it, as I myself had made no such plans. For about a year, I was getting a natural sudden craving for green vegetables and salad. I definitely listened to that craving but didn't stop eating non-vegetarian food completely until quite later when I saw dreams with blood and flesh of chicken and naturally found no appetite for meat as a result. Also, I notice that my food habits are seasonal. In winter, my body needs more warmth and more food too. Who knows whether my body needs these dietary changes temporarily or for good, as I had recently gone through a lot of changes physically and emotionally. I will just listen to my body. **No one but my body can tell me what is best for me. Don't do things just because**

others are doing them. Really tune in to what is right for you. Do get information from outside and then listen to what your body is saying. Develop an authentic relationship with food, your body, and your mind through Meditation, and regular, healthy sleep patterns, to really get a grip on your health.

Over the years, I also gravitated to soya milk, rice milk and other alternatives to milk. I started to notice that my digestion was sensitive and I needed to find something light, as the milk that I was used to in India, seemed quite different to milk in the UK, which was processed. Strangely, it's legal to sell raw milk in England but not in Scotland where I am. Initially, after giving up milk, I did feel less bloated and felt lighter and more energetic too. But recently my body has accepted heavier food and I do use milk on and off. I also, through my own inner guidance, was led to information about two years ago on Leaky Gut Syndrome that strangely a Psychic told me I was suffering from. I didn't know that it was actually a medical term, so I ignored it for years until I prayed one day and immediately received an email with the subject 'Leaky Gut Syndrome', which explained that this was what I was going through. Now I had no clue what this was until then. It's usually a problem with digestion of milk, sugar and bread. Staying away from milk and bread for more than a year helped me a lot. I stopped taking sugar with teas and coffees some years ago. I have also tried gluten-free food. In my experience, it's best to have natural organic food as much as possible. Now I do love my pizzas and cakes and really do enjoy them, but I know it's a treat and not daily food for me.

I would highly recommend staying away from microwavable food. For a start, research appears to have shown that once the food is heated in a microwave, it is not something our human bodies accept very well. Usually in the West, microwaves are used to cook ready-made meals. But when we buy more natural food, it's not only good for us, but we support our local farmers, or retail sellers rather than making the big brands rich by serving us processed, packaged food that is not really good for us. It is hard to see that these days we have to fight for the natural food that is our birthright. I would rather have earth-covered potatoes than the clean packaged ones if I had a choice. It's still easier in the part of India where I grew up to see local farmers selling fresh vegetable and fruits at almost every street corner, but in the UK, I often have to order online to get fresh organic vegetables from a local farmer, and also have to pay more than the usual supermarket prices because of their unhealthy domination over the food market. Sometimes, if I haven't had organic food for a while, I literally start to feel a craving. My body talks to me! And so can yours, once you create the habit of listening to your body.

Talking about listening to your body for food, you really cannot get the full feeling about what your body wants unless you cook yourself, if not every day, then certainly on most days! I grew up in a country where, traditionally, almost all men don't cook! But in many other parts of the world, men and women are both equally engaged in cooking. I feel rather sad at how much men are missing out through cultural ignorance. I am not the world's best cook but when I am tuned into what my body needs, I know what to put in my pan and in my body. It's different from day to day. It's like creating a relationship with food. Also, you try new things as a result and become really fine-tuned to the way you like your food. When I was in India, I saw food being cooked mostly by servants, often not to the taste of their masters. Owning the kind of food you eat is also about owning your power. Food is so crucial to our balance of mind and body. I was lucky that my mother chose to cook herself all the time rather than getting servants to do it. Parents are, of course, the best judges of their children's health.

I would like to share a story my old school friend, Sucheta Rawat, had told me about her grandmother. Sucheta is also a food and travel writer and blogs at http://www.goeatgive.com:

"While my granny is 80 years old now, she has had no major health issues in her life. She has an active lifestyle and a sharp mind. She looks youthful and wins beauty contests too! So what's her secret?

Everything in moderation: My granny loves to eat. She likes her sweets,

177

chocolates, fried foods, ghee, etc. and still continues to enjoy them, but only in moderation. Sort of like the French women do. A small piece of chocolate every day to satisfy the sweet tooth, balanced with lots of fresh fruits and vegetables. Her meals include balanced diets - occasional meats, lots of greens, yogurt, whole wheat breads and fruits for snacks. When I tell her about the latest diet in America, she laughs it off and cites herself as an example of someone who enjoys everything, has never dieted and keeps good health.

Move it: Her second tip is to keep moving. My granny has never set foot in a gym in her life and believed yoga is for yogis. Her take on physical exercise is walking before and after every meal (long or short walks depending on how much time you have). She would also move her arms and legs in the morning and be on the move constantly around the house. Housekeeping is a great way to stay in shape and save money too.

Occupy the mind: My granny has been a social worker all her life. She was involved with the blind school, orphanage, Red Cross, Rotary, Innerwheel, Servas, children's club and many more organisations. A key to having a youthful life is to have a youthful mind. If you keep yourself occupied with new things, interact with people, learn and be open to new experiences, you will never feel old and weary."

I really agree with Sucheta's Grandmother. I have seen this example also with my ex father-in-law who always said that walking kept him healthy. He is still practising as a Doctor after retirement and walks to work. My mother always believes housework keeps her moving.

I so believe in the importance of keeping positive, healthy thoughts in mind: an idle mind and gossiping (i.e., indulging in negative talk about others) can really lead to stress and issues of weight too. So do focus on occupying your mind with the right thoughts. Remember as I mentioned earlier, one of the most important secrets to weight loss is to be relaxed and stress free which really comes from being, talking and feeling positive about things and situations in life. And let us not forget that a great way to keep the mind clear is through Meditation! I often feel that my weight balances itself through Meditation in stressful times.

YOUR WORK TODAY

1. Exercise! If you don't already exercise, then find an exercise routine that suits you to start this week or just check to see if you need a change. Start with the pace you are comfortable with and increase it slowly. Keep at it regularly and keep reminding yourself until you become consistent, but don't be angry with yourself for doing less or forgetting. It needs to be a happy process. Listen to your body, and if you are tired, don't overdo it: you can even skip it if necessary. But stay honest to your body. You can't fool it. Your body needs you to have an authentic relationship with yourself, and once you do, it will respond beautifully.

2. Start observing when you are not eating healthy and start replacing it with better food habits. Ask your body in a prayer or simply through Intents, as some given below, to just guide you to the best form of exercise suited to you for now, and also for your diet. Keep questioning your Heart for more direct answers. I do that all the time, so it's not a one-time process. It's a habit! Your body is not a machine, it needs different kinds of nurturing all the time.

Start being aware and ask your Heart and body to guide you to what type of food is best for you. You will find that some food will make you feel energetic and some lethargic and moody. Try cooking if you are new to it! Notice when you are eating unhealthy food or over-eating! Try healthy snacks like some yoghurt with fruits, nuts, oat biscuits with some cheese and a topping instead of a bag of chips in the middle of the day. And never let yourself go hungry. I really don't believe in dieting. You can eat light by having a big bowl of soup for lunch instead of a heavy meal, but never skip a meal! You will put more weight on when you eat next time as you will be hungry and will over-eat!

3. Also question about how to dress your body best and pray that you are taken to the right clothes! Dress the way you would love to but perhaps don't! Start your new relationship with your body in every way. The body is part of you and all the answers for it lie within you. Other than losing weight, I changed my self-image to a great extent through my Intent, visualisation and by looking for answers within to the way I wanted to look like, to the extent that my own parents thought I looked like a different person.

4. You can also work on these following Intents today and every day.

I call on the I AM Presence to direct my Higher Self that:

I AM guided to all healthy food and the amount I need for my healthy body and ideal weight.

I AM guided to all exercises and ways to look after my body that I enjoy and find beneficial.

I AM eating food that is healthy and right for me.

I AM eating right-sized portions and enjoy taking responsibility for what I AM putting into my body.

I AM eating healthy and tasty food.

I AM always led to the right clothes that I enjoy wearing and look good in.

I AM grateful for my beautiful body and look after it through all ways.

I AM tuned into my body's needs and I ask regularly and listen to feelings, hunches and all intuitive knowing.

I AM appreciating my body's wisdom within.

I AM always keeping myself relaxed in mind and body with right positive thoughts.

I AM keeping an eye on my stress levels by doing regular Meditation.

I AM having a good sleep pattern and am guided to how long my body needs sleep.

I AM meditating everyday.

I AM visualising how my body looks like as I am changing.

EXAMPLE 1

Alisha wrote:

"This time I followed your advice and didn't listen to music, I decided to focus on my body instead and decided to breathe deeply and feel where I felt the stretches and the muscles. It was a really new experience for me as in the past I have always had headphones on with music to avoid feeling the exertion of the exercise, but ironically it seems so much better to be connected with your body and feel what it's feeling instead of being buried inside your mind! So thanks for that advice!"

EXAMPLE 2

Mary Ann wrote:

"I already have an exercise routine that I love, and if I miss my weights workout or my Qi Gong (Tai Chi), I feel sluggish, lethargic and a bit miserable. I am a strong believer that exercise makes you feel happier and more alive and I couldn't be without it! I have been doing weights in a small gym with staff that have become my friends for 3 years and I do Qi Gong at an evening class. If I am having a bad day or need a lift, I head for my gym and I know that I will feel better and can get my stress out of my body.

I am very keen to work on my diet now so that I lose weight. I have shaped and toned up since doing weights but the gym staff told me I need to cut down on my excess food if I want to lose weight. I would love to do even more exercise per week and really want to do more yoga in the future too as I absolutely love it.

I went clothes shopping on Friday for the first time in years and loved it! I told my partner that I wanted time alone and I had a very relaxed afternoon browsing for clothes. I have started to pick out clothes with colour too (I normally wear black) and I am picking out feminine styles too. Clothes-shopping is one of the most stressful things for me as I don't know what suits me and I feel so daunted by all the patterns etc. Suddenly I seem to know what suits me and I am wearing patterns and colours. My partner loves the new me! Where is this new knowledge coming from? It is part of my dream to have nice clothes so maybe there is my answer."

In the case above, Mary Ann is relying too much on advice of the gym staff. I should really like her to first herself tune into her own body's needs. If she feels inclined to check in with an expert, then that is her intuitive guidance which she needs to follow.

Please add appropriate I AM Intents to your list of things to do from today's topic. As you get stronger in body, the strength literally shines in every area of life. It brings vitality and joy into your life. Happy exercising, eating well, and looking beautiful and handsome, gals and guys!

Love,
Robin Bela

DAY 19
WHOM ARE YOU STILL BLAMING?
SET YOURSELF FREE FROM THE PAST

Today we are continuing with some more work along the lines of clearing the past. It's time to let go completely of old, past melodramas from our lives if anything is still lingering about. Check to see if you are still blaming the past for things not working out today, or even blaming people around you or yourself? This means you have to let go of the habit of blaming the past or people around you for who you are today. If you have been doing this, it also means you have given away your power and you need to reclaim it and put an end to the old story.

You have already decided to let go of a lot when you cleared fears, but if you didn't touch upon any issues of forgiveness, or were simply blaming the past experience as a block, then it's important to work this through. If you believe someone around you didn't let you do what you always wanted to do, then you are the prisoner of your story. Set yourself free by deciding that you have full control over your life now. So if you believe you cannot win the competition because you lost last time, clear that old story and get a new story - You can do it! It doesn't have to be harder or easier because of the past. You are now presented with a clean slate. What are you going to allow on it?

For me, it was a revelation to discover that an old pattern of failure as old as first grade in school was still giving me fears about success. I had just joined a school in a different city where a different language was spoken and its standard of education was much higher than the earlier one, so my parents were advised by the class teacher that it was better that I repeated the class 1, and thus had to redo the whole year! I was just 5-6 years old and probably never understood at that time what it meant. But its stigma remained for

183

long in my mind, implanting in me a subconscious belief that it's hard to succeed. I was never able to have firm confidence in success in many aspects of life. It came to a point where the image of me as a failure stood in my way. I really had to let go of this old story.

So far as these "old stories" are concerned, the most important part is to realise that this person - in my case the "failure" - is not me, rather it is my history, my "old story", and I can let it go, put it behind me and make my own "new story. That "old story" is not who you are, because you are born perfect. These are just experiences and certainly not who you will become! I can tell you from experience, that usually these stories of the past are the kind we love to spice up with emotions, so that when things go wrong we lay the blame on our history. But the more we talk, the more that belief just grows within us. So the sooner you start talking more of the New story of good things in life that are to come, the better!

I want you to notice this week as to which statements you make repeatedly or you use commonly in conversations, which block your power to achieve the New You in your life, and see what happens. Some examples: - My parents never showed me enough love so I am closed to other people. Or I am always careless, I always drop things! Or I have always been fat! Or I don't trust people easily because of my past hurt. How you think and speak is really important. These statements show that you are still stuck in the past image of self. And you have to rewire yourself by really not allowing yourself to use statements that make you feel less deserving or not good enough. You need to make a new story. **Whenever you catch yourself with your old story, simply breathe it out in one breath and intend the positive again.**

Ask your family and friends which statements you always make which show you are not capable, or are not confident about yourself, if you are unable to yourself observe these or if you would like to gain further insights into your habits of speech. Check if you think you have been using such statements since you started this Programme.

Also notice how often you are catching yourself in the past, or focusing too much on the future. The key to success lies not so much in reaching the goals you aimed at, but in the process of reaching. The more you stay in the moment, joyful, and focus on simply enjoying this moment, the more you are then truly 'living' the life that you came to live on Earth. With worry, you are merely existing and missing the moments of precious life that you could live instead! It's never easy I know, but it's a practice that grows with conscious self-reminders. **The best way to cultivate 'staying in the moment' is by asking your Heart every day 'How can I bring myself more happiness?' And do what the Heart says!**

Not letting go of the past was illustrated by the case of Susie, a client of mine. No matter how much clearing we did, she always came up with fresh issues to clear, and blamed it on the past, that it was causing all problems in her present. I had to tell her that her core problem was not the past but her not letting go of the past. Instead, she needed to look at things positively in the present to allow anything good to come into her life, including the healing she wanted physically and the happier relationships. Staying in the past was blocking her from simply living and carrying on with her life!

YOUR WORK TODAY

1. Notice if you are still dragging some old stories along. Even though you are anchoring positive Intents and breathing out past issues, sometimes you need to let go of the blame and just forgive. It can be forgiving self for blaming, or even doubting self that you cannot lose weight or get the right partner or job, happiness etc. From today, what you are is because of what you choose to be. For your past story, thank your soul for the lessons you learned and allow forgiveness and grace to come in by simply saying:' *I AM calling on the I AM Presence and I ask the I AM Presence to direct my Higher Self that I AM forgiving and letting go of the blame against this person/situation___, for____ I AM at complete peace and that all is well at this moment of time.' Just sit with it and breathe till you feel lighter in heart and body about this issue. And focus on the Intent: I AM good enough to achieve all I want. (You can name them).*

185

2. Also, as you are letting go of the past, I would like you to *retrieve 'the part of you emotionally and psychically'* that you may have lost in that past situation. Usually, people who say 'they were never the same again after that', need to Intend to call back the part of themselves, their soul they literally lost in a situation by breathing and saying, e.g., I AM bringing back that part of me that feels I cannot trust any more from that situation when I was left alone as a child. And say I AM now trusting people around. And breathe till you feel lighter.

3. If the situations involved other people, *visualise your new picture with them as happy and peaceful.* On a soul level, we are all connected and you might even feel that the people you are working with in this image may feel it too, and their behaviour towards you may start to change. For a week, see these people with you on the sofa, happily sitting or hugging, or doing whatever you feel comfortable with. Bring your pets into this image too if you like. You can even include people who are deceased to start healing issues about them within you. In my opinion, souls always live and you will feel immense love from them as you do this.

When we forgive someone, we are not removing from our consciousness the deed they did, but rather the resentment we are carrying within ourselves about the other person, or even the resentment and non-acceptance of 'our own self being wrong'. In fact, the only thing you can change about a situation is 'your making peace with the situation'. The peace of mind within yourself is all that is important. You will notice that when you do so, usually the other person responds quite well on his or her own when you meet next. The person forgiven in your mind can usually feel the change in the way you feel energetically and respond better. It can be on an unconscious level or the person may be sensitive to and perceptive of your change in feelings about him/her.

4. *Also, notice if you are holding on to things because you are addicted to 'victim mentality'* and often like to be pitied, and feel good when someone says, 'poor you'. I once knew a client whose main issues were all cleared emotionally.

But somehow she still kept saying that something was wrong in a part of her body. I checked her energetically and asked her all sorts of questions till she herself couldn't find any excuses. Then I felt I should ask her to let go of the 'victim mentality'. Then there was a sudden shift in her body and she could also feel the clearing. So she was not allowing healing just because she was addicted to the behaviour of looking for attention and it had stemmed from lack of attention from her mother during childhood. Check with yourself if this pattern exists within you.

5. A FORGIVENESS TECHNIQUE:

You can make a list of the people you would like to forgive and also try this other technique if you feel the need for the same.

I would like to share a powerful Hawaiian healing technique called Ho'oponopono. It is very simple. You should sit and say the following line in your mind repeatedly:

"I AM Sorry. Please Forgive Me. Thank You. I love You." (You say this again and again till you feel better about the situation.)

It doesn't matter if you are responsible for the situation, or are the victim of a certain situation. You take the full responsibility of the experience to attain your peace of mind. Saying this again and again, you will feel lighter energetically about the situation in body and heart.

I once read a quote by Kahlil Gibran, *'To be able to look back upon one's life in satisfaction, is to live twice'*. I love that we always have a choice to live our lives with regret or to choose happiness. We can look at past with peace and focus on the good things. **Focusing on the positive should not only be practised for a better future but also to make peace with the past**. Even if I had a dispute with someone in the past, I would rather focus on good things about the person and celebrate the wonderful moments rather than focus on some regretful ones!

EXAMPLE 1 by Rhonda on how she formed her statement to let go of her past:

"I am calling on the I AM Presence to direct my Higher Self that I AM forgiving and letting go of the blame against MYSELF for being jealous and expecting abandonment from my partners, past and present. I AM at complete peace that all is well at this moment of time."

EXAMPLE 2 by Seema:

"I notice that I have a habit of starting questions or statements with "sorry" e.g. 'sorry to disturb, sorry I can't, sorry but ...' when the situation really does not require any apology. Another habit is my use of BUT e.g. 'yes, that's a good idea BUT..'. I have become more conscious of this throughout the course in my effort to be more positive and I am getting better! I also often find myself saying things like, 'if there's a wrong way to do it, I'll find it' or 'silly me' so I will be more aware of that now.

The visualisation tasks have been interesting. I seem to find words easier than pictures in my mind. I may be trying too hard to 'see' instead of being appreciative of my ability to 'feel'.

I have worked a lot on letting go of the blame and forgiving. I read somewhere that forgiving is not forgetting the deed but just intending that I am no longer going to carry the hurt associated with it. That works better for me. There have been many things I have been able to let go and I intend to do more work on this. Learning to forgive myself for some 'wrong' decisions over the years has been a challenge!"

EXAMPLE 3 by Pam:

"I had psychotherapy for 2 years, and this was basically what it was all aimed at, but I like that it can be done in ways that are painless and forgiving, and visualising is a simple process. I like that we don't have to understand it and just forgive and send love and peace. I am sitting with my older brother on the sofa this week. It is so uncomfortable, it always is and always has been. It is getting better everyday. I will continue this and see if it gets any easier. Also, writing this has reminded me of some school friends (well I used to see them as enemies) and for past and current boyfriends. I don't want to have any negative memories or feelings to carry around. It is a powerful exercise. I moved out of home at 19 years old because of my brother – this is 19 years ago!!!! Ever since we haven't spent much time together and only ever once or twice alone: to visualise him on my sofa with me every night and hugging! It is really hard. I will continue."

***

Once you change your story of blame, it gets easier to change yourself to positive frequency. If it requires a few more reminders, you can do so by allowing your Inner Self to remind you, that this old part of you is gone now! And you have received your power from this person or situation or behaviour completely. Intend that and breathe into that.

See you tomorrow! In the meantime, have a lovely, peaceful day.

Love,
Robin Bela

DAY 20
WHERE HAVE YOU GIVEN YOUR POWER AWAY?

Since I lost weight, I have changed my wardrobe and have started to see the way I'd like to be dressed. In this process, I started wanting to wear high heels. Now I had not worn much heeled footwear for literally a decade. First of all, I had a hairline fracture in my foot that came about through an accident, which occurred in India while participating in a rowing competition. Also, I had a knee dislocation around that time. Later, I married a guy who was my height, so I didn't feel the need to wear heels at all! So when I started playing with my new-found freedom of wearing heels, I actually took it really seriously. I started believing that if I cannot wear the really high pencil heels, I'm not truly connected to my power. Since I was new to that, I was not good at choosing the right pair and I ended up getting blisters and had a painful experience. I felt I had lost a race as I saw my friends wearing heels so easily. I knew that my older injuries weren't an issue as my legs were now strong with all the exercising and healing. I was just choosing the wrong types of heals. It took me a while to realise that I had given away my power of feeling good to the success of wearing heels. When I thought about it, I felt annoyed for doing this to myself. But we do these things so often in our lives. And it's important that we don't give away our power to things, people, situations etc. So I made peace with wearing heels and decided I will buy and wear heels that I am comfortable with. Sure enough, I soon found them.

This situation happens many times to us, when we often say, "I will only be happy if I get that job or am accepted by this person or have more money." When we do so, we are only introducing an element of fear in our progress and creating a kind of attachment to certain things as a condition of our happiness. Are you too attached to the outcome of your Intent? It's important to know what we like, but not give away our power to it for the sake of our present happiness. I know plenty of people who just stop their lives for such things, as they wait. I always tell those people, "Keep living your life, because you cannot control anything but yourself and your feelings at this moment." In the past, I have dealt with liking a person but not getting the same attention back. When I was younger, I had a tendency to sit in that misery, but now I am able to live with it because I shift my frequency and focus on myself through all the techniques we have talked about in previous chapters. I know that only I can make myself always feel good.

Let me reiterate that the relationships outside of us are always a reflection of our relationship with self. So, as we focus on ourselves, everything around naturally balances accordingly. Happy energies attract only positive outcomes of old situations or bring in new and better ones. I can expect all good things, money, love etc., and I look at it with excitement, and live my life as if it were already abundant. I don't stop in my life and wait for it to happen. The energy you are in now is what will increase tomorrow. So, what energy would you like to be in, so that you attract what you really want? Would you like to be in happy energies, or miserable ones that you are not loved, not attractive, poor, not good enough etc?

Whatever the nature of energy you are in, is exactly what you will create more of in the future. Here, recall the exercises we did in an earlier lesson on finding things to love and creating the fertile soil for love and positive feelings. That is the key to happiness and to take back your power to create anything you want. It also helps us to stay detached to the outcomes of all our Intents. Further, it's when we breathe in a relaxed way that we allow more positive and happy energies to flow around us. The energy now moves in a relaxed way. Universe naturally responds to that energy, increases it and reflects back to what you are Intending and feeling, which is to be more happy! Universe gives you all you want! Just Ask and Intend as if you have already received!

Also notice the small things you have given your power away to: for instance, some people expect the décor in a restaurant to be a certain way. If they don't find it that way, their whole experience of the evening is ruined. On the other hand, their companion may have had a great time because the décor of the room wasn't the focus but instead, the conversation was. If you focus on creating good feelings, and choose to see, think and feel only what's positive, rather than dwelling on not so positive things, you are naturally likely to be in good spirits and have a happier life.

Sometimes, we give our power away to others for approval, so much so that we lose touch with our own power and our own feelings! What will others think? We live according to what should be accepted, speak what sounds like perfect etc.. Living in that artificiality will give you no real appreciation back and also no real love and friendship. When you say anything out of love, it is always more real and authentic, as you speak for yourself rather than saying what you think should be spoken. Also when we seek approval, it's because we haven't fully accepted a certain aspect of ourselves, or a choice we've made. We doubt our abilities, judgement or worthiness, so we look to others to validate us. The approval from others is never guaranteed but what really matters is validation from within oneself. When you embrace yourself and your choices, your inner natural confidence, power and strength will appear.

Here I would love to share a story of a client from India who has given her power away by being unauthentic to her feelings. She once contacted me saying she had caught her husband with a prostitute, and she was not worried so much about the fact that he was going to her, but rather she was more concerned about putting the prostitute in jail, and worried about the money her husband was spending on her. I told her the first thing that she needed to work on was her relationship, or leave him if it wasn't working. But she wasn't even addressing that as a problem. Or rather, she was trying to stay blind to the real issue of love and understanding missing in their relationship and directing her rage at the other woman. She is a well-educated working woman but is also probably affected by the cultural influences in India. She was more concerned about having enough money for her children's education, and it appears that she and her husband were more concerned about the financial and social aspects of the situation. Everything from outside should look perfect in their family, but what was going on within wasn't important! I was really surprised, as I would feel it to be so fake, unauthentic.

There are many people living artificial lives who are truly unhappy to the core. Yes, you can heal and bring your relationship to balance if both partners are ready to do it. But it is so important to stand true to what is acceptable and what is not, and not compromise on your happiness. It is important to stand by your authentic self bravely even if it means to separate and go through a change to begin with, which may initially seem fraught with uncertainties. This is all in order to protect yourself, and for your true happiness and self-respect in the long run. I am not sure whether my client took my advice, but I do pray that their relationship is healed and happy as she's still married to the same man. I know she is trying to save her marriage for the sake of children, but I hope that she addresses the root cause of her husband's behaviour as to why he needs to go to a prostitute. It could be a habit that he needs to eradicate, or a past issue that he needs to heal, that first made him start going to a prostitute and continue despite having such a loving wife and beautiful children.

Being educated is empowering, and it is never too late to start educating yourself. In so many countries, elderly students are very common. So your education doesn't end after 21 years of age when you are supposed to have completed your degree. You can design and shape your life even at 50 or later! Why not! I know someone who's about 40 and is doing business relating to properties but doesn't have an architecture degree because his parents couldn't afford or rather didn't bother to send him to a University. And now I would love to see him do what he really would like to have done, mainly because he has given power to the fact that he's not educated enough and feels something is missing in his life. Either he makes peace with the thought that getting a degree certificate is really something his ego wants, or he can say, no I really wanted to do it, and I will. But he needs to take his power back either way and make peace with it.

YOUR WORK TODAY

1. Check with yourself and write where in life have you given away your power? What are the things that make you feel less good about yourself because you have given away the power to be happy to somebody else? I would like you to try breathing out such things that make you feel less good and Intend the opposite with I AM statements and add them to your regular I AM Statements' list.

2. Simply focus on the Intent, *'I AM taking my power back from____'.* Anytime I feel someone intimidating or threatening my peace and happiness, I say that in my mind, and instantly I feel my abdominal muscles relax.

3. Also ask yourself regularly every day, *"What would I like to create for myself today?"* and act on whatever answer you get. This will get you into the habit of creating happiness yourself rather than feeling the need for it to come from outside. As you do this, it will bring you more love, as love within shines through you and naturally attracts the 'like' by law of attraction.

EXAMPLE

Lisa wrote:
"I give my power away when I look for approval outside of myself. The things that make me feel less about myself are talking badly of people or myself being critical and loving with my words or thoughts. Wearing clothes that don't suit me or feel scruffy. Overeating. When I get drunk. When I argue or become aggressive. Not being fully honest. Doing work that doesn't sit right with me ethically and morally.

I can feel a shift but there still feels like so much releasing and forgiveness work left to do. I will continue with this. Also I realised that yesterday I was saying my Intents almost obsessively and it was from my head. It feels like every area of my life needs releasing and forgiveness work, so I am just going to stay with this for as long as necessary. The breath work when I am releasing through the mouth feels strained and uncomfortable. <u>Also, I have a question. I have 10 sides of A4 paper filled with I AM statements. Is this ok or do I need to narrow them down?</u> I have read through them and they all connect and feel relevant so I am not sure which ones I would let go of. Is the aim of these Intents to become part of my normal everyday thing so one day they will be automatic?"

My Reply to her:

"You don't need to breathe through your mouth all the time, just 1-2 times and then through the nose is what I have asked you to do. 10 pages is a lot. Yes you may wish to narrow it if you feel some things have cleared or are repeated. If not, check in another few weeks, some may be ready to go. You can add or remove as per how relevant they are for you at this moment compared to when you began saying those Intents. Under Day 30, I ask you to always check yourself consciously where you stand with regard to your Intents. And also check with yourself if you are holding yourself back from believing that you are moving forward."

Also, the following Intents were given to her:

I AM eating only what I feel is right for me.

I AM consciously making decisions to eat and drink healthy.

I AM dressing in a style that I AM comfortable with.

I AM working honestly in a way that my conscience is comfortable with.

I AM communicating peacefully to all under all circumstances.

I AM going at a pace that is comfortable for me with this 30-Day Programme.

I AM believing I AM moving forward."

***

I hope you are enjoying the work so far in the Programme with me, and enjoying the changes you are bringing in with the inner work or self-introspection that you are doing. Please do keep reading your daily I AM Statements, continue doing daily Meditation, exercising and writing your daily thoughts about each day's topic in your journal. See you tomorrow!

Love,

Robin Bela

DAY 21
PUT YOUR WINGS ON AND SAY 'YES' TO YOUR FLIGHT! TRUST YOURSELF

A quote I read somewhere: "A bird sitting on a tree is never afraid of the branch breaking, because her trust is not on the branch but on it's own wings. Always believe in yourself."

I love Angels and Fairies and collect many nice decorative items representing them. I have also been gifted many of these. About two years ago, within a period of two days, four of them fell down and one of the wings of each got broken! One was just a key-chain and the wing broke in my bag on its own! Now that was a clear message I was getting from Universe. I do ask for signs to provoke me to search, get more guidance on my path, and I also ask for signs that I can easily notice. I remember a week before this incident, I actually wanted more messages about what was happening in my life, and I wanted clearer signs. And I sure did get the signs repeatedly as you can see!

Now as I meditated and Asked my Heart, what were those repeated signs trying to tell me, I got a clear message that I was not showing real trust in my inner strength, and hence was not ready to fly or go for what I truly wanted. I was therefore wavering in my decision, and was not really in my full power to start working towards my goal and achieving it. Metaphorically, my own wing was broken and I could not fly to where I wanted! I was told by my inner guidance to forgive myself for not believing and trusting myself by acknowledging that it was hard to manifest what I wanted. I did that and then I was told to just state my Intent of what I truly desired: I don't have to know the 'how' to start believing. So just like a baby bird taking its first flight, you need to take your new flight without knowing how it will go or where it will end. Just say 'yes'! We limit ourselves to not receiving, simply because we don't have the guts or the drive to see beyond our previous experiences. And it's time to just say yes! **When Universe receives a clear 'yes' without 'ifs' and 'buts' and justifications, it simply delivers.** So Ask and demand without any hesitation! Take back your 'power to receive'!

We are in such a habit of trying to control everything in our lives including the future we Intend to create. Let me now give you another tool, which is to learn to work through your 'Inner Guidance' and not control things through your mind. **Real trust begins when we learn to listen to our inner voice.** We are body and also Soul, or you might call it Spirit or Higher Self or the Intuitive or Inner Voice or Inner Being or Inner Self. For the convenience of using one or two words for this concept, I will use words 'Soul' and 'Spirit'. But you are welcome to choose any word or words that are comfortable with you for referring to Soul, Inner Voice or Spirit etc. Your Soul or Spirit is the channel or medium through which you receive your inner guidance and reflect upon things deeper. The body deals with all the materialistic things in the world like eating, breathing, thinking, talking etc, and the Soul or the Spirit deals with the part of us that we cannot see in our physical plane, but usually sense it with feelings and Heart. That includes manifesting things that we have no way of controlling, as there is no proof of how things have happened or can happen. Most of the time, people try to control results that are not in their hands, and don't want to see that it's humanly impossible to do so. Hence they worry and end up anxious, depressed and even ill, e.g., worrying about a result of a job interview. You can't do anything about it now, so just stop worrying, stay in good energies and enjoy life. Your positive natural energies would create best results before and after the interview when you are not trying to control results, and thereby, not blocking positive energies.

It is important to realise that if we start learning to rely on this very powerful and intangible part within every human being, called Soul or Spirit, it results in tremendous trust and power within ourselves. This is the closest connection to our divinity, which is our true essence within, away from ego and our personalities, who we really are behind the human body, and it is ready to assist us if we allow and ask it to do so. Thus, you can literally get onto your soul's pathway. Those who don't are those who we would describe as living a soulless life, without passion, love, joy or peace. I wouldn't consider these to be mere emotions the brain emotes; these are functions of the Heart which science finds hard to measure. **Our Soul needs to be a part of our lives just as much as the qualities of reason and logic of the brain.**

Say, for example, I have done marketing work such as advertising etc. for my business, but energetically, if I am worried about whether it will work, that energy will go straight back to Universe as a negative message that I may not get clients. In this way, you just create a negative situation. But instead of worrying, I recognise my Spirit as an equal partner to my body and mind, and trust that it will support me to create things, although as yet, I have no clue how. All we have to do is to give it an assignment, because only if you Ask, do you receive! In fact, once a young girl asked me as to how she could increase the energy of 'receptivity' in life. The answer to that question is simply to 'Ask' more for yourself in prayer and through Intents. Every day in the morning, I ask my Divine Self, Spirit and other helpers to help with the things I really want to create; for instance Money, relationships or to help me write something creative etc. You remember the chapter about prioritising? Well, just think of the 3 things and then say "My Spirit, I ask you to help me with this..., thank you." And let the magic roll in!

We are supposed to live with the assistance of our Soul, but somehow we are on manual mode and not on autopilot as we should be. Somewhere, our humanity stopped giving importance to our 'Spirit' or 'Soul'! I think it's when the age of reasoning came when we needed proof of everything, for instance an apple falling is due to gravity! So anything we cannot reason with, started leaving our lives, and this sadly included our Souls! Some call this new age the period of Enlightenment: well to me, it has been the dark ages, and now the new era is coming back where we are giving importance to our Soul again.

By allowing yourself to have spiritual connection within, you create more trust in your inner messages, gut, feelings, visions, asking, actions and the unknown. We are not machines that can work certain hours according to mechanical or quality management principles. We are human beings with feelings, and our productivity can vary depending on how our day is going, our moods etc. Without our Spirit's participation, we are only living to half or even less of our highest potential. Accept your Spirit as part of you and see how your life becomes magical and easier, by simply asking its assistance, and breathing with it. This is when you live a "spirited" life. Our mind and Spirit are both equally important. Do what's possible and trust the rest; perhaps the result will be perfect too. You may have heard people commenting that someone is so bright and spirited. This is exactly what I wish you to be throughout your life.

To connect to your Divine Spirit, first of all you need to know what things you love and want in life, and forget about the things you 'should' do. When we do what we love, we are at our best and at our happiest, which is really the purpose of every Soul to achieve on this planet. Follow your Heart and you are then connected to your Soul. To me, Heart is the most magical organ of the body. It's where we experience magical love. When you are tapped into that fertile soil for manifesting, which is just love and joy without fears and doubts, you are tapped into the very energy you would always want to access, and I call that 'being in Spirit'. From this fertile space, you will be able to give a crystal clear message of any feeling or thought you hold to Universe, as there are no fears and worries you are sending along with what you are Asking. Universe then just delivers what you Ask, by law of attraction. To tap into that Heart space, remember the things you love, and indulge in them, ideally on a daily basis, count the things you are grateful for to connect to that Heart space. You can also connect to Heart energy naturally with your Sacred Altar Within technique taught to you in Day 6, Meditation taught in Day 5, Stillness practice from Day 7 and 17, connecting to nature, singing, dancing, everything you enjoy and that we have talked about in the previous chapters.

I know that often some healers think they are offering healing to the whole world, when they are actually sitting in a state of fear while they send their healing energy, so really they are spreading the energy of fear of whatever they are praying for along with the peace. That is why, it's important not only to speak, but to think and feel positively in your Heart, to attract the like. In the first chapter, we talked about 'appreciating your goals'. When you do that, it naturally opens the Heart to feeling love and brings positive energy around your desires. Universe and our life mirror our thoughts and feelings. Yes, we get influenced by others' thoughts, but by and large, we are in charge of most of our experiences through our conscious Intentions and feelings of what we want to create in our lives.

Also, be careful not to wait for signs to take action on what you want. I have seen some people give away their power to receive what they want by waiting to 'receive a sign' before they do anything. Signs support our inner guidance system, our Soul's wants and needs, just as I received in the above case with the Angels' broken wings; but truly, I first look within to get a clearer picture and to make my decisions. Signs may appear to support me but my life does not stop or stay in a pause button whilst I wait for them. Some people start looking for meaning in everything around their life and thereby actually lose control over their own inner guidance and Spirit, and as a result, life too. But when you get an answer to your question like I did through clear signs, I found it was helpful and I didn't need to wait for more things to break around me to understand what the signs were telling me! I was quick to notice and search its meaning through ways explained below. It is important to take action straight away on what you have realised you should be doing, otherwise your inner guidance system thinks it is not being taken seriously and stops responding, or rather the intuitive guidance can get muddled up with our over-analysing, doubting and worrying mind.

To understand our signs, we can find out about our needs by simply placing hand on Heart and asking our Spirit - My Spirit what is it that you want next? - and see what you get. It is a similar exercise like you did with Heart at the beginning of this book, but now you are more consciously connecting to your Spirit with the information in this chapter. Perhaps you can feel more confident that you are already getting and listening to your inner guidance. Try speaking aloud, try writing, whatever works for you. Ask frequently, so that you are always in touch with your Soul's needs. All answers are within. This way you are never out of your Soul's alignment in life and are connected to your Soul's purpose and also in complete touch with your Power within. This also will help you to learn to do the things you 'want' and not what you 'should'. I believe this is the new age thinking that is so needed, especially as the economy is breaking down right now and people are losing jobs. This is encouraging people to start their own businesses, which is perhaps what they always wanted to do, but never found the courage to take the first step. **When we deprogramme the thinking that security is important, we are then able to try new things in life. We didn't have the concept of salary a few hundred years ago. Today's economic structure, which is dominated by big brands, has kind of enslaved us into the thinking of security, while in reality, we humans were born with the idea of never knowing what's next. Life was always exciting, and everyone believed that what they were doing 'today', could be easily replicated.**

In the course of the Online Programme, I had an important conversation over emails with Tanya on Spirit/Higher Self that I would like to share here:

Tanya: I am not clear on connecting to Higher Self or the Spirit that you call.

Me: *Think of a Being without a Heart. We would say he's soulless. And think of someone full of love and joy. We always say he's spirited! Well the Soul or the Higher Self or the Spirit lives in the Heart. That is why I teach the concept of connecting to love through Sacred Altar Within technique, things you love doing etc. They are practical ways to connect to Heart or Spirit or Higher Self. Our emotions reflect the state of how we are connected to Higher Self. In a state of problems, if you stay calm, you are connected to the Higher Self.*

To understand what kind of emotions you are going through, you need to keep a journal. I usually tell you to draw the Sacred Altar Symbol on your Heart to stay in connection with your Higher Self in times of emergency. Placing hand on Heart is a sign to feel your Soul/Higher Self too. That is my number one priority when I need to ground and centre myself immediately under stressful circumstances. I always ask my Spirit/Heart to lead my day daily so that my ego stays out of the way. And I speak to it, I ask it to help me every day with the things I want help with.

In reply to that, Tanya had asked her Spirit for guidance and one of the things she got was:

"I also feel guided to drink more water - and I am not doing it. I think I should remind myself repeatedly until I start to drink more water!!!! I know the benefits - I also feel guided that a hydrated body vibrates better and I am permanently with mild dehydration. To increase my own vibration I need more water in my body. I even had a dream where I was told that I am killing myself (or shortening my life), by not drinking water like I should do. And that I would manifest more easily with a body that has enough hydration- but not just any water, the water has to be good enough to drink! Funny thing is I know our oldest dog Pluto is allergic to our water supply, it has been tested safe, but it has meant that I have done lots of research into water and it's properties and I'm sure that the problem with our water is a fusion of iron and copper making some sort of 'super' molecule which makes Pluto poorly. Anyway, enough of that - but I do know better! This is coming through so strongly for me that I don't really understand why I am not acting upon this!

I have more questions, why do we have a Higher Self? What are its functions? Is the Higher Self a part of us (as in, is the Higher Self a part of me?) or are we just a part of it? Can we access information via our Higher Selves and if so, what information would this be? Is the Higher Self a part of us or more like a separate entity e.g. like spirit guides etc."

My Reply:

Why do we have a Higher Self? - *If we didn't, we would be robots! Imagine us without Heart and love! Love is Divine! When we are in love in our Heart, and do everything from Heart instead of fear, we are acting through our Higher Self.*

What are its functions? - *It helps us stay in love with life, with our self, away from fears and when we are connected to it, we can hear our inner voice/Spirit/Higher Self or you may even call it God as we are all part of God - just as you heard the message about water! That's divine guidance from your Spirit/Higher Self.*

Is the Higher Self a part of us (as in, is the Higher Self a part of me?) or are we just a part of it? - *We are part of Higher Self. Our Soul has lived many lives but our body is always new. Some people as they connect to Higher Self more, may remember past lives too but really it's not important unless you have a block from past lives. It's a good thing not to get too obsessed about past lives. I have seen some people blame everything on past lives and stop living their present lives. There have been some cases where notified Past Life Regression therapists like Brian Weiss have healed situations in the present lives and it wouldn't have been possible unless you went to the past life for that person. But the need to do this would usually be rare. Normally all our healing is connected to the present life. Often we may find that we are naturally good at some things from a very young age which other people may take a lifetime to master. This could indicate that it is something that we were doing in past lives, as for instance, I did healing and teaching work from my early 20s and I know it's what I did for sure in past lives!*

Can we access information via our Higher Selves and if so, what information would this be? - *You were already doing it when you asked your Higher Self for answers to your questions, for example when you found information on water. The words you receive are very neutral, and are not trying either to please you or to make you feel wrong about yourself, but are usually to the point without stories, and most importantly resonate with you and feel true.*

Is the Higher Self a part of us or more like a separate entity, e.g., like spirit guides etc? - *Our Higher Self is the first guide to us as it's part of us - it's our Soul, it's who we truly are. Other Guides outside us can be, Angels, Gods and Goddesses, past loved ones etc.*

YOUR WORK TODAY

1. *Every day, in the morning, Ask for signs when you feel you need more guidance and assurance.* Pay attention to repeated words, images and incidents. They may occur not immediately when you Ask, but perhaps days or weeks later. Ask Universe to show you signs that you can easily understand.

2. You always deserve to receive. Just Intend, *'I forgive myself for not Asking for all abundance due to my limiting beliefs of what I can Ask for and receive. I receive all I Ask now. I AM safe to Ask and receive. I thank you God/Universe!'*

3. *Ask your Spirit and Divine Supporters you work with, to assist you* with the things you would like help with every day/morning, perhaps as you read your Intents. Breathe with it for a couple of minutes and then relax, it's all taken care of!

4. Connect with your Spirit as was explained in the chapter for any questions you may have. And start connecting to all the answers within you. You can ask "My Spirit what is it that you want next?" Try speaking aloud, and then writing it in your journal, Ask frequently, so that you are always in touch with your Soul's needs.

5. I should also like you to *say 'Yes' to your flight for things you want this week and allow yourself to find trust within yourself.* Simply say, I say yes to money today! I say yes to love! I say yes to just being happy! I say yes to feeling good! I say yes to new love! I say yes to me looking great today, I say yes to some wonderful surprises today! **Demand your needs today without any guilt or feeling that you don't deserve this instant gratification! Yes you do!! Dare to say 'yes' unconditionally without limitations of 'ifs' and 'buts' and of knowing 'how' and 'when'! Just leave it to God/Universe and YOUR SPIRIT to bring you what you want!** You are then at a frequency of positive energy for that goal unconditionally, and simply attract the same. Don't wait to be ready! You are ready now at this minute! Say 'Yes' and see the magic start!! I am so excited for you!

204

EXAMPLE 1

Margaret wrote to me:
"I have been saying yes this week and have had a jam-packed week with different experiences. I had tickets to see a singer and my friend dropped out so I went alone rather than not go - had a nice time and was glad I caught up with friends and family, been to zumba, and went to a new energy healing circle today to give and receive some healing.

The thing that has been different was that I did not have much money in the bank and I would usually say no as a result, but my Heart told me to say yes and the angels told me to have blind faith so I did. I have been having ideas to get the money to pay for things and I am just working on releasing the fears. It was a big step as I have been intending that I am responsible and that I am having a respectful relationship with money right now, so part of me wondered if this was irresponsible but I had an underlying feeling that I am doing the right thing. Almost like now is the time that I have to take this risk and just believe. I have had a great week as a result."

EXAMPLE 2

Dawn wrote to me:
"Have become pretty good at setting goals and Intentions and believing they will manifest. It worked with me winning this course with you and many other things. It always used to happen until about 15 years ago when I just stopped dreaming and went on call for work 24/7 and became very ill. Have learnt my lesson now very painfully. You have taught me how to ask God for what I want so I don't have to worry about things as I know they will work out for the best."
***
I wish you magic every day in your life!

Love,
Robin Bela

DAY 22
IT IS SAFE TO BE POWERFUL

After yesterday's lesson on simply saying 'yes' and 'receiving', is it still hard for you to affirm your Intent regarding your goal/desire, and to believe that you will get it? Is it difficult for you to believe that you are powerful enough to do this? Perhaps you do not feel secure enough to be your most powerful self? Are you afraid that people will ridicule your ideas? What others think and say is a reflection of their thoughts, their dreams. Once you are immune to their opinions, you don't need to be a victim of this suffering. You simply accept people as they are. And are you afraid that people will take advantage of your power? Remember you have the right to say 'No' then, and set your boundaries. Is it that you do not accept your power because you think you are not good enough? At this point, you merely need to remember that you are living according to your highest values and full potential, which are unique to you, and that make you who you are; and as long as these are coming from a place of love, truth and peace, you are perfectly safe!

I have intimately felt what I have said above because I truly suffered from the fear of not being safe, or from insecurity. It showed with knee dislocation at the age of 13, which recurred when I was in my early twenties. The second time was really hard and I couldn't walk properly for almost a year, which resulted in me looking deep within myself for answers, as I found that any outside help was not helping my knee. Over the years, my knee strengthened as I had started connecting fearlessly to my true inner values, becoming authentic, and listening to my feelings. **Feelings are the deepest words of your soul.** I heard it loud and clear, and realised that I was moving in the opposite direction to where I wanted to go in my career. To me, the problem in my knee was a blessing in disguise as it helped me learn to look within and hear my true desires for my life's pathway. Earlier, I wasn't truly listening but was focused on going in the opposite direction to where my true desires lay, with the result that the two sockets of my knee literally moved in different directions and dislocated. I then left my job, which was a great one by the way. I was even offered a house and a car with it. After these early years of being ambitious with regard to my career in marketing, I completely switched to just following my Heart, my inner knowing, instead of following my head as I was so used to doing. So my normal language of talking turned to doing what I 'want' rather than what I 'should'. I felt safe to follow my path in Energy Therapy and Coaching work simply because I was happier in my Heart and I realised that I alone was important to my Soul.

Money and status cannot on their own create real inner happiness, they can only add to it. For me, the happiness within is the compass for showing me directions in life. Sometimes, what happiness means to my Soul, may mean that initially I accept less money for doing what I love, but aim to earn more in the future as I grow. For me, it has also meant choosing to be alone for the first time in my life in a different country, separating from my ex-husband to start life again, or simply praying and listening for guidance to help me lose weight. I had no proof beforehand that I would be safe in thinking like this or that, and then being able to achieve it. All I had was the inner knowing that it was right for me: I didn't feel suffocated any more, I felt peaceful. In my experience, the end result is usually much better than when choosing the safer options. This is when you are truly living a Conscious life.

Even later, after making the decision to be authentic, I was haunted by many images and visions of the fears deep within me. I would see people attending my programmes falling down the staircase and whenever I wanted to see myself as happy, I was haunted by nightmarish dreams of myself being hit by a car, or my legs simply crumbling like powder. I had to start questioning myself really deeply as to why I was unable to visualise myself as happy and strong. Really, it was me just wanting my power to be happy! At that point, I did my 'clearing' for merely the fear of 'feeling unsafe to be happy'. It was as though I felt an inner nudge that I just needed to simply Ask for what I wanted. It's as if I knew that it was coming. I saw glimpses of this even earlier in different ways.

I realised that the power of getting what I wanted was within me, not outside. I truly needed to feel the attention, the love, the peace, the abundance inside me first, before it could reflect outside of me. I also realised that only if I can learn to stay happy in the moment 'now', will I be able to create more happiness in the future. This may sometimes mean opening yourself to smile, to do something for fun - like for me, it's fun to cook and eat my favourite food or watch the moon etc. - to get your mind off an upsetting situation for a start. But as you become accustomed to repeating this, you will find that you do move towards accepting your stronger, powerful self. Once you are in a better state of mind, start tuning into your inner guidance and trust it. And really, neither antidepressants nor anyone but yourself, can help you there! My friend, Dawn Gillespie from creating-harmony.ca has shared her experience with antidepressants below:

"I can share with you my personal experience of what pharmaceutical drugs did to me last year. Although they were a different type of drug, I do feel that any type of drug used could have negative effects on people. I need to start by sharing that I am Clairaudient (so I hear my guides, spirit). After my late husband's passing, I was on antidepressants, muscle relaxants, sleeping pills, to help me cope with his loss. I had some experiences where I thought I was having a heart attack, after many hospital visits and doctor appointments, I found my heart was okay but my doctor at the time kept prescribing me more meds. (I really was over medicated). For about a month, I then started hearing and seeing very scary evil things. I was harassed by these entities for at least a month. I thought I was going to die. I probably called the ambulance at least 6 times and finally admitted myself into the Psychiatric ward for a week where I was taken off all meds. I learned through a private session with Deborah King that I was tapped into the 5th dimension (I think that is what you call it). This is a place where there can be light and dark energy. With me being on this medication, that is how I got stuck in this reality for a while. I wouldn't want anyone to ever have these terrifying experiences. I do hope that people really pay attention to the amount of medicines they are taking and ask that you reconsider taking any type of street drug. Thank you for allowing me to share my experience, I hope this will help others to reconsider taking any type of drug not prescribed by a medical doctor."

If you are going through an emotional loss or are overwhelmed with disturbing emotions due to whatever reason, do remember that this is how our Body and Soul naturally release the old and let in the new. It's like a tidal wave, it comes as a high and then calms down. We must stop running away from emotions and from fearing them. It is a blessing that these are about to clear when you have started feeling them. Breathe with this wave, work with Meditation, Stillness practice, prayer, gratitude and do your journaling. Know that if you can allow it to flow through you, it will be easier than resisting it and remaining stuck. And it gets worse, as Dawn talks above, when you take drugs to numb the emotions.

Recently, as I was writing this Book, I was also having dreams that I may hurt people with my power, or do something wrong with it. My fears were stopping me from finalising this Book. Of course, I was clearing all my dark shadows, for feeling safe in order to connect to my full power within. Accepting power is being truly authentic, sincere and responsible for yourself, and also your relationships with others in your life.

YOUR WORK TODAY

1. Notice if you have had problems with legs, hips, feet. Most likely, at such times, you have had some issues with regard to feeling safe in your life. It is connected to your "root chakra" in energy healing terminology.

2. You may have some issues about feeling unsafe to accept your power. Perhaps in your family, you were brought up in such a way that you came to believe that accepting your power and shining in all you do were not right or safe. Check within to identify the root causes of this for yourself.

3. It's important to see if you have any fears about accepting your Power. Check with your Heart or Spirit whether you deserve all happiness and live

your best, and write down if the answer is no, and why. I discussed some possible fears of power in the first paragraph of this chapter.

4. See also if you are afraid of feeling your emotions. We cannot avoid them and so we have to learn to face them in the most peaceful manner, focusing and knowing through our inner self and positive Intention that we get a clearer picture at the end of whatever we are searching.

5. *You can make the following statements as your Intents for today* and repeat these later if you feel the need to work on them more:

I AM calling on the I AM Presence to direct my Higher Self that (Breathe as you Intend):

I AM safe to be happy now.

I AM safe to receive love now.

I AM safe to receive money now.

I AM safe to follow my dreams now.

I AM safe to look good now.

I AM safe to speak my truth now.

I AM safe to just be peaceful now.

I AM safe to connect to my Heart now.

I AM safe to connect to my inner wisdom now.

I AM supported by Universe to be happy, to receive love, money and all good things in life now and it's a ceaseless flow of supply.

I AM safe to trust in the uncertainty.

Literally feel and visualise your legs and feet strong, standing tall and firmly on the ground. When you are ungrounded, you could have shaky legs, find yourself faced with trips or falls or have some other problems in legs and hips.

I also recommend exercising with some weights for 5-10 minutes daily, perhaps of about 2 kilos each. It really helps to strengthen your power centre, which is in your abdomen and is called "solar plexus chakra" in energy healing terms. As you start building power on the outside, it also helps within. It really tightens the muscles there and builds up your strength. Go for some training if need be; even a couple of classes is enough to give you the confidence to start on your own if you feel uncertain.

EXAMPLE 1 - Psychic Attack

Sarah wrote:

"Dear Robin,

Thank you for your email, I have very much enjoyed the e-course and it is good to have the extra tools now for times of need. Do you recall after one of your healing courses I attended with you, I began to see moving images of beautiful tigers and other creatures when I first awoke in the morning and sometimes during the middle of the night? These visions stopped following my treatment the 2nd time I became ill and never returned until, that is when I was doing your 30 day e-course! About two weeks into it the tigers, apes, birds etc. all returned and I was delighted with this. However, I then started to be attacked - three times when I failed to protect myself before going to sleep. It has been truly horrendous - something has leapt upon me - on my back one time. Another time it came up from my feet and at the same time claw-like talons dug sharply into my arms and I think the worst one - I felt something pull back the bed covers and get into bed behind me and attach itself to my back - this one I could not shake off until I called to Archangel Michael and let out a huge scream and finally threw it off - this has all been very scary indeed.

I know that this is because the energy work I have been doing on the course has reawakened my senses, but of course this might happen to someone who does not realise what is happening. So I thought I would share this with you and ask if there are any protection techniques for those working on the goal on opening up their psychic senses."

My response to that was:

"Dear Sarah, Thank you for sharing your experience. What you have written is interesting. Many of the participants usually focus more on things like money or relationships but you were focusing on the spiritual aspect, and you really got what you asked for! Congratulations on getting that back first of all. But now we have to address the fears of it. Over the years of doing healing work, I have learnt that the protection really comes from feeling deep within that I AM safe, but things like putting protection from outside are just a way of helping us connect to that feeling inside so that we can release our own blocks of insecurity. Energetic protection techniques that I teach in programmes are more like a band-aid, and not the real healing. The real healing for you in this situation would be first of all to accept your gift of clairvoyance. Secondly, question yourself using Day 2 work as to why you fear the connection to Clairvoyance? Keep asking why to every answer you get till you reach the core issue. You may even end up in a past life situation where for instance you were afraid to use your power. Then I should like you to breathe it out with Day 3 work. After that, use positive Intents regularly as needed so that you can firmly anchor what it is that you wish to create instead. I have put down some obvious statements, but you may have to add more depending on what fears came through for you.

I AM calling on the I AM Presence to direct my Higher Self that:
I AM safe to be clairvoyant.
I AM allowing only positive and peaceful images and experiences to come to me psychically.
I AM having peaceful sleep and dreams that support my happiness.
I AM always in light so only positive psychic experiences come to me.
I AM strong and safe as I stay in this light."

In reply to that, Sarah got back after a few weeks:

"I followed all your advice and did the I AM Intents for protection and am pleased to report that the bad visions and dreams have stopped. I also searched back - Day 2 and 3 of E-course - could not get back into prior lives, but my childhood was filled with fear and I believe this is where it all came from.

I did actually get very distressed during this healing and do you know what happened to me whilst I was doing this work - my body began to tingle and the most beautiful vision appeared in front of me - try to imagine one solid wall made up of fluttering butterflies in beautiful colours then a heart shape was cut out of the centre of it with the odd one of two butterflies flying across it and this hole was filled with the wonderful green light of Archangel Raphael - an amazing feeling of deep peace passed through me whilst I watched this and as it faded I was so sad to see it go. How amazing is that? And you know after that I was completely healed of any fears and I now can move on with what I need to do."

In the above experience, Sarah was challenged to look within herself for the fears of being psychically attacked. *It takes a lot of courage for the recipient of healing to be open to the idea that the cause of feeling unsafe does not come from outside, but lies within. People usually look for quick fixes from outside when really all answers and healing again are within. Our outside world is a reflection of our inside world.*

EXAMPLE 2

Dawn wrote,

"When I wake up every morning, my feet ache as if they are so tight- This is a new sensation: I have only felt this in the last couple of months. I should look into my feelings of safety. I know for sure I am still anxious about keeping myself financially afloat and safe from being emotionally hurt by my partner. I found the hardest to say 'I am safe to be happy'...this surprised me, but it nearly made me cry. I said them over and over and it felt ok after a couple of times.

In my family and in Australian culture generally, it is not seen as a good thing if you are powerful and want new challenges and strive for success.

They think you are a "try hard" or "wanker", which is really saying you think you are better than everyone else. It is the tall poppy syndrome and my Father and both brothers are kings of this philosophy. That is why I feel free of this cultural barrier being here in Britain. Also, my mother has a tendency to expect the worst, so this is really debilitating as well. I do think, 'what will people think of me, or will they take me seriously.' I am working with this. I am powerful and I deserve to be, as I am a clever, bright, happy, successful, loving, attractive woman. There!

I really don't like using weights, but I will try!"

My reply to that was:

"Great! You can also add the following Intents to your list:

I AM comfortable with new challenges and feel great about striving for them. I AM compassionate to my mother's opinions and rest of my family. I choose to stay in my own positive feelings."

****

I hope you are all enjoying the daily lessons so far. I shall see you tomorrow.

Love,
Robin Bela

YOU ALWAYS HAVE THE POWER OF CHOICE : LISTEN TO YOUR HEART

Welcome to DAY 23 of the 30-Day Programme

You always have a choice to wake up early in the morning or not, to exercise or not, to smile or not, to be honest or not, to believe in yourself or not, to be conscious of what you eat, to say and do what you like at every moment of your life. It is important that you live consciously as you can choose to do things every day that can change your life completely to the way you want. Having this is a gift and a responsibility and also a conscious process to attain your goals.

You can choose to be positive or stay in the negative, fearful thoughts that only increase as you continue to dwell there. But you can reduce the negativity and completely remove yourself from the energies of whatever you are fearful of by 'choosing' to think and feel positive, perhaps by reminding yourself of the things you are grateful for, or by staying connected to things you love as explained in the previous topics. I know someone who constantly worries about what would happen if violence were to break out, or if her son were to grow up to be bad. The interesting part is that she being so fearful of all this, actually lives in an area that is affected by such things. She has neighbours who really are the very kind of people she would despise in her fearful world. It is so important to understand that what you focus on, whether good or bad, only grows and seeps into your life.

There is a person I know, who when she's busy or upset with something in life, walks around in her daily life with a sad face. On the other hand, I have seen people who have gone through so much in their lives but always have a happy face, and usually the latter get through to the positive side much quicker. A great example would be my friend Natalie Smith, who in a span of few years, lost all her family and relatives through various deaths and tragedies, yet I always saw her smiling during that period. It all happened in a very short time. She told me she gets through it quickly because she tries to get back into focusing on being happy no matter what. **It is important to let your emotions flow through you and not block them, but at the same time, you should choose to look at the bright side constantly to help you move to a better feeling.** I chose to show a happy face too when I broke up with my ex-husband, and also Intended to feel happy during the phase of my separation. It surprised many people, including some friends common to me and my ex and some did not like it at all. They probably thought if I liked my ex at all, I should be miserable. But strangely, my ex and I are good friends, and we probably came to terms with the separation much quicker than the people around. My ex always has a happy face, and I am sure that influenced me over the years to be the same.

So many times, 'feeling sad' or 'being upset' is the standard expectation that we should have in our lives when certain incidents such as 'separation', 'death' or any loss take place. Yes, you do mourn in the way you need to, but at the same time, are making a constant effort to heal and let go of as quickly as possible by always seeing the bright side of life. You take the effort to smile, to choose doing things that make you happy, so you can heal. The longer you moan and groan, the more you get into a state of depression, which won't help solve anything really; in fact your negative thoughts create negative experiences and energies around you even more, which will make you feel worse. I really feel sad when I see a person go for antidepressants, as that can become a vicious cycle preventing you from getting your real life back. They are the ones who cannot see the bright side of life easily, due to circumstances they may be facing, or are not strong enough as yet, or are not ready to face their fears and pain, to heal and let go! The work on breathing in Day 2 and Day 3 is crucial for them to start learning to see the brighter side of life again.

So you have a choice at every moment to wonder if your life could be full of fearful events or happy ones. Those stuck in thinking that life is full of fearful events will have a tough time to grasp that they can choose to shift to the positive way of thinking. It requires a conscious effort at every single moment. Similarly, you need to reinforce this by constantly choosing positive actions along with the positive thinking. In the beginning, it's always tough; it's like creating a new habit, it takes time and effort, but soon you won't have to be really that conscious about it: it will become second nature. But you have a choice about how you get there. I have certainly seen people heal quicker than usual when they are more positive about life.

When we realise that our lives can be sculpted to the way we want, the words 'Yes' and 'No' are very empowering tools. It is very hard for some people to realise that they can actually say 'No' to others, declining to be their doormat and be pushed around, or on the other hand say 'Yes' to getting more out of life. You can say 'No' to being stuck in life, waiting for someone, and allow yourself to say 'Yes' to your life instead.

Several years ago, just a couple of weeks after I had started dating my ex, a very attractive young man had asked me out, in front of my ex. He was my ex's friend, but did not realise that I was my ex's girlfriend. I was overwhelmed with the situation as I had just started seeing this very nice person, and here was someone I did not know at all but to whom I had suddenly felt very attracted. However, I said nothing as I really couldn't say Yes or No and just stood there feeling shy. I would have felt guilty saying 'yes' as I would have hurt my ex then. I now know that it is so wrong not to hear your own truth within, but I was also scared to say Yes in case I was making a mistake, as I couldn't see the logic in liking someone at first glance. I used to think logically about everything, but unfortunately I learnt the hard way and now I know that I just have to listen to my Heart! Later I knew that he would have been right for me. Had I got the guts to be authentic to my feelings and had the experience in listening to my Heart more instead of my fearful mind, I would have gone past those initial fears. It has been my Soul's lesson to learn this. It is unfortunate that my relationship with my ex did not work out, but I am glad that I stayed authentic to my feelings later about separating, and made the right decision, however hard it was at that time. It was us being honest to ourselves rather than staying in denial.

YOUR WORK TODAY

1. How would you *rate yourself* for being, feeling, speaking and thinking positively since you have started the 30-Day Programme? Rate yourself on a scale of 1 to 10. Check with your Heart (or Spirit) by placing one hand on it.

2. *Where in your life can you say more of 'Yes' and 'No' to yourself and others?* Make a list. Have you in the past said no when you should have said yes and vice versa? If so, how can you rectify this? Take the courage and pray or Intend for answers if you are lost about how to go about it. It may require a lot of courage at times.

3. *What choices do you have today?* You will be surprised to discover that you can change the day completely in some way you hadn't thought of.

4. Take a breath and pause as you *decide to choose to say 'Yes' or 'No' from now on.* Listen to your intuition, your heart, your gut: what does it feel like when you are deciding? - good or uncomfortable? You will know what to say then. Practice this consciously today and in the days to come.

5. *You can use the following Intents for yourself:*

I call on the I AM Presence to direct my Higher Self that:
I AM making my choices consciously.

I AM choosing to listen to my intuition, my feelings.

I AM choosing the options that make me happy now.

I AM choosing to stay and feel positive.

I AM choosing to smile today as much as I can and share with others.

I AM choosing to see my life, my future and the world positively.

EXAMPLE

Julie wrote:

"I am saying yes - I was asked to join friends for lunch, I said YES, I was asked to do a reiki session, I said YES, I was asked over for afternoon tea, I said YES, I have said YES to a new career, I have said YES to a positive view to everyday, I have said YES to meeting up with new and old friends, I have said YES...I love the OSHO song "Just say yes"...see it on youtube...I was playing it all morning when I opened your email. And I danced around the flat - very invigorating!

I know doubt is still lurking around a bit in the background so, this is a reminder to move forward and be positive and OPEN.

Not knowing HOW is ok. This helps with the responsibility factor: in the past I would be so hard on my self to work everything out and blamed myself for making wrong or silly decisions: handing it over to Universe makes me a happier, lighter and more positive person :) Thank you Universe, Lovely!"

***

I hope you are reading your daily Intents and continuing with other usual morning practices like Meditation, Exercise etc. It will keep you focused and grounded through all the changes you are making in your life and it will also give you more stamina and energy to make more changes and choices quickly. I look forward to bringing you the next lesson tomorrow. In the meantime, have fun choosing what your day should feel and be like.

Love,

Robin Bela

DE-CLUTTERING TO BRING CLARITY AND PEACE WITHIN

Welcome to DAY 24 of the 30-Day Programme

When I say de-cluttering, I am referring to our physical surroundings. Clarity of mind will be easier if you are in an organised environment. You will naturally be able to make your decisions quicker, and any kind of work will be done more efficiently in organised surroundings. As we organise, cleanse and bring peace within our environment, it naturally creates harmony within our inner lives and offers peace.

I have learnt this not just from my mother but also my father. I have seen my mother being the most peaceful when she is ironing or just organising the house. Similarly, I know my father is very conscious of keeping surroundings very clean, literally shining and organised. He doesn't sit down to do any work unless this is the case.

I read in Mahatma Gandhi's autobiography of how he would visit sick people living in poor areas of India, and would simply tell the people to clean the surroundings and thus help restore health to the sick person. Usually, the person would get better quickly. Feeling good is the key to ultimate happiness and well-being. But feeling good within is hard if our environment does not reflect what we want, i.e., health, peace, love, harmony, beauty etc.

After living in the UK for about a year after I first arrived there, I went back to India as planned. But I soon realised that I wanted to return to the UK. However, my parents were not keen that I should go, as we are a very close-knit family, and I, of course, did not want to upset them. I then connected to some insight I had gained through a reading from someone that helped me to use the concept of de-cluttering to gain inner peace, and also I later manifested what I wanted. This illustrated that de-cluttering helps one to gain clarity peacefully and to focus better with crystal clear Intention for manifesting:

I cleansed the room I was living in at that time. I cleaned it so much that even all the switches were shining. As I did so, I felt love and peace at every moment. In fact, all my anxiety about going back to the UK had gone, as I just knew within that all was well and in perfect order for my happiness. I was simply in the moment, just enjoying the peace. Cleansing, de-cluttering is a very healing experience and also an additional technique to what I speak about in Day 17 on Surrendering in return of peace. I also sprayed beautiful fragrant perfume or incense, and the room had literally become a sacred space. I remember doing continuous cleaning for 2 days, not just for an hour, but spending many hours each day. For me, it was as if, through inviting the experience of what I wanted, it was already present in that moment. Truly, I was experiencing the saying, 'Cleanliness is next to Godliness'. I had stated my Intent to Universe and had released what I wanted. In fact, I had forgotten all about it, as I was so enjoying the moment of peace I had created. In the evening of the second day, my mother entered the room and could feel the energies created in that room. It was vibrating with such peaceful energies. At that point, my father came home and he too entered my room. My mother then told my father, I think she should go back to the UK, and my father simply said ok. I had been trying for months to get them to agree: it was so perfect and natural. I didn't have to say or force anything. We really don't have to say much but Pray/Ask and work on ourselves; this alone can change the people around us. It is the opposite of trying to control things and people. In this way, our goals are manifested. Truly, our power to manifest is through staying in the moment.

I have also come to realise that whenever there is chaos in my life, that is when I recognise that I am not aligned fully with what my Heart wants. I tend to become disorganised in both my inner being and surroundings. It is good to be aware of this sign! A good start to help bring clarity into your mind, is to start de-cluttering your space: to allow any new energies into your life, you have to make space for them. So think about whether you have kept bills from years ago, or old letters, which neither increase your happiness nor serve any kind of purpose at this moment? Do you have clothes that you have not worn for a year or more? It's time to go through everything and have a clearance by giving them away to charity or dispose them of in some other appropriate way. Perhaps some activity such as ironing of clothes can help to bring peace of mind for a start! Is your room always cluttered with things lying about? It is really hard for our minds to focus on anything in that kind of environment. One of my clients said she never gets the time to tidy up and clean and so her house is constantly cluttered, but at the same time, she is also not able to think clearly about what she really wants in life.

I once lived with a person whose room was always cluttered, nothing was where it should be. The chaos in and around her was reflected in her lifestyle. She would change boyfriends every month, have a very chaotic lifestyle and was always ungrounded. I have been in situations of being disorganised in life myself, so I sympathise with those who are going through this phase. At that time I was not happy, and was unclear about my life; so my confusion started to be reflected in my environment.

You can bring a space of sacredness into your home. We talked earlier in Day 6 about how to simply have a Sacred Altar Within you through a Sacred Symbol of your own which brings instant peace to you as you connect to your Heart. I would highly recommend that you also have a physical place for a sacred altar in your house. It can be simply lighting some sage or an incense stick or a candle. Feel free to walk the house with the incense stick or sage intending what you like your house energies to be before placing it on the altar. You can probably create the sacred place on a small table. It could have all your favourite things that are dear to you, and you could place some pictures of Gods or Angels or pictures of the Earth, Nature, whatever you feel connected to. You can place flowers there and crystals too. Feel free to place the collage you did on paper the other day there as well. If you sit at your Physical Sacred Altar everyday and say your prayers or read your

Intents, that place will become very powerful. That sacred place will now be vibrating with high energies after regular prayers, and meditations. Whenever you feel low, if you just sit there, you will feel instantly at peace.

YOUR WORK TODAY

1. De-clutter and cleanse your space with the intention of achieving a peaceful mind. **Clearing the old means you are creating more space for bringing abundance into your life. As you de-clutter, you will notice you are de-cluttering your mind in the process; it will bring clarity and focus within your mind.** You will find you are more at peace naturally. Don't rush this process like a chore. Enjoy it, it's almost like doing a Meditation and it puts us in the state of mindfulness.

Also, you can state your Intent to bring more clarity within your mind, about anything you require, as you de-clutter. It is a very therapeutic process. Or set the Intention to create the energy for what you want in life through this process of cleansing the room as a sacred place. You are literally filling the room with the energy of the Intention you carry in your mind, just as I did with regard to going back to the UK. You could be tearing the old bills with the Intention to bring more money, as when you create space, more can come. You will notice as you keep clearing, at one point you will forget the real Intention and become really absorbed in the cleaning: that's when you are really letting go and allowing yourself to relax and allow things you want to come to you easily.

2. I would love you to create a Physical Sacred Altar as explained in this chapter.

EXAMPLE 1

Lorna says:

"I have been aware for a long time of the therapeutic effects of scrubbing the kitchen floor – my mum used to say it helped her to get rid of all her annoyance with something, and I have followed her example. I started clearing out my bookshelves so that I have space for the new books I have collected since becoming interested in expanding my spiritual growth. I have been having a busy time doing things with family and friends so have not yet done a serious de-clutter. There is a load of stuff around me which would be better put to the charity shop for someone else to benefit. I have a habit of hanging on to things beyond their usefulness "just in case I need it". I guess I have used material possessions as a type of security blanket."

EXAMPLE 2

Marina says:
"I am working on de-cluttering my bedsit room at the moment and have recently sold some of my possessions at a car boot sale. It felt good to get rid of them. As soon as they had gone, I realised I didn't miss any of them and they are merely material possessions which can always be replaced.

I am working on creating my sacred altar very soon and am excited about it. I have a "mini altar" at my partner's flat. We have written down our Intent for a baby and placed it under a vase of flowers. My altar is going to be very special to me and I want to clear space in my bedsit first before I create the altar."

***

We just have a few more days left for this Programme. So, if you are reading today's lesson, you have done quite well in sticking with the Programme. And if you have been slow, it doesn't matter. What matters is that you are going at your own pace. The mantra is -'Keep Moving!' whatever your pace is. If you don't move, that's when you have given up. To bring change, action is crucial on your part.

Love,

Robin Bela

DAY 25
NON-JUDGEMENT AND COMPASSION

I had been working very hard for some time and when I met a friend whom I knew through another friend, she looked at me and said that I wasn't glowing the way I was when she had met me earlier. I told her that yes I had been working extremely hard, meeting some deadlines. I thought that should have fed her curiosity about me looking tired, but unfortunately, every time I met her that week she kept repeating it in front of people. At the same time, she also complained about how everyone judged her and told her things about which she then got very emotional. She didn't realise that people were reacting, sometimes deliberately, to her judgemental comments. I was glad I got the reminder from her that I needed to take rest though. But if I had absorbed what she said, through my ego, I would have been hurt and sat in resentment of the way she spoke to me not once, but quite a few times, even after I had taken her aside and explained that she was close to being rude! Since I like to work through non-judgement, it was easy for me to see that comments from people really don't mean to be personal, rather she was saying whatever came into her head, and after a couple of hours, I managed to let it go.

This incident also made me wonder why I attracted this situation: yes I did need to recognise when I was tired, but I also realised how judgemental I had been with myself. After all, what's outside of us is usually a reflection of what lies within. When we decide to bring changes into our lives as I did, we can get into the notion of having to be perfect, and hence we question everything about ourselves, become hard critics of ourselves: perhaps that is why I was overworked at that time. **'Comparison', 'Competition' and being 'Critical' are the 3 Cs that I would say are toxic to our mind, soul and also health.** It has been found time and again that people who judge themselves and others all the time and indulge in negative gossip, are prone to suffer from loss of peace of mind, irritability, stress, depression etc. and consequent ill health. But sadly, comparison and competition are ingrained from childhood when people start comparing children's grades. Once some people are labelled with low grades, they may carry this with them as a value about themselves for the rest of their lives.

I know a young girl in college who is very bright and doing well in terms of getting jobs on the side, but is not confident about getting good grades because of the fear or stigma ingrained in her by her parents who made her feel she would never be good enough to do well. I told her that she didn't need to believe what others thought of her, but concentrate on what she thought of herself. We can choose our present. Her beliefs were constantly recreating low grades. **If you have been in the habit of judging, it is time to recognise this and stop it each time. It takes a constant reminder to change. Everybody is different, and we are meant to be so. So there cannot really be a comparison.** All of us have unique gifts. If you are terrible at science or mathematics, maybe you are a genius artist or a writer, or an actor, baker or a therapist etc. Never limit yourself to fit in a few categories. Be open and creative about life.

During this phase of being over-busy with so many different activities, I was lately recording some meditations, and noticed that technically, the recording was not going well. At the same time, an important website page stopped working. Then I wasn't getting the response I needed for some programme I was doing. In the process of all this, I felt myself suddenly critical and judgemental of myself, and doubtful of my own abilities. It was interesting that during all of this, I was aware of these feelings, and at the same time my inner self was wondering how to get out of this counter-productive energy state. I knew by experience that if I didn't, the energies of all the things around which were not working would remain and increase! So I thought, if all the recordings went well and my website page worked, life would be back on track as normal. It was just a glitch and I looked at how my life and I were already doing well. I really needed to be grateful. Sure enough, by the end of the day, everything fell into place with my positive outlook. But I know, that had I carried those energies of lack and inadequacy, I wouldn't have created anything better. I needed to feel good about myself, to create my Intent about the outcome and be assured that it would come about through Intent/Prayer. But make sure that your Prayer or Intent is not a complaint about why things are not going well. You should thank God or Universe that all is well. It is really important to be grateful that what you are Asking has been received.

Non-judgment comes from being compassionate to our own selves, showing kindness to people around, and instead of sharing the problem further, share some joy instead. In fact, I had a very good friend who loved gossiping and saying rude things about people, and even about me in my presence, as a joke. After years of friendship, I finally got so tired of this behaviour that I had a fight with him saying, 'I don't want to be friends with you if you are not going to learn to be positive and not be so judgemental about others.' Until today, he has not spoken to me. We both know I had a valid point and that we still care for each other, but the problem is he's judgemental and so he continues to carry the resentment still. I was standing up for self-respect and being compassionate to myself by not letting others take me for granted through their ill judgements or gossip.

So next time a sales person calls or knocks at your door, be compassionate and refuse him with kindness in your heart and speech! Otherwise, in terms of negative energy, you could end up carrying the frustration of speaking rudely to the sales person as well as the frustration of the sales person himself. Small acts of kindness help to make your life happier and peaceful.

It is our job to look at ourselves with the eyes of self-love and compassion. When we do that, we are naturally generous and caring about the feelings of others. And we learn to receive for ourselves. It is a very important step for those who find it hard to receive love or abundance of any sort. When we let go of judgement and accept our mistakes, delays and even what is lacking in our lives, then we don't need to prove anything or please anyone including self. We accept ourselves completely. 'I AM who I AM' statement helps to anchor this. The need to please others and stick to our titles comes from the need to fulfill our own insecurities. These insecurities are often caused because we feel we are lacking in something within, and hence look for outside power. We just need to look within to connect to our own power for happiness and peace.

When we start becoming authentic in all areas of our lives, we do so by following our hearts, we are naturally more certain of what we want, who we are and what will bring us happiness and confidence. But I know it's hard in the beginning, especially if you are trying to be authentic about your own feelings, which may be in conflict with those of others, in your perception. In such moments you can try the following technique, which I use and find really powerful. I just keep saying the words 'Mercy' and 'Grace'. It's the way how I stay kind and compassionate to myself instead of getting upset that I am still stuck somewhere. It helps me stay non-judgemental, prevents me from being overpowered by high expectations and helps me centre very quickly when I find myself under the influence of the feelings and emotions of others. Repeating it in my mind, also helps me stay humble, and keeps me aligned to my soul with confidence when I am feeling down. So when you feel you are not doing this Programme well, or simply feeling low, or even anxious about something, just start Asking/Intending for Mercy and Grace, with compassion for self.

YOUR WORK TODAY

Please take your time with the work today, if needed.

1. *Write in your journal what judgements are you carrying about yourself?* Are you critical, always competing and comparing yourself with others? Are your power, your confidence and self-esteem simply depleted from thinking you are not good enough? You really cannot compare or compete with anyone; everyone is born unique with different circumstances and interests. Our job is to appreciate the diversity.

2. *Repeat the words 'Mercy' and 'Grace'* when you feel low about yourself in

any way or anxious about things. It can even be when things are going well but you start to doubt if that will continue.

3. *What judgements are you carrying about others?* From now on, see if you can catch yourself whenever you are passing a judgement, be it on yourself or on others. When you do, stop yourself, and instead be compassionate: you, or the others you are judging, are doing the best in the circumstances. If you are not able to complete your 'to do list' but did your best, just be generous to yourself and do the rest the next day instead of beating yourself up about it.

4. *You can Intend the following today:*

I AM calling on the I AM Presence to direct my Higher Self that:

I AM compassionate to myself for everything.

I AM loving and kind towards myself. I AM who I AM.

I AM compassionate to others for everything.

I AM loving and kind towards others.

5. *You may have noted some patterns about yourself that are negative.* Make sure that you don't let these patterns stay within you: change them to positive I AM Intents and add them to your daily I AM Intents sheet. But before you start adding these new Intents, as usual, do take time to clear those core negative beliefs through the Soul Clearing Technique under Day 3, which *may involve forgiving some old judgements you hold against others or that were made on you.* You cannot develop anything new if you are still holding something back inside and don't really believe in what you want to create. No amount of positive Intentions will work without this inner soul clearing. Also, you will often find that no amount of medicines will work to treat an ailment, and you will be compelled to look within.

Sometimes, long-term illness is just a disguise for the need to look within, and there comes a time when no amount of pills can bury those emotional issues you are hiding and not letting go. As an energy healer, I have seen this many times over the years. Problems of body and mind are always related to emotions within. Once we make peace with our long-held emotions, miracles occur, lives change, people change and create the lives they really want. Simple fever or illness can sometimes be due to overwork and allowing no time for self. Rarely do you get ill in the relaxed periods of your life when you are taking care of your health and are happy. So when serious illness takes place, think of what more there may be beyond stress and simple tiredness that you may have been holding on to. This may be a pattern that repeats itself in your life. Free yourself of all the unnecessary emotional baggage you are carrying now. Feel free to keep working on today's work for days to come if you need to let go of some judgements that are causing toxic emotions within you, and as you go about the other lessons in this Programme.

EXAMPLE 1

Nicole wrote to me:
"The 3 Cs really are toxic and I have been doing all 3 on a daily basis for as long as I can remember. I have been working on affirming I AM who I AM. I have been feeling, thinking and being positive but I have not always spoken positively although I am choosing to be gentle with myself about this as I have been consciously opting out of gossiping for most of the time and tried hard not to speak badly of people. It has been hard though as I am finding people around me are doing this a lot. I am hoping that as I become more non-judgemental and loving towards myself, and my words are kinder, that will disappear around me."

EXAMPLE 2

Pam wrote to me:
"This is a very important thing for me to learn, because I am so sensitive to

my environment. If I go out when I am not grounded, I end up having arguments with people on buses, in the supermarket etc and I feel really angry at the world. I have really tried to become more aware of this and I don't go out, go to the park instead where I can be alone, or re-schedule with friends.

I also am the kind of person who says "whatever suits you" when I am planning to meet friends.....so I end up compromising time, energy and happiness due to not being clear about what I want or would suit me. I am really working hard on this. My friends are not used to me being assertive though, so I can see that they get a bit put out as they are used to ruling the social outings. I also have a weakness, something I have had since I was a child, where I don't call people because I think they are too busy or wouldn't want to talk to ME. I usually wait for others to call me and arrange stuff. I am better than I was, but I am still weak in this area.

Now that I have a baby to work around, it forces me to be more decisive and clearer, because I am doing it for her. I should try and make decisions for me as well though, I know. Today I emailed a friend and invited her out to a gallery with me on Friday. She replied and said she would love to and was really appreciative and excited. It made me feel good and in control, but still in the back of my head I was thinking "I hope she likes it, what if she doesn't enjoy it.... etc. I can see that I hand over the power to others to avoid being held responsible or to blame."

My response to her was to work with the following suggested Intents:

I call on the I AM Presence to direct my Higher Self that:

I AM accepted.
I AM peaceful with my environment and compassionate to people's differences around me
I love myself.
I AM comfortable to let others know of my needs as I will enjoy their

company better, and I let my friends know the reason so that they appreciate it too.

I AM here to share love and as I do, I AM at peace with the people I AM with.

I AM connected to people with love, and it's a joy to share unconditionally!

I AM loved and safe amongst people.

I AM smiling and just getting more from the people around me!

I AM flexible and open to all new ideas to socialise and share with people.

***

See you in Spirit tomorrow, my Lovely Empowered Friends.

Love,

Robin Bela

DAY 26
OPEN YOUR HEART TO RECEIVE

Welcome to DAY 26 of the 30-Day Programme

If your Heart is closed, you cannot create anything, but when your Heart is open, you can give and receive easily in life and create any form of abundance with greater ease. If you put up barriers to giving and receiving love in general, it can affect your general flow of receiving and giving abundance with money too, and I shall explain this more in this chapter.

A Heart needs to be open to 'giving' and 'receiving' love to 'Self' first, which means offering time and care for Self, asking more for Self, listening and following your Heart and setting boundaries by saying 'yes' and 'no'. The second main requirement for an open Heart is 'giving' and 'receiving' love to and from 'Others' equally, and not being drained in giving too much or being blocked in giving, which is mostly noticed amongst people who may have been hurt in the past and don't share much to defend themselves from any future hurt. Notice whether your Heart is closed in any way. We will discuss more ways to see if your Heart may be closed, later in this chapter.

A closed heart can be opened by bringing healing to any past hurt to oneself. One has to be able to forgive and set oneself free from the memories that are holding one back, to simply be open to the wonders of life such as nature, the beauty around us etc. to begin with, so as to start receiving love from Universe and life itself, and create more joy in life. To learn to 'receive' love in life, I would like you to check how open you are to following your own heart, to trusting the people around you, to opening yourself to new things and people, and even to receiving money, because I know of people who feel guilty about receiving money. I had blocks against receiving not just money but also love, as I talked in the previous chapters about the images I had of falling and having an accident, as soon as I tried to visualise myself as happy in any way. In this example, my heart was also just not open to receiving love

233

for myself. It was as though I could not believe that it was possible to always be both happy and abundant. After clearing out old memories and Intending, 'I AM deserving love', 'I AM deserving happiness', 'I AM deserving money', 'I AM safe to open my Heart to receive love and abundance' and 'I AM safe to open my Heart to give love and abundance', now I imagine myself being happy with all abundance, and I no longer see images of myself being hit by a car or my feet crumbling.

If you think Money is impure or bad, are you not thereby blocking it even more? If you have been receiving or abusing Money in corrupt dealings, then you are becoming the source of receiving back conditional love. It's a sign of a closed heart. As you know, any conditional love does not last but is temporary. You are not creating and receiving any real and lasting happiness. Yes you can have a lot of money and feel happy for sometime too, but you have to deal with Money in the right way, with a clear open heart.

Here is a detailed checklist to find out if your Heart is fully or partially closed to 'giving' and 'receiving'. Feel free to rate yourself from 1 to 10, with 1 as the lowest score and 10 as the highest score, as you read along the points below:

1. You are not giving yourself enough time to enjoy the simple things in life. The reason could be that perhaps you are a workaholic or simply that you never thought about it. Do you have time to smell the fresh air, spend time with family and friends and do the things you love?

2. You are not open to trusting new people in life or ready to get intimate with anyone.

3. You are not trying new things in life because of fear of losing or because you are not used to them. You are simply not asking for more from Universe!

4. You are not willing to try again.

5. You do not love yourself unconditionally and feel you don't deserve more, e.g., I will feel good about me only if I lose another 10 kilos. You have to start loving yourself right away and not postpone it! In fact, losing weight comes easy to those who already appreciate and respect themselves as they are; everything you do is for you, not to prove something to any one else. You have to love your body now to appreciate it more. If you cannot imagine and feel it now, you cannot create it. It is really important to open your heart to loving yourself. When you do that, you get into the right flow for everything in life: work, relationships etc. You naturally feel deserving of everything in life.

6. You are not taking responsibility for taking care of yourself unconditionally. I know of someone who liked taking care of others and felt empowered about being responsible, but was in no way able to take care of herself. This is also connected to self-respect and loving yourself. This kind of person does not mind being the butt of jokes.

7. You are not letting go of things in the past that might still have a hold on you. This may be blocking you from loving yourself and others unconditionally. It can also include being judgemental, and unforgiving.

8. You are trying to control the people and situations around you instead of simply going with the flow and staying in the moment.

9. You are always exhausted in general, perhaps through constantly giving to others or looking for attention from others.

10. You often feel lonely and scared to step out to meet people because you are too stuck in your own ways or just afraid to allow people to come too close to you.

11. You are not able to trust in the future that all is well. It is important then to connect to your own reservoir of love that all is well, through techniques taught for connecting to your Heart.

12. You are not speaking your truth.

13. You doubt you can do it.

14. You just cannot say 'Yes' to things you want because of all the fears you hold about if or whether you can have them.

15. You are a perfectionist and too critical about things. An open-hearted person is more concerned about experiencing happiness now in the simple things rather than fretting about looking good in the eyes of others, and more concerned with relaxing and enjoying life rather than being rigid about things to be done. Your spirit is tired and does not feel like doing anything that is not in accordance with its wishes.

16. You are not doing what you love at work. There is no joy and excitement in life as a result.

17. You are not honest in your relationships.

18. You are not listening to your Heart's yearnings.

19. You feel you are just 'existing' and not 'living'.

20. You don't feel deserving of happiness, health, abundance, money and love.

If you scored low, that's ok as you now know how to set about writing your Intents to correct the situation. You can write the Intents and work with Soul Clearing Technique if needed, for all those points where you scored less.

A person with an open Heart is full of joy and has a sparkle in the eyes. This person doesn't get too tired giving time to self and others, and receives gratefully. This person also has a brave open heart and is happy to try new things, unconventional things and most importantly, follows his or her Heart in doing everything in life. An open Heart is honest and sincere to self and others. Having an open Heart means allowing more people into your life and also allowing intimacy. You may feel that you have an open Heart sometimes but a closed one during another time. It is important that you recognise where you stand, so that you can find out where and why it started, and clear what you need to.

You can help open your Heart by simple things such as watching nature as I mentioned. I can see a cherry blossom tree from where I am sitting. Its beautiful pink flowers just lift my Heart! Another way of doing it would be through music, which can help open your Heart. Make sure that you choose soothing, loving and lively music that opens your heart and gets you instantly in a better mood. Be responsible for everything you put into your experience. I once knew a person who suddenly stopped talking to me. This person was moody and thought it was ok to disappear suddenly. To me, that is lacking in thoughtfulness and is not a conscious or responsible way to behave. An open heart would realise that yes 'I am moody and not in a position to talk to the people around me, but I am conscious of how that upsets people. So I will tell them, I need my space and will get back to them when I am ready.' An open heart is responsible and can be relied upon. An open heart is not afraid to tell the truth, whatever it might be. We all may go through various situations in life where circumstances cause our heart to shut until we can process our emotions slowly. But the key is to process slowly and focus on opening our hearts again soon. <u>There are many ways to stay open-hearted as I explain in the list in the following paragraph.</u>

Sometimes, our Heart shuts temporarily under fear of overwhelming situations. I have talked to you about various tools to help you stay centred in your Heart. These are also the tools you need to stay open-hearted whenever you feel worries, or are fearful or stressed: – Meditation; Sacred Altar Within; Stillness Practice, journaling, list of things you love doing; going outside into nature; exercise; being generous to yourself; gratitude; your daily Intents; prayer; being mindful and enjoying the simple things in life; speaking daily to your Heart or Spirit by placing hand over Heart;

staying in your energies by keeping the focus on yourself and the positive; remembering as you encounter fear, to breathe it out, and it's safe to feel the fear as that's how you let it go; setting boundaries by not paying attention to outside influences and most importantly, simply learning to feel the peace within by letting go of the fear of the outcome and trusting that it will all be taken care of. So please check with yourself how often you use these tools, and if you forget, just remind yourself. Write down this list somewhere for easy reference. This is your survival kit for times you are in doubt or fear.

Trying new hobbies, different foods, meeting new people, seeing things differently, staying flexible and living in uncertainty are some of the things that are part of the lifestyle or behaviour of an open-hearted person.

I have come to realise that whether it is in my work of helping people or simply in my personal life, that unless I love myself completely, I am not offering my authentic Self to any relationship. At work, I really don't want to over-give my time and be drained. I really had to learn to love myself and at times learn to say no; otherwise I would be offering half-hearted service. Also in my personal life, I realised that loving myself is truly important so that I don't need to look at my relationships to feed any insecurities. **I always need to offer my love to others unconditionally and for that, I have to be really content and happy with the way I am. It means really having strong boundaries and not over-giving, or also over-receiving**. Notice if this becomes imbalanced, it's then time to look within, to open your Heart to yourself more and love yourself completely as you are now. When you are ok with the moment and accept it, it will be easier to allow change. **A change is really a way of looking at life differently right now.**

The process of receiving naturally involves the requirement 'to stop controlling and to trust in the process of Asking Universe' and 'involves keeping a playful and joyful attitude'. Receiving is all about knowing how to say 'Yes' to your wildest dreams first and then allow the process to take place. In my experience, as I start believing and stay focused on what I want now, the next steps come naturally to me. Your path becomes clearer as you start. That is when you really have to go with the flow and keep your heart open. To a great extent, you work through your gut feeling, your Heart and your intuition. The mind is there to analyse and help you choose your options but it has not always been the deciding factor for me, as things that are not created yet cannot really be proven in my head: it's the Heart then that gives me the courage and joy to go for it. I have always made decisions by placing my hand on my Heart and asking 'What do I want next?' When you keep the focus on your Heart, you are surely and simply going to create in accordance with what your Heart really wants and also what feels right. **Unfortunately, what we want does not always resonate with our doubtful, fearful ego minds. So it's best to keep your mind away and stick to your brave Heart.**

Trust that you are safe as you open your Heart now and experience new things in this process. We have already used some Intents on feeling safe in Day 22: as you keep using those, you will feel relaxed about opening your Heart. Remember, you are strong enough to discern what is right and what is wrong; so don't be afraid of taking the bold steps towards believing what you feel is right for you.

I know a woman who is about 30 years of age and her father left her family when she was very young. This experience clearly had shut her Heart to men. Today she has plenty of boyfriends but as soon as they start growing intimate, she feels unsafe, fearing that perhaps they will abandon her, and breaks up with them before it can go any further. But strangely, she cannot even live without the attention of men, as her insecurity is fed artificially by their physical presence. So I have seen her with a new boyfriend literally every month if not even more frequently! She even once said on one unusual day when she wasn't with a guy that it was so nice to be with someone even to watch TV. So great was the extent of her insecurity that she just didn't know how to be on her own for a while. I would say, it's not an easy place for her as she cannot get close to anyone, and also chooses to be with someone just for the sake of company and feeling loved for the moment. This need of hers really has left her with no boundaries. She would sleep with her best friend and at the same time have a boyfriend. Her issues with intimacy, are really deep. She even admitted that she had issues with intimacy like her dad. If she clears and heals the root cause, she can rectify this imbalance in her behaviour and also open her Heart in the right way and learn to say 'yes' when she really should. She would then feel safe to have an open Heart, which is not dependent on conditional love from others for reasons such as security, but instead simply for sharing love with the one who is right for her. I even saw her later with a new boy friend for a longer term, but that was not a relationship of mutual love, rather the guy was needy and her role was more that of a carer, and I could catch a glimpse of her wanting to take care of her dad there as she would often tell me how her father needed help, and was not good on his own.

Often people close their Hearts to the various aspects of life as though they simply don't know how to give or share. Usually, this happens as a defence mechanism because they think it will help them to remain safe. Perhaps they were taken advantage of or had been cheated or betrayed. I had a friend who just had no clue what the word 'sharing' meant. She would cook something and I am sure intended to offer it to others to share, but just didn't know how to go about it, so she would come across as rude. She also didn't like to have people around her intruding her space. She would live in her own world and was quite different from the other woman I talked about earlier, who came across as an extrovert. But both have closed Hearts and they neither allow unconditional love into their lives, nor are feeling safe to give unconditional love. It is important that they should feel safe to step out to people and frequently affirm the Intent "All good and loving people are in my life". What you Ask is what you receive, and what you fear is what you receive too. So choose consciously if you notice these tendencies in yourself.

In general, a closed Heart is not a good receptor for the good things in life: abundance, enjoying work, love, happiness and money. It is important to be in the flow of enjoying, sharing life and experiencing it with an open Heart. I know that when I first focused on increasing that process of sharing and receiving, I felt quite vulnerable initially. It takes courage and I approached it one step at a time. I still go through uncertain phases, but now I recognise them and keep moving. You can Intend daily: "I AM open-hearted, and lead myself to a full 360 degree open Heart." This is what Jesus is considered to have had, a heart that is open 360 degrees. Love really is the real power. It is also the real power to heal and be healed. I talk more about it in the next chapter.

YOUR WORK TODAY

1. *Do go through the list given at the beginning of the lesson to see if your Heart is closed in any way.* Do you feel your Heart is closed to giving and receiving? If so, 'why'? Clear that with Soul Clearing Technique as explained in Day 2 and Day 3, and you may want to form Intents to keep anchoring the new beliefs within yourself. And work with all steps talked about in helping you to have an open Heart, e.g., being in nature, Meditation, journaling etc.

2. *Ask yourself and write down in your journal for more clarity:* Are you truly open in your Heart for change without knowing the entire process of the 'how'? What little steps are you taking daily? Do you daily ask your Heart, or your Spirit, what one to three things you should focus on? Only the Heart can truly connect to your Heart's desire, not the mind. Please don't tell your Heart what to do if you really want to work with your higher intuition. If you have asked your Heart a question, notice what answers you get when you listen to those subtle hints and feelings. If you have not asked regularly, just do it now. Place one hand on your Heart and ask 'what is my next step, my Heart?' And your Heart says...? Did you take any action on it? After this, were you afraid or did you procrastinate about change or still went ahead in taking that step? Check with yourself every morning.

3. *And most importantly, ask yourself how can I 'joyfully create' and do what I want to do today?* When you do things out of joy and excitement, you are naturally open to receiving the best. Let your Heart lead the way, allowing the trust to grow.

4. *You can breathe and Intend the following Intents to have an open Heart,* so that you can move confidently towards your goal/s:

I AM calling on the I AM Presence to direct my Higher Self that:

I AM open to giving and receiving love unconditionally.

I AM deserving of receiving love.

I AM deserving of receiving money.

I AM deserving of happiness forever after.

I AM safe to receive.

I AM open to sharing my love with others unconditionally.

I AM having an open Heart and it is safe for me as I have strong boundaries to enforce by saying 'yes' or 'no'.

I AM open to going with the flow with little steps towards my goal to achieve____.

I AM strong enough to discern what is right and what is wrong for me. So I AM safe to keep my heart open to new things.

I AM appreciating the progress I have made so far. I am compassionate to myself.

My heart allows new things in life.

I AM keeping my Heart 360 degrees open.

I AM filled with gratitude for all things in my life.

I AM open to love and loving experiences.

I AM doing things out of a place of love and passion always.

I AM open to allowing new people and situations to come my way that will bring me more joy in life.

I AM surrounded by loving people.

I AM letting go of the past and any lack of forgiveness.

EXAMPLE

Mary says that opening her heart to others meant being kinder to others in a way that she realised she wasn't before. She talks of her experience below:

"I know that I have softened in a lot of ways over the years, especially since I found my true spiritual path in the last three years. I now make a conscious effort to soften the tone of my voice when I talk, and how I say things. I used to be quite abrupt as I don't think I thought about what I was saying and I used to hurt people (they told me). I can say the same thing as I used to but the reactions of people are very different now and they accept what I am saying without thinking I am being nasty. The difference in the way they talk to me and treat me is incredible. I feel like I am truly loved by my friends now and have a number of friends I could call close compared with a few years back when I didn't.

I think my work is going to continue after this course finishes and I have processed all the wonderful information. I do check my heart for goals when reminded by you and the answer often comes straight away, like it was waiting for me to ask and had its answer ready.

Little steps I am taking daily are: repeating my Intent on my journey to work, praying to Universe to take my worries away and telling them specifically what they are (and being grateful for this), meditating whenever I can, morning and evening, taking quiet time. Reading my Intentions and reading them out loud whenever I can. I am not sure if I have been acting on what my heart tells me but I have made note of it every day and thought it was amazing to talk to my heart!"
***

I wish you an open-hearted day where you receive and give immense love and joy.

All my love,
Robin Bela

DAY 27
LOVE IS THE REAL POWER

Welcome to DAY 27 of the 30-Day Programme

When I say that power is really inside you and not outside, I am emphasising that you should connect more to the state of Love, to your Heart, in order to connect to the real Power. When you do anything out of love for self and others, you cannot go wrong. So, when you wish to say something that you are scared about, if you connect to your Heart, the seat of Love, you really cannot say anything to hurt anyone or even look foolish while doing so. **If you feel Love in your Heart as you speak your inner truth, you are truly accessing the most authentic and powerful part of yourself.** This will give you real confidence in self in personal and work life, and also help you pass easily through many tough situations while pursuing your goals that make you happy.

Many a time, I had decided to do things that my Heart wanted, which didn't appear logically feasible, and I had no idea how to go about the same. But I would stay true to the Heart, and it would show me the way and provide me all the answers, including instant manifestations of money, offers of such freebies that I wouldn't be able to afford otherwise or had missed bookings for events etc. on time. I really don't know at times, 'how' that happens. I listen to my Heart and ask Universe, that's all! So we understand, that it is very helpful to stay more and more in the state of Love and surrender to our Heart and Spirit to guide, especially when we feel confused, fearful, doubtful, worried and unhappy. I reminded you yesterday of all the techniques we have learnt that can help you stay in your Heart, like Sacred Altar Within, Meditation etc.

Staying in the Heart, i.e., in the state of Love, gives a certain kind of strength, whereby people around you will respect that you are sincere, and open their Hearts to you naturally. Also, you are peaceful even at times when you take steps that are not born out of logic and may look scary. At every step of the changes I have made in my life, the direction I was following was always new to me, and often a disfavoured choice, or rather new to the people around me. To connect to my inner belief that this was right for me, I had to tap into my source of Love, my well of Love. The famous modern Indian spiritual guru Osho, really knew that a person who is truly connected to his spiritual side can be abundant in every way, and to prove it he even once owned 93 Rolls Royces. He had said, "*Love will give you the courage to move out of the patterns of logic. The person who lives in logic is a coward.*" Of course, logic has its place, but to access Love and true Power, you have to go beyond logic. That is the place from where genius, intuition and original, creative and inventive ideas come from.

A great way to connect to Love, is to simply do this exercise:
When you inhale through your nose, Intend in mind or say aloud, '*I breathe in Love*' and as you exhale through your nose, Intend in your mind or say aloud, '*I breathe out Peace*'.

Doing this exercise for a few minutes, and thus focusing on Heart, is a great way to connect to the Source of Love.

In my own energy healing work with others, I know and use several techniques, but when everything fails, I just Intend Love to pass through me to the other person, and for me, this has been my most powerful healing tool to date.

I would like to share a story from my father's life. In fact, it is through him that I have learnt the power of Love. He is now a retired Police Officer. Around the time I was three years old, my father handled major communal riots in Kanniyakumari District in southern India. In India, there are so many languages, and my father did not know the Tamil language spoken in that area very well, so he had an interpreter with him all the time. He would stand in front of highly agitated or fear-stricken crowds to calm them, and he says he would simply look at them with Love, as words were of less use to him. He said he could feel that they felt the Love. The words he spoke came from his Heart, full of Love and compassion, which had a telling impact in calming frayed nerves of the violent mobs. In a very loving way, he helped defuse the riots with minimum use of force. He was extremely popular and was loved by the people in that District and is fondly remembered even today. He had later used this compassionate approach in effectively dealing with terrorists. He has told me several stories about speaking to dreaded terrorists and he did not need to threaten them or use force to make them talk, he simply communicated Love and compassion and they would pour out their whole life story to him and reveal vital secrets and leads for investigations. I truly admire Mahatma Gandhi for showing us the non-violent path to any conflict. Gandhi would say that Non-Violence was nothing but Love, and that Love and Truth were two sides of the same coin. We should understand from this that Love takes birth only in a truthful Heart. My Dad has been influenced greatly by Mahatma Gandhi, with whom interestingly, he also shares his birthday!

Whenever I have come across people who don't resonate with my ideas, I know that fighting or arguing with them will only push them further away from me, so it is better to stay peaceful with Love in my heart and just send love in prayers to such persons, and usually they come around. I once had an Aunt who was upset with me. I sent Love and peace from my Heart to hers, simply because I knew my words wouldn't make a difference to her at that point. In a few days, she herself called me and I was surprised that she even apologised.

The power of Love is truly how you connect to your true 'Power'. Everything you do and say, if you do it out of Love, you are safe and right. This is how I was able to make some important transitions in my life and work peacefully and confidently. I also noticed that when I connect to Love, the tension which I sometimes would feel like a knot in my abdomen, loosens and relaxes. It reduces stress too. When I became good at this process, I felt myself literally losing weight from my stomach. We know stress can cause weight gain, and what better way to tackle it than by simply staying in the state of Love.

I would encourage you to say your Intents by first feeling Love in your heart. When I do that, I always connect better. I already feel peaceful about what I want, so it's easy to manifest what I want. **We cannot create anything if we are in a fearful state at the time of Asking. What we feel is literally also what we Ask for. So, it's important to Ask with Love, and have faith that everything will be taken care of. If you allow fears to creep in, they will block what you want, and therefore, it is important to realise that Love is the Real Power.** It is not easy to be always free of fear, but with the techniques we discussed for staying connected to the Heart centre in this and the previous topic, it is possible to reduce our stress and anxiety, and connect more quickly to a peaceful, loving state.

Real power is first tapped into through self-love. This is such an important topic. I have come to realise that unless I focus on attaining that, I just cannot realise Love and happiness outside of me in reality, as the outer reality is a reflection of what my inner thoughts and beliefs are. So it is crucial that I choose to be happy consciously even under circumstances that are making me feel low. It would only help me to move to the positive light quicker.

I know of someone who just could not find the right guy as a partner, as the guys would either leave her or she would discover that they had some really dark secrets such as that they were married and had not told her etc. She never had confidence in choosing and doing the right thing in life. At the same time, I have another client of mine who just feels it's hard to take care of herself and needs support from outside. She just cannot feel self-sufficient and feels her parents should have taken care of her from the beginning. In both cases, the well of self-love and self-worth is empty and they become needy and create unauthentic relationships with people and also don't find the right way to sustain themselves and take care of themselves emotionally and physically. In both cases, there was lack of love in their childhood, or lack of appreciation of who they were, from their loved ones. So the confidence in them to be happy and to sustain themselves, which stems from self-love and self-respect and develops mostly during childhood, was not there. It was important for me to help them achieve peace with their past and to invite a new way of thinking for themselves through Intents. It is the start of unconditional love for themselves, and also true power, and listening to their inner guidance to discover what their Hearts truly want. A person who doesn't love and respect self, usually cannot hear what his or her heart wants and always says, 'I don't know what I want', 'I am afraid to make the wrong choice'. If you are maintaining your journal everyday, you should be already on the way to self-discovery, self-love and listening to your Heart, as all the answers lie within. You should respect what you hear in those writings, as important inner guidance will always come out clearly and repeatedly.

I would like to share an example which shows how listening within and appreciating your needs is important to your happiness.

Rita wrote to me:
"I've been invited to apply for a job in Tanzania. A local Tanzanian agency requested my services for a one-year contract, which can be renewed. I was looking for such a job for next year, as working for a receptive agency is what I should really like to do. But they need someone in June. I can't be there for June. I asked them many questions and the facts are: they would pay me better than my present job, they would give me a resident permit so that I would be a legal worker, they offer me accommodation in their home for the three first months or the possibility of renting a studio while waiting for me to find my own place if the studio doesn't suit me. The lady is French and about my age. The company is registered in Tanzania. This is a new challenge for my brain!! I have just arrived in Carcassonne, where I like living but don't enjoy the job that much. And I have now the opportunity to do the job I really would like: being abroad and taking care of French guests + being a specialist with sales in only one country (here, Tanzania).

If there were no "if" and "but" and if I didn't care about what people would say, I would go. But the reality is somehow different in a sense that I would have to resign this job, only 3 months after I've started. My boss would have to find someone else, train her or him again. I feel uncomfortable about putting her in that position. On the other hand, I feel, as though this could be

248

a once in a lifetime opportunity. When I left for a five month trip to India, I had the same issue: I was offered a job in an agency. But I chose to go to India. I do not regret this choice, but I remember it was hard to choose because, you never know if you are making the right decision. You cannot foresee what will happen after you say Yes or No."

My reply to that was:

"I am sad to see that you are struggling between your heart and head because you should always follow your heart and not worry about what others say. It is best to be honest, authentic about what you feel in any relationship including work. You and also your employer are not going to work best together if you are not interested. They might as well get someone who is. So be kind not only to yourself but to them. If you didn't take the offer out of guilt about hurting others at your current company, you would be depressed for not even trying. I think you have been gifted with the offer of a great job. It's come in response to your prayers, and it pains me to see you are not jumping to take it! You really should live your life and go for it."

After this Rita followed her heart and went for the interview. Unfortunately, she did not get the job but at least she won't have the regret that she did not try. Having an open heart also means accepting rejections courageously. She is happy to have honoured her Spirit's needs. And recently I heard she managed to get into another job she likes!

YOUR WORK TODAY

1. Write down what are the things you think you can achieve if you connected more to the state of Love, away from fear?

2. Try the 'love and peace' breathing technique mentioned in the chapter to connect to Love.

3. I would like you to take action on all the messages you have been getting in the last few weeks with real Love and appreciation in your Heart. Think of

a couple of things you will do today and this week, e.g., speak your truth to your friend, and staying in Heart. You can pray that you get the right words to do so, go out and put flyers around for your business where your Heart feels right, meet people with Love in your Heart, show more compassion to self this week when you have low self-esteem etc. What are the things you would do out of Love this week?

4. Also, this week, I would like you to say the below statement several times to yourself:

'I Love You'!
Look in the mirror if you can when you say as Louise Hay, the amazing teacher, author and publisher would do!

EXAMPLE

Susan says,
"I can say that now, I say "I LOVE YOU" in the mirror and believe it truly. I feel lighter in my body and happier with it. I am still working on being confident with food but I've lost this "guilty" feeling I had while eating.

I feel stronger with all the I AM sentences. I feel I have created a shelter inside me. I needed it so much, now I feel so safe. I am not scared any more of my emotions because I know I can sit and hide to find peace and calm inside me. This is the most beautiful gift of this month."

***

Thank you for joining me today! Have a loving day today and I shall see you tomorrow!

Lots of love and blessings,
Robin Bela

DAY 28
WAIT PATIENTLY AND ENJOY THE MOMENT

Welcome to DAY 28 of the 30-Day Programme

Patience is something that I have not been good at for much of my life. I always wanted everything now, and believed I could control things. But I have learnt that more than reaching somewhere, it is the meaningful and enriching process of reaching, that is crucial and a rewarding experience in itself. That is what makes us who we are, and also it is often that which makes us worthy of achieving our goals. Unless we allow ourselves to be moulded and changed, we cannot really reach where we want to be. Frequently, before we get somewhere, we are expected to go through a learning curve, perhaps build new skills to get a new job or learn to simply let go instead of trying to control everything.

So, what is the secret to patience? The only secret is to start learning to enjoy every minute of 'this day'. Mostly, it's about our everyday work. Focus on just today, and be excited about all that you are doing today and are going to achieve today! This way, you are taking baby steps towards your goal, and also are really measuring your success on a day-to-day basis, e.g., checking your weight regularly or taking time to draw your paintings for the exhibition or simply noticing how peaceful and positive you are. That can be a task for many who are not familiar with this way of thinking. A large part of this process of patience is the act of surrendering the anxiety and simply making peace with it: it's all fine; just take your action steps joyfully one day at a time.

If you find it hard to surrender your anxiety, you can say the following Intent/Prayer:

'I Ask/Pray to Universe/God to please take away this anxiety and worry I have about ... and offer me peace and trust instead.'

251

Just sit with it for some time with your eyes closed. You may notice you start feeling peaceful too. Use this whenever you feel anxious and impatient. If you are still not used to the idea of prayer, you can simply say the above like an Intent, and ask for the support of Universe.

When we are impatient, we are really not in the right frame of mind to achieve anything. We do not trust the support of Universe, and this can lead to a state of losing hope and giving up. **Remember, happiness and peace are really states of mind. Many a rich and successful person can be seen in a state of depression, and I have seen unconditional love and smiles on the faces of children in the slums in India.** I think also of the many people who have gone through difficult stages in life where they just don't know how to lift themselves up from despair, and wonder if there will ever be light at the end of the tunnel. Having been there, I can say that the only way to keep moving is to keep focusing on enjoying just today, by staying present in the moment, and give our hundred percent to our daily tasks, and keeping the torch of hope lit in the meantime. Soon you will get there!

Seeing uncertainties lying ahead is to be expected when you start working on your goal. It's the sign that you are changing, you are growing and ready to be something more in life. There is always some fear when you move forward, and you may be feeling impatient and anxious to prove yourself. Be compassionate to yourself whenever you feel you are being too hard on yourself or are being a perfectionist. Just do it for the experience, whatever your goal is, not to impress self or anyone, but simply for the joy and happiness of the 'moment', not even of tomorrow!

When I left my job to start my own work, I had no clue how I would follow my Heart in the work I do, but step-by-step, it just grew. The main fuel behind was my deep burning desire to do what I loved doing, and I did not focus on proving anything to my family and friends, but just did it for my own peace of mind. **When we focus on what we like doing, it is easier to find trust and faith in self in being able to do it.** At those times, when things were dull at work, in terms of income or simply growth, it was my love for what I did that kept me going. Had I chosen my profession just to make money, it would have fizzled out soon, and I would be meandering somewhere else by now. When I realised what I really wanted to do, I just couldn't be happy where I was working at that time. I could see that I was merely existing in life and not living. If you are in that phase of life, you really have nothing to lose. Move on fearlessly with your Brave Heart that you can access anytime! You are safe if you feel good about it in your heart. Once you take action daily or continuously as much as possible, that's a success! If you are still not sure what you want to do or how to do it, just Intend the answers to come to you from within and outside.

Patience involves letting go, and sometimes, trying again and again. I recently lost all the files in my computer when it crashed, and I hadn't saved the last 5 topics of this Programme on my back-up system. So, it is interesting how I have been tested with patience myself, as I was working on this chapter. Sometimes, to get anywhere, we just need to breathe and stay in the moment, with no rush to be anywhere. I still enjoyed rewriting this. The process of trust also includes learning to trust in the unknown, while we still keep the belief alive within. It is sometimes simply allowing ourselves to be led by the Higher Self, and believing that there is something better ahead.

So how do you stop yourself from thinking constantly about reaching the end, but instead stay peacefully in the process, and actually feel that being present in this moment, is where you need to be? You keep alive long-term Intents, and then simply focus on each day. Prioritise your daily 1 to 3 goals. Speak to your heart for more intuitive wisdom about what you should do each day. As you focus on the day and keep moving, you are in the flow towards your goal. You will know and feel it too, and this will bring you immense joy! Many of you will start seeing that people around you notice what you are feeling, and also you may look different each day. You will already start radiating what you have Intended to become. For example, even before I had begun to lose weight I started getting compliments. I would focus on the Intent: *'I AM truly grateful that I am radiating and glowing and living each day with the excitement of feeling good about my Body and Spirit.'* I would appreciate my body even if the scales showed no results, but maybe I exercised for several days in a row or simply looked after my diet, and that's an achievement in itself. I would appreciate how strong, light and happy I felt to be in charge of myself. It is the experience of enjoying the process that brings success. Hardship at the cost of happiness is never the way, nor is working late nights all the time, at the cost of your health and happiness.

I once noticed a little girl trying to get her mother's attention to listen to her stories, but the mother was not paying attention but rather looking impatiently at her watch so that she could leave the restaurant. By choosing to not stay in the Now, the mother was missing out on precious moments with her little girl. Really, what we strive for is happiness with our loved ones, and that is what was available right in front of her. Instead, she was probably worrying about getting some things done. I have often noticed people acquire the habit of looking busy all the time. Impatience becomes their second nature as they are always pushing; they do not know how to let go, how to wait to receive and simply be: live! It is as though they are in a 'pause' moment of their life which often ends sadly. Soon, the kids are grown up, their passion for doing the things they always wanted is delayed by years and sometimes it is just too late. When we die, we do not carry wealth with us, but we do carry the contentment of how much we loved and have received love from our loved ones, and how much we enjoyed our life. If we can understand that there is really no rush to get anywhere, but rather our job and purpose is just to be here in the Now with joy, then life will really go well.

For anything I am working on, I have to do step 1, step 2 and so on, and just live each day to get there. Sometimes, the process simply requires letting go and waiting, but that doesn't mean I hold my breath in fear and anticipation of whether it will happen. But instead, I am patient, with trust that what I love doing will be successful, and most importantly, will make me happy and satisfied. I ensure that I remain positive about the outcome and focus on taking the steps I need to.

Here are my feelings and also *Intent about living in the moment and being patient.* You are welcome to add this to your Intent list:

'I AM always focusing on living with passion right now. I AM creating more love and joy around what I want now. Everything I create is out of love, and joy results in a positive outcome. I AM living for today in full faith of a wonderful tomorrow! It feels very empowering as I appreciate each day that I live to the fullest.'

With a patient approach, you appreciate and enjoy all you do each day, not just for the pursuit of your main goals but also simple things like washing clothes, washing dishes, getting grocery etc. It's like a mindful meditation in itself, as my Mother would say. It becomes part of your daily life and you want to bring your Spirit alive in all aspects of life now, to be mindful and enjoy it. Staying centred in your heart helps you to do that and keeps you away from worries.

Patience is truly a virtue and if you are mindful of all you do, you can choose to be patient with yourself and others. I once had a client called Pauline who had a lifetime of healing issues but had no patience to let the healing process take place. She would be disappointed at her slow progress, but in my eyes, she was doing really well. The healing of a body is an organic process. Pauline also required clearing of some of her beliefs and fears in the process. But she would slow down her healing progress simply by worrying that it was taking so long, and then she would have negative thoughts that she would never get well. Pauline really needed to look at the positive in all that she was gaining, and not look at what she had not yet achieved. I told her to keep saying the word 'DELETE' to all her worrying negative thoughts and instantly breathe and Intend the positive instead. To remain patient, sometimes you have to choose consciously to calm yourself and know that all is well, even though there is no real evidence of it yet showing. If not, you are simply delaying the process.

YOUR WORK TODAY

1. Check with yourself, how patient are you with yourself about your goal? Do you still feel anxious for some reason? Or you still feel you cannot trust that all is well now and will also remain in future? Please then try the following Intent/Prayer we talked about earlier:

'I Ask/Pray to Universe/God to please take away this anxiety and worry I have about ... and offer me peace and trust.' Just sit with it for some time with your eyes closed. You may notice you start feeling peaceful too.'

2. Are you able to focus on your goal one day at a time and prioritise every morning as soon as you get up, the 1 or at most 3 goals that you want to focus on that day?

3. Notice today and this week, if you are able to stay in the moment and be mindful about all you do joyfully, without worrying about when you would reach your goal.

4. How would you rate your passion for your goal from 1 to 10? How else can you increase it? See how you can get yourself more excited about it. Perhaps dream with your eyes closed and put some music on. See where you wander off to.

5. Also reminding of the Intents mentioned above - *'I AM always focusing on living with passion right now. I AM creating more love and joy around what I want now. Everything I create is out of love, and joy results as a positive outcome. I AM living for today in full faith of a wonderful tomorrow! It feels very empowering as I appreciate each day that I live to the fullest.'*

I would like to leave you today with an old but very inspiring song; it is really nice as you can really feel the passion when Jimmy Cliff sings – "You can get it if you really want". You can access that on the Internet through YouTube, or through a music store near you.

The words of the song go as follows:
"You can get it if you really want
You can get it if you really want
You can get it if you really want
But you must try, try and try
Try and try, you'll succeed at last

Persecution you must bear
Win or lose you've got to get your share
Got your mind set on a dream
You can get it, though harder them seem now

You can get it if you really want
You can get it if you really want
You can get it if you really want
But you must try, try and try
Try and try, you'll succeed at last
I know it, listen
Rome was not built in a day
Opposition will come your way
But the hotter the battle you see
It's the sweeter the victory, now

You can get it if you really want
You can get it if you really want
You can get it if you really want
But you must try, try and try
Try and try, you'll succeed at last

You can get it if you really want
You can get it if you really want
You can get it if you really want
But you must try, try and try
Try and try, you'll succeed at last

You can get it if you really want - I know it

You can get it if you really want - though I show it

You can get it if you really want

- so don't give up now"

EXAMPLE

Rosalind talks about how she is learning to stop controlling everything in life and be patient with her process with self and others.

"I believe in my heart that I am truly ready for change but am not 100% sure at the moment about the "not knowing how!" I have always needed to know how, where, when and why. I never thought of this as control before though until I read this chapter.

I joined this course as I really want the help to change my life and get out of the same old patterns which bring the same old heartache and negative patterns.

I think it's hard to see your own faults until you start being asked specific questions (like on this course) raising things you hadn't thought of about yourself. I have really enjoyed finding out more about myself.

I have been having some strange "moments" recently, which I have put down to shifting of energies? On some days I have been "up" one minute and "down" the next. On Monday this week I was 'down' all day and evening but I just trusted that I am going through energy changes and lots of healing and I have chosen to change and improve my life so I have to go with the flow! It doesn't feel like a bad thing and I am aware of healing crises and how they feel.

I admit I like to control certain things and in the past I have tried to control my Sister and my Mum (and they have told me this) and previous partners. This has meant having to lose relationships so it is hard to accept the process without knowing "how" as most of my life I have wanted to know "how" so I could control it"

***

I hope you are noticing changes within yourself and how far you have come since you started this Programme. Recognition with gratitude of what is good around us simply gives us patience that the rest will be fine as well.

See you tomorrow with an interesting and a very important lesson to support you before the 30-Day Programme is completed.

Love,
Robin Bela

DAY 29
STAYING AUTHENTIC TO YOUR FEELINGS : THROUGH JOURNALING AND SPEAKING THE TRUTH

Welcome to DAY 29 of the 30-Day Programme

We have talked about how it is important to be authentic in every relationship, whether it is in business, with others, or with our selves. This requires two things: one is to be clear in 'listening' to our feelings, our inner wishes and truth at all times, and secondly, is to 'speak and live our truth'. If communication through 'listening' and 'speaking' is suppressed, it can affect our throat and can also cause physical problems there.

'Communication with our own selves' is about listening to our needs in life, and it's important to cultivate self-love and self-respect to allow this 'listening' process. This is how we know what our true desires and needs are. If we are unclear of what we want, it would naturally affect our communication with others too and the outcome of our entire life. I was on the borderline for thyroid problems, and had put on weight, until I really communicated my feelings to myself and came face to face with all my fears, especially about my marriage, and then had the courage to articulate them to others. I went through a big clearing around my throat then.

Often, we have no clue about what is happening around us, and we suddenly become emotional and ungrounded, and people don't understand us, and in this process, neither do we understand others clearly. There is a total lack of communication as a result. **Proper communication begins, most importantly, with communicating our feelings to ourselves. When we are firmly connected to knowing our inner self, then whatever others say or do, cannot overwhelm us.** It is easy then to stay neutral, as you do not feel threatened. You just listen, and choose to do and believe what you like, peacefully. If not, you would face discontent and boredom with life, and you may start looking for happiness through others, through material things and even through food, alcohol and smoking. In this situation, we are dependent on others for our supply of happiness.

When feelings come by, usually it takes time for our brain to process and understand what we are feeling and why. It is then that writing helps us to manage emotional issues. This can really help all the highly clairsentient people who may feel others' energies and get upset easily. This process helps us to be real, honest and authentic about these intangible feelings, and also gives us strength to tackle any difficult emotions from a place of consciously aware and calm self rather than in a disturbed state. To connect to your inner peace centre, I highly recommend having a daily journal where you just simply write what you are feeling.

I usually write my journal before I go to sleep or in the morning, when I just scribble a page or so. It helps me understand my inner journey much better, and also to stay focused and notice if there is anything that I need to address. This writing is for no one, but for my eyes only. Often those emotions which you cannot normally understand, become clearer when you write them down, and this actually helps you feel better instantly. When you go through this process, it will make you speak clearly and objectively of what you are feeling, without any emotional clouding, and may even help you to stop feeling over-sensitive to issues. **Journaling is a very healing and empowering tool that keeps you firmly connected to your true voice, your authentic power, and it cuts out all the melodrama that could drain you. It also is a process which gives fuel to imagination for creative ideas at work or for solutions to ongoing professional or personal issues.**

You have already been keeping a journal in this 30-Day Programme, but I have been leading you through with daily questions. From now on, you should just write daily about what you are feeling. If you have any pressing questions, you may write that on the page and ask your Heart or Spirit, 'why?' or 'how?' and see what comes to you. Keep questioning and asking 'why' or whatever other questions you have until you receive all the answers. You may often feel emotional without knowing why: just write down about it to receive clarity and see what comes. This process keeps you clear about your inner feelings and in touch with your inner guidance on what it wants you to do next. It can really keep us one step ahead of what is to come and can help us to manage our emotions and clear them quickly before things become worse. Such a focused journalling process can tune you into your intuitive genius, and thereby push you far ahead in the pursuit of all your goals.

There is no point in denying that feelings are a fact of our daily lives. They are what make us human. And let's not forget that our skin is the largest organ of the body through which we feel 24 hours! **Feelings have a purpose. We are created to have them, so the need is to listen and understand them. Keeping in touch with inner feelings will help you to accept your limitations, and also to become constructive in releasing and creating space and energy for those things that you really need and want more in your life.** Being sensitive is truly a gift, as you already feel uncomfortable when things aren't going right and gives you a clue to look into it and find out why. But if you don't know how to handle this sensitivity and instead keep burying it down, it could become a problem for your complete well-being. So keeping in touch with our inner thoughts, looking at our dark shadows face to face through writing in a journal on a regular basis, ideally daily, really helps in overcoming inner obstacles. Through journaling and checking within, when you know what it is that you need to do next, you are empowered to take the next step. And when you can comfortably talk about those things, you are truly empowered.

Those who are extremely sensitive to feelings and are clearly Clairsentients, are truly receiving clear inner messages, but maybe are overwhelmed by so many wordless feelings. They often shut down in their own world, or may create intangible shields, which prevent people from coming close to them. That is why, it is so important to come face to face with those feelings, to understand and recognise them on a regular basis, and one way to do that is through journaling. In fact, it is truly a gift to be a clairsentient as you are receiving intuitive messages of what is right and what is wrong. Soon, when you come to grips with your sensitive emotional feelings, you won't feel so intimidated to connect with people or shy from intimacy.

Keeping a journal can help you connect to your authentic voice for business as well. You simply write a page describing whatever problems you might be facing or simply that you are doing today. Many leading businessmen rely on this ability to listen to their gut and intuition. The ones who are good probably don't even need to write it down. They just feel it and they do it! Here is a quote from Losing My Virginity: The Autobiography that shows how Richard Branson, one of the most famous entrepreneurs right now, gives credit to his gut instinct or his intuition for his success:

"In the same way that I tend to make up my mind about people within thirty seconds of meeting them, I also make up my mind about a business proposal within thirty seconds and whether it excites me. I rely far more on gut instinct than researching huge amounts of statistics."

Richard Branson, a high school dropout, escaped being schooled to use a purely analytical approach in life and business, and so naturally uses his intuition too. We do not have to try to control the way the intuitive insights come or to make an effort to move towards them. We are naturally endowed with intuitive abilities. But these may be lying dormant. All you need to do is to trust. You can develop this part of yourself by listening first to your inner feelings through writing in a journal, and then by acting upon them by prioritising at least 3 steps for today, everyday. They might be what you 'feel' would be right to concentrate on today. Soon you may know you are quicker and do not require to write in your journal every time.

As you write, you might begin identifying specific blocks. When you start noticing them, you will be able to release any trapped emotions such as jealousy, or any judgements etc. We don't stop feeling these emotions in our life, but if we carry them for too long, they can cause serious emotional, and sometimes, physical problems also. I have always found that diseases have been triggered by unresolved emotions. Once, a 39-year-old cancer patient, who belonged to Ukraine, was my client. He was very unhappy because, having studied Engineering in the UK, he was unable to find a suitable job in there appropriate to his education. Instead, he was doing other work which he didn't enjoy, and felt very undervalued. He and his lovely partner were living together hoping to start a family. Suddenly one day, they found that he was in the late stages of cancer, and he then went on to suffer a stroke. When I told him what I felt to be the real reason for his agony, and suggested that he could be flexible and look elsewhere for the job he wanted, perhaps in his own country, he suddenly felt so relaxed as the whole burden of struggling to trying to fit in this country went away. But unfortunately it was too late, he died 2 weeks later, when I was away on holiday. When I came back, I was told by his partner, that he had been asking for me. I remember I felt really awful, and helpless. I could see that he had become internally open to healing after the main block was opened by our simple dialogue, when he had wept, and I remember seeing peace in his eyes; but his body was too weak to recover in that late stage. Had he dared to look deep within into his stuck emotion about being a failure, he might have realised that he truly wasn't. He was just not looking at things in the right way, perhaps out of a stuck ego, determined that he wanted the job in the UK more than anywhere else. Writing a journal might have helped him become aware of his issue way before his body began to suffer due to his emotions.

My teacher and mentor, Deborah King, healed herself of cancer and feels that she was able to do this through Meditation and through constant journaling that opened up her buried emotions and let them free. She found out that the root cause of her cancer was the sexual abuse she suffered from her father and her subsequent debased actions and lifestyle. And as yet, I haven't met Louise Hay, who for many decades has really been a pioneer in the New Age world for inner work and empowerment, but she too says that she had to identify her emotional problem in order to heal the cancer that she suffered, and the reasons she found were quite similar to those of Deborah King.

My own very close Aunt who lived in USA, died of brain cancer at the age of 54. She had migraine throughout her life as far as I can remember, but she ignored the reasons behind her migraines and never took proper rest. She believed in popping a pill and continuing to work like a machine. So the headaches turned to migraines, and the migraines turned to brain cancer. She just did not know how to relax. As a child, I used to hear my parents tell her to learn to relax. A couple of years before she died, I had just got into the field of healing work, and I remember doing a healing session with her a year before she developed cancer, and I found her energies extremely blocked. She carried so many emotions and resentments about the past. When I told her to start working on them, she ignored me and still wanted the secret to feeling good and finding healing. She was so tired of her work and just wanted to retire. But she told me she wanted to work for 2 more years so that she could get full pension and insurance etc. Unfortunately, she did not live to see that as she kept working and never really bothered to take care of herself physically, emotionally and spiritually. Writing a journal and Meditation would have done wonders for her. She could have realised and resolved all her issues way before they engulfed her.

I seriously believe that diseases like cancer can be turned into a blessing in disguise for people, a prompt to help them realise that they cannot pop a pill to solve all of life's problems, and live like machines or bury their unresolved emotions. You really have to face your issues, and there is no magic pill waiting to take them away. Most often, the pill that is needed is just forgiveness or realising and making some changes in life that have not been healthy for them. Having a cancer is a way for the body to tell us that something needs to be seriously looked into within, that's it. We really have to search deep inside, not outside, for the answers and the power to heal. I do believe that medicine is extremely important in supporting our lives, and in many situations, can be a life-saver but we really need to start working more on prevention rather than cure, especially in those cases where there is no cure at all in medicine!

Keeping a journal can help bring the changes within you easily and smoothly and it starts reflecting in our behaviour and moods for a start. As you come face to face with your issues, turn them into positive 'I AM Intents'. They are the Spiritual pills to heal you. Use these spiritual pills or the Intents regularly. You can delete the Intents and add new ones in the future as required. That way you will always be in charge of your inner world and that reflects in the outer world. I highly recommend that today, and definitely after you have completed this Programme with me, you should keep in touch with your inner feelings through this practice. By doing this, you will always be empowered and you can carry on the work we did together, on your own. On a lighter note, I am smiling as I say this, it's like you, having become a graduate, are now progressing on your journey by yourself, but fully equipped with the tools and techniques to stay always aligned with your most authentic powerful self within.

Now I would also like to touch upon the second part of communicating your feelings on how to also stay authentic to your feelings as you speak. It is natural to speak your truth well if you first communicate with yourself and gain clarity on your feelings. It is also important to speak your truth to others without melodrama. You can pause and breathe before you say anything and stick to facts rather than invoking statements that might come through your ego state with anger or resentment, perhaps like 'How could you?', 'You cannot do this'. This is laying blame and provoking rather than creating a constructive resolving statement about what you observed and are querying. Instead, you could perhaps say some peaceful resolving statements as, 'What do you think?' Or 'Would you like to try this instead?'

How often are you really not doing what you want to? That too is not expressing your unique self in your life. I now know that whenever I don't say or do what I want, I just feel I cannot breathe and my throat feels choked. I am so sensitive to my feelings that I can see the inner reaction going on within my body. Years ago, I truly wasn't the one listening to my inner world and was not flexible in listening to my needs. I was just running a mad career race and working through the check-list I had created of what would look good on my CV. So by the time I was 24, I had worked in 2 multinational companies, had 2 Post Graduate Diplomas in addition to my BA degree, and also an MBA degree from the UK. I was very competitive in college and received various awards. But then one day, I dislocated my knee and couldn't walk properly for almost a year. It forced me then to look within, and soon I connected to energy healing work and to my passion to heal and help people. It felt so natural to be doing it. I remember feeling so suffocated by feeling myself to be in the wrong job at that time, and I would come home in tears every day at the agony of not being able to do what I wanted. It felt like a prison to me.

Around that time, I met a psychic, who said that it was as though I had a line in my throat cutting and preventing me from speaking my truth. I said yes, I needed to take the step and do what I wanted to, even though I didn't at that point know the 'how'. My choice to follow my path was for my peace. I was happier with lesser income as I had started to do what I loved. I really did not care anymore about status or all the things I'd been running after before. Since that day, I just try to do what my heart and my conscience feel is right. I had to speak my truth to the people around me and to my ex-husband. I kept staying away from the drama, tried not to always seek approval and remained focused on the next step. That was just the start of me opening my throat chakra. Some of the blocks there continued as I still had unspoken issues I had not addressed until I dissolved my marriage. After that, I felt immense clearing in energy terms around my throat during my Meditations, to the extent that my neck could not move for a few days as it felt so raw with the clearing. It felt to me as though my throat had literally grown slimmer, and my collarbone, which had not shown because of my excess weight, was once again visible to my delight! But I know that no amount of healing for my body would have helped until I removed the core issues, addressed them and did something about them instead of just living with them.

YOUR WORK TODAY

1. Notice if you are usually overwhelmed with situations, are out of touch with your feelings and become ungrounded easily? **Acknowledging this sensitive side of yourself can be a relief, as in the real world you are**

generally taught to hide it. It is highly imperative to acknowledge it so that you can make peace with it. Feelings are a natural way for human beings to receive information, but unfortunately our society has taught us to hide them and not talk about them.

2. *Write regularly, ideally daily, your feelings in a journal* especially when you are going through a tough time or if you are really focusing on achieving something. You will feel that you are clear about where you are going and will also have more trust in the steps you are taking. You can start just now and get a feel for it by writing a page about just how you are feeling today.

3. *Check within to see how often do you speak your truth to the people around you and ask for your needs to be met.* Once you start writing and becoming real with your truth, you will find it easier to articulate it and tell others. You can even pray/Intend that the right words come out of your mouth when you talk about a difficult situation. I often ask for that when I have had an argument and would like to stick to my truth peacefully.

4. *If you have a health issue, talk to that part of the body where you are having the problem, and ask 'why' is this problem here? What is the message for me?* And then see what answer you get. Our bodies are very wise and have all answers within. You can keep asking 'why' till you get some direction or answers from it. You will then need to clear your core issues with breath and Intent work as explained under Days 2 and 3, and start saying your positive I AM Intents regularly to bring about, firstly, inner healing, and then physical healing. Also ask your inner self if you need any other support for physical healing. Perhaps you will be directed to see a specialist or guided to some other forms of healing along with your work on your Intents. Once a core issue is cleared, I notice that physical healing speeds up. I have seen this both in my own experience and that of my clients.

5. *You can say the following Intents: Breathe and Intend:*
I AM calling on the I AM Presence to direct my Higher Self that:

I AM connected to my feelings and truth through keeping a journal.

I AM staying aware and conscious of my feelings.

I AM always speaking my truth to self and others.

I AM speaking my feelings courageously and peacefully with emotional detachment.

I AM always in touch with my inner world and my inner guidance.

You can help open your throat chakra through chanting and singing. It's the best exercise for throat.

EXAMPLE

Sarah wrote about today's topic in her email:
"I have been journaling for many years and find that it helps me immensely although I have started doing it daily now. What you said about clairsentience really resonated with me - I do feel overwhelmed by situations and get ungrounded quite easily. I am a therapist and I find myself becoming wrapped up in my clients' feelings, and feeling scared about empathising too deeply in case I become consumed by my clients' feelings as this has happened before and I burned out. I work with suicidal clients on a daily basis, and I want to meet them at a deeper spiritual level so I can truly understand how it feels for them, but I am scared of not knowing how to do this or of losing myself.

I was concentrating on staying centred in my heart and keeping my thoughts positive and my energies high. One day last week I finished work and felt my energy was low but I wasn't sure what was wrong, so I came home and meditated and then decided to write about it to try to figure out what was going on. I used a technique that I have tried before: that is writing a question with my dominant hand and answering it with my non-dominant hand. I was very surprised to find the answer- I wrote quite angry words and I realised that I had been changing my thoughts to positive ones without acknowledging how I truly felt first. So after this I now acknowledge the problem, then say to myself I AM choosing to release this with breathing work (as explained in Day 3), and then I would Intend the opposite such as I AM patient and tolerant towards others and I AM patient and tolerant towards myself. This has helped me to feel more authentic, like I am noticing but taking my power back and choosing to do it differently. After realising this my energies returned to feeling more clear and bright."

***

Tomorrow will be the last day of this 30-Day Programme. Yes, it's almost the end. Time just flies. But we have done so much during this period. I have a special last lesson coming up, so stay tuned until the next page!

Love,
Robin Bela

DAY 30
OWN YOUR POWER BY BEING CONSCIOUS THAT THE POWER TO CHANGE IS WITHIN YOU

Welcome to DAY 30 of the 30-Day Programme

Yeah! You have done it! Congratulations on this journey you have taken with me. I am so grateful that you allowed me to support you on your path. If you are on this page, I greatly appreciate how much you have done for yourself.

Today, we are simply being conscious and accepting, as to where we stand in truly owning our power! This requires you to be 'conscientious' about your actions. You have the power within to always know what you need to change, and to make a conscious and conscience-based decision.

I've noticed several examples of owning power when I use public transport, for instance, it is so easy to see examples of people tuned into their power in a bus. I see power in the old lady over 80 walking with her shopping bag and getting on to the bus. I see power in the mother who managed her four children with such assertiveness in the bus. I also remember once a driver not being kind to a teenager and no one in the bus stood up for him including me, as at that time I did not have guts. I know I made a mistake! That's not stepping up to power! We all make mistakes, but staying conscious of those mistakes is what helps us learn and truly step up to the power within. So many times I have been engulfed in fear, and then I return to the peaceful state where all is well. Really, we are all "work in progress", for something new in life that may just come to us through our situation, or we can choose consciously to improve our situation, and connect to the power within to create the life we want. But please let's not get stuck and make it into a regular pattern!

I have a simple exercise to help you check and see, as to how you are doing with some of the things we started working on, throughout this 30-Day Programme. But you can always apply these questions to anything you are

271

aspiring towards in the future. **Remember, the first step to connecting to your power within is about recognising and owning that you need to work on something within you that needs improvement, change or healing,** e.g., getting rid of some undesirable core beliefs or fears, losing weight, or working on the need to raise the quality of your personal inputs into your new business enterprise. Then you will find that things start improving as you become more aware of the process, and consciously start working on yourself as outlined in the Programme. You will find that you are naturally taking better care of yourself, as your conscience would prick if you did not. Perhaps at times, you may require more nudges, but be patient with yourself: look at the positive side of how much good you are achieving, rather than berating yourself or worrying about what is still to be achieved. Otherwise, the whole purpose of this process and this 30-Day Programme will be defeated. Being aware of your progress and enjoying each step, without being judgemental, is important for any growth. You are already a step ahead in the journey by noticing it and in being excited about the new you that you are bringing in your life.

YOUR WORK TODAY

Place your one hand just above your navel, which is where your power centre is based. This Programme has been all about this energy centre, really. It is called Solar Plexus Chakra in Energy Healing work, and the origin of this concept is in Vedas, which is a large body of texts, originating in ancient India. This chakra is also called Power Chakra. This power centre is about self-confidence, self-esteem, strong will and your true power. I would like you to speak to this part of the body and ask the following questions, and if the answer is no, ask why, and start Intending the opposite through your Intents, if you have not been assiduously working on them already. Perhaps, you have felt a distinct improvement there through the work you have been doing?

Feel free to rate yourself on a scale of 1 to 10, '1' being poor and '10' being excellent. You can add some comments below if you like. It will help you understand and own your truth about how you are doing. Ask yourself the following questions and write their answers:

1. Is there anything still blocking me from connecting to my full power of living joyfully and following the excitement of my heart's desires?

2. Am I connected to the power of speaking my truth?

3. Am I connected to the power of listening to my inner guidance?

4. Am I connected to the power of feeling safe?

5. Am I connected to the power of having an open Heart to try new things?

6. Am I connected to the power of trusting my inner guidance and being able to surrender my goals for results?

7. Am I connected to the power of having the courage to take action on my goals?

8. Am I connected to the power of asking and accepting support from others and also through Asking or Prayer to Universe/God?

9. Am I connected to the power of standing up for myself?

10. Am I connected to the power of freedom of choice or do I always choose what I 'have to' or 'should' do?

11. Am I connected to the power of accepting abundance of all forms in relationships, money, health, success, love, and friendships?

12. Am I connected to the power of being able to stay in my own energies and have strong boundaries?

13. Am I connected to the power of being mindful and staying in the moment rather than in the past or in the future?

14. Am I connected to the power of Love and can I easily get centred again when I become stressed, perhaps through tools such as Meditation, keeping a journal, Stillness practice, Sacred Altar Within, Prayer, positive thoughts, remembering what you love, listening to your Heart, prioritising your daily work or through other ways?

15. Am I connected to the power of happiness and joy?

If you have a pressing question which you know is blocking your power, please probe yourself deeply about it, remembering to ask "why?" and to search for the time you first experienced the fear or unpleasant feeling which is now blocking your power. Follow the process you learnt in Day 2. Then do the breathing work as explained in Day 3 to clear anything still causing a block. It just means you have more work to do, and you need to give yourself time to breathe and be with the situation, to come face to face with it. You can write it in your journal to get more clarity. As you write what you are going through on a regular basis, it keeps a check on what is going on within as discussed yesterday. You will know exactly where you *power is 'leaking'*.

In general, ask yourself how do you think you have done this month? Have you changed in any way? Are you consistent in keeping your journal?

By reminding yourself and questioning yourself, you will be able to increase your progress. The more you notice the positive steps you have taken with regard to achieving your goals, the more you strengthen your confidence and faith in yourself. You do have all the tools you need to stay on the path now. Keep clearing any blocks, and anchor in the new beliefs; your power centre will simply strengthen, and then you will step into your true power. Intend, 'I AM in full Power now'!

EXAMPLE

Nicole sent her scores and answers. The questions may slightly vary as the layout above has changed since it was an e-course:

1. Is there anything still blocking me from connecting to my full power of living joyfully and following the excitement of my heart's desires?   7

This is about me feeling safe to be powerful and knowing that it is safe to be who I am now.

2. Am I connected to the power of speaking my truth?   5

Not fully yet. There has been a shift so it is easier, the more I write and get in touch with my truth the easier it will be accepting myself as I am. Detaching from emotion here is important and so is feeling safe in speaking my truth. Knowing I AM heard is also important.

3. Am I connected to the power of trusting my inner guidance and being able to surrender my goals for results?   2

This is a low score as I still worry that I haven't listened to or heard myself properly or that I haven't taken enough action or the right action - it is self-doubt and not trusting myself enough.

Robin replied:
Here use your tools as Journaling and question 'why' to your doubts, work with Sacred Altar Within Technique to help you tune into your Heart better and also connect to things you love to take your mind off the doubts, and just focus on doing the things you want instead.

4. Am I connected to the power of having the courage to take action on my goals? 4

I have taken some action but for some reason I haven't been writing action steps everyday. I have found that exercise, Meditation, I AM statements and prayer is taking over an hour each morning so I have been getting up much earlier than usual. I have been enjoying this but also feel like there is such a lot to squeeze in to that time, so writing the action steps is the part that has fallen by the wayside - I suppose I haven't been fully trusting my inner guidance.

Robin replied:
It should not take more than 15 minutes reading your Intents. Ideally you should be scoring off Intents which are similar, or duplicates and things that you feel you do not require any more especially if you have been saying them for more than 21- 30 days. If you feel the need to sit with them longer, you just need to build up the faith that what you are Intending is already true. Remember stating an Intent requires stating only once with your full open heart. Universe picks up as you speak and feel it. Thinking about what you want to focus on for the day should not take more than a minute, and in that time you should be able to hear what your heart says. Writing it down is not necessary. It's just a case of getting your mind to focus on what you know within yourself is important and then giving it due attention for a couple of minutes. Yes, Meditation, exercise and saying your Intents can take up to an hour or even more. I think that this is the most important part of the day for

me, when I take a little time to do all these things for myself. If you think about it, it's quite a short time out of 24 hours to be doing something for yourself. But this is necessary if you want to lead a "spirited" life, rather than merely existing bodily. I know for a fact that if I miss my daily routine, my whole day is less productive and I can feel myself not the most efficient. So to have a good day, I make sure I find the hour for myself to do those things.

5. Am I connected to the power of asking and accepting support from others and also through Asking or Prayer to Universe/God?   6

I am connected to asking for support from God but need to be more peaceful and clear in my prayers. I need to open myself up to trusting others more so that I can ask for and accept support - at the moment I do not do this unless absolutely necessary. I feel this is because I relied on my family for financial rescue and so feel that I have to do everything myself now.

6. Am I connected to the power of standing up for myself?   8

I am definitely more connected to this and have been focused on doing it from the heart and trying to detach from emotion. I am much more clear with my boundaries now but I need to learn how to do this but still be loving, open and non-judegmental.

7. Am I connected to the power of freedom of choice or do I always choose what I 'have to' or 'should' do?   5

I don't really know what this one means. If it means freedom of choice to behave and believe what I want and that all choices are open to me then yes I am connected to this. I am connecting to the freedom of making choices that are for my highest good. I need to be accepting that others also have this right of freedom of choice.

Robin replied:
YES you got it right!

8. Am I connected to the power of accepting abundance of all forms in relationships, money, health, success, love, and friendships?   7

Health - yes, money - yes, relationships - yes but I need to do more work on intending that I AM connecting with a partner who fits easily into my life, as I have worries that I would have to change my daily rituals and compromise what I have built up so far if I let someone in my life. Success - yes but I need to keep intending that it is safe for me to be successful. Friendships - this is the one I need to work on - I need to open myself up to close friendships with like-minded people as at the moment I feel like I am on the outside of my friendship group. I don't enjoy drinking alcohol as much anymore and I don't enjoy going to bars as much anymore, my friends do not have the same beliefs as me and sometimes they laugh or make fun of me in a way that from time to time borders on being disrespectful, I don't want to lose my friends but I want them to accept me for who I am now. I also would like to extend my social circle to include friends that choose not to drink alcohol and to do other things instead. As I have made changes, my friends think that I have become boring and think that I am better than them. This isn't the case but I just feel like they don't really understand me and feel threatened by the changes that I have made. I have prayed for healing with this.

Robin replied:
You don't need to, also you cannot force others to accept the change in you as I explained in Day 16 about changes. If they don't accept you, you move on! It is as simple as that: do it as peacefully and lovingly as possible.

9. Am I connected to the power of being able to stay in my own energies and have strong boundaries?   4

Yes I am learning and am trying to find the balance between having boundaries and being guarded. I need to have boundaries but with my guard down.

10. Am I connected to the power of being mindful and staying in the moment rather than in the past or in the future?   4

I am learning and am more able to do this and to focus on not thinking beyond the day, as I have spent so long thinking and worrying about the future.

11. Am I connected to the power of love and can I easily get centred again when I become stressed, perhaps through tools such as Meditation, keeping a journal, Stillness practice, Sacred Altar, Prayer, positive thoughts, remembering what you love, listening to your heart, prioritising your daily work or through other ways? 8

Yes, I am breathing out fears, doing Meditation, Sacred Altar Within, focusing on gratitude. I do still get caught up in some drama but am more easily able to speak my truth and get back to feeling centred in my heart. I am very aware of feeling centred in my heart much of the time. I love this change and I feel calmer and more grounded as a result.

12. Am I connected to the power of happiness and joy?   7

Yes I am finding it more every day and in every day things. Surprisingly I am feeling it more through the week when I have my daily rituals but feel it less at the weekend when I feel as if I am just waiting to get back to work. This is because 1) I am waiting for financial flow to manifest and so have been spending time just in my flat and 2) the weekends include drinking alcohol if I socialise with my friends and I am trying to cut down on this.

13. As my rituals become more established, natural and easy I will feel more peace and happiness.   6

Overall I am working on forgiveness, releasing the three 'Cs', and anchoring the new beliefs deep within myself. I am truly grateful for this course and the changes that it has already brought. I feel like it has opened me up to life again. I am excited about my life and it feels amazing to finally believe that everything I want to have is achievable. I have surprised myself by how much I have committed to this course and even though it has taken me longer than the 30 days, I have done it at a pace that is right for me. I really do have the tools now and something within me has shifted, I am more trusting of life and see life as a team that is working with me for my happiness and peace rather than conspiring against me trying to trip me up. I know that everything I need is already within and I am continuing to remove any blocks that stop me from realising this.

Thank you Robin for giving me this life-changing opportunity and I look forward to the day when I am able to meet you personally and work with you."

****

So I hope dear reader, you have scored yourself well. If not, do not worry, at least you know where you are aiming to reach. **Keep up the good work and all the practices you have built up through this Programme as firm habits!** Ensure that as you step back into normal life, the new way of living and being sees you through all the wonderful times in life, and even strongly through any tough situations easily, effortlessly and gracefully. You can always browse through the chapters to keep reminding yourself of the places where you want to put in more work. Also, you can always redo the whole Programme with a completely new goal to achieve! I am sure it will be a completely different experience.

Thank you for taking part in this Programme and taking this journey with me. I truly enjoyed creating this and I hope you too have enjoyed your time with me in breaking and changing your old patterns and connecting to your power within to create the life you want.

Gratitude and Namaste!

Robin Bela

EPILOGUE :
CONNECTING TO THE GODDESS WITHIN!

The food is so lovely that I cannot stop eating. I just had freshly made spaghetti with salmon and salad on top. Trust me, it just melted in my mouth. I am sipping on my drink and watching the crowd go by at the cafe restaurant on Macmillanstrasse at Augsburg in Germany. I am now trying my best not to finish my fresh cream tiramisu. I'm all on my own for the first time on a holiday since my separation from my ex-husband. The waitress reminds me of a lovely friend called Anique. She smiled every time I ordered food. We liked each other. I was surprised to find that I didn't feel anything missing. It was great being alone, just by myself. It was perfect. I could see a man far across, watching me all the time, but my peace, being content on my own was so good. I was comfortable, with no husband, friend or laptop or even phone around me. I was ok with me.

It was interesting as I could feel the excitement in my spirit, and felt confident to walk without a map. I felt that excitement as a reminder of my childhood days. I had an exciting day visiting an old BC church and walking about the cute little town, Augsburg.

As I was sitting there, looking forward to a weekend workshop with my teacher and mentor, Deborah King, I had no idea of what was to come.

About a year earlier, I had decided to write this book and I wanted to call it 'Connecting to the Divine Goddess Within'. I remember that my father had asked, "Why Goddess, why not God within", and I had laughingly replied that I am a woman in this life! Back then I used to Intend every day –"I AM a Goddess", so that I started attracting whatever I needed for the book. But what I experienced just a year later in Germany, I am sure, was beyond my wildest dreams. I really questioned myself whether I should include this experience in the book. But I think it all happened so sequentially right after I had completed writing the 30-Day e-course, and was in the process of converting it into this book, that I thought it most appropriate to narrate the episode. I have been so open about all my experiences in my journey to connecting my Power/Goddess/Source/Spirit that this too had to come. Though I had thought about writing the book a year earlier, it remained on hold for some months as I separated from my ex-husband and also went through a personal transformation of image, with weight loss and inner changes. All these developments were facilitating me to connect to my most authentic self spiritually, physically and mentally, through the processes of consciously Asking, Intending and taking action steps, on the lines laid out in this book.

Early that year, I had met the wonderful Sonia Choquette, author and teacher, at one of her programmes. She brings great inspiration to the topic of connecting to things you love through your Spirit. She told me that this was the year I needed to focus on Connecting to my Power. Sonia's words had sunk deep in my subconscious. I ended up making that as a part of the title of the book. But I had no clue then that the process initiated by her remark and its culmination would be so dramatic. Nine months had passed since I met Sonia Choquette and the first draft of this book was ready, yet I was hesitant and kept questioning whether I really had the right to call myself 'powerful' and teach others to become that. All this had made me go back and forth and I certainly had no idea then about the way this book will conclude.

It was during that stage of my own growth story that I had decided to go to Augsburg in Germany to see my teacher and mentor, Deborah King. In all my time in the field of energy healing I have not found anyone whom I wanted to follow more than Deborah King. She has dedicated almost her entire life to the field of energy healing work and has grown her work with such transparency, authenticity and clear conscience that she is truly the epitome of Power to me. It was during Deborah's programme in Augsberg that this amazing experience took place. I was called on stage with regard to some question I had asked, but none of us had any clue of what was to come. I was standing there while Deborah was clearing some of the blocks she felt I had, and also a hex which since childhood I had been aware of having been placed by someone who was jealous of me. Now this information is getting very esoteric and I beg the reader's indulgence, open-mindedness and some imagination that anything is possible in this world. As I was standing there with about a hundred participants witnessing this (many of them are my good friends now) - I looked out at the people in front of me and a huge sense of energy came over me and made me feel very good. I remember smiling. People said they felt the energies of the Madonna. Then Deborah said that the energy of another form of Madonna, popularly known as Goddess Isis, was being transmitted there through me. I had never heard of this Egyptian Goddess, but yes I sure was intending that 'I am a Goddess', sometime back when I was planning on writing a book on 'Connecting to the Goddess Within", which was a year before this incident with Deborah King took place. Interestingly, my only link to Egypt till then was belly dancing, which I had learnt that year! Deborah said I was also a queen and a member of royalty in many past lives! I didn't feel surprised by this at that time because I remember that as a child of 5 years or so, I used to say that I was a queen! But what followed, astonished me. At the end of the session, Deborah made participants kneel in front of me and said this is what people did for me in the olden days. It was an utterly amazing experience for me. Deborah hugged me and told me that I was very powerful and that I should use this power. I think that is what I was striving for to hear, and this became a kind of culmination to my book. It's as though I needed to hear this from outside of me too.

I was absolutely amazed and I also went through a phase of feeling overwhelmed with this powerful experience, and felt that what if I made a mistake and went wrong. The chapter in this book on 'feeling safe to be powerful' reflected the processes of the experience I went through in that phase, after the above episode. It took me more than a year or so to meet Deborah again in US. I was then feeling quite unsafe. I think that at the back of my mind, I wanted her and everyone to forget that experience so that I could feel normal in the class. It's quite rare to be initiated again with Deborah, but there I was back on stage again, and this time, clearing my fear of being powerful, and knowing that I am in Light, and no darkness can rule me. At times, all you need to move forward is to hear it from outside. I could easily go about talking about Goddess energy with this experience. But my aim is to show you that we can invite our most spiritual sides into our normal lives, and anyone can. After gathering all these experiences, let me just be the channel to tell you dear reader, that you are safe to be your most powerful authentic self and to shine in your unique light.

Talking about shining light, let me mention that my picture on the cover of the book was taken right after the day of my second initiation with Deborah King. It was from my phone camera, and really, the way this and a few other pictures came, I felt were representing my journey and experience to coming to my full power and light. I had no doubt in my mind, it would be the cover of my book! Thanks to Deborah King that such an amazing experience became a culmination to my book.

I was bowled over by both these experiences, I still am. I hope you found it entertaining. My life since these experiences has been pretty much on a different channel energetically. I am still catching up on how the energies have changed within me and have changed my life since then. Now I hope you will take your Intents more seriously! I intended, 'I AM a Goddess' and boy did I get that experience! The sky really is the limit. What do you want? I truly believe that to manifest anything in the world, all you need to do is to Ask and speak positively until Universe gets used to it, or rather until you start believing in the process and you start receiving what you are Asking for.

In my experience, the process of Asking regularly really speeds up the process of receiving. Sometimes you get things almost instantly if your Intent and belief are strong, just as at the beginning of the book, I felt unsafe and afraid and my bank balance went to zero and I then had to change my thinking consciously. You will find that as you keep using your Intents, things start happening. Sometimes, when working on manifesting what you want, you may have to take a step back before you return to a faster speed.

So don't give up: stick to your belief as firm as rock! Soon you will be on your supersonic jet flight: remember to enjoy the journey as that only is really our goal in life. Truly, the Power to achieve happiness, lies within us.

Thank you, my fellow beings. I am eternally grateful for this opportunity to share this book with you.

Love,
Robin Bela

SOME COMMON INTENTS YOU CAN USE

ISSUE/PROBLEM	INTENT REGULARLY
	I AM calling on the I AM Presence to direct my Higher Self that:
I am having bad days due to all **people and situations around me.**	I AM surrounded by peaceful and positive people, and environment. I AM happy and peaceful within.
I have **no time!** I am also struggling to find time to read this book.	I AM always having all the 'me time' I want, easily and effortlessly. I AM working through the Book to clear all my fears with ease and grace. I AM ready to bring change!
I am always in **pain in body.** I cannot focus on anything.	I AM feeling great in my body, and I can do everything I want with ease and grace. I feel more energy and vibrancy in my body (Name where) I AM led to all I need to, to have a healthy body. Thank you Universe!
I am **pushing/pulling too hard** to make happiness happen.	I AM happy and peaceful within, therefore everything outside of me is wonderful. I AM simply focusing on me enjoying my day, my time with my loved ones and in focusing on doing all I like to do. I AM having _____ in my life and I feel wonderful, grateful, content and peaceful.
I don't have enough **money!**	I AM abundant in Money and it flows to me naturally in numerous ways. I ask Universe today for more money__ to come to me. Show me Universe what would it take to bring that to me easily and joyfully.
I need **better understanding with people** around me.	I AM connected to all like-minded, friendly, positive and lovely people.

You can create your Intents to change any experience in your life.

YOUR INTENT SHEET

YOUR INTENT SHEET

YOUR INTENT SHEET

www.ingramcontent.com/pod-product-compliance
Lightning Source LLC
Chambersburg PA
CBHW051414090426
42737CB00014B/2658